New Jews

New Jews

The End of the Jewish Diaspora

Caryn Aviv and David Shneer

NEW YORK UNIVERSITY PRESS

New York and London

NEW YORK UNIVERSITY PRESS
New York and London
www.nyupress.org

Library of Congress Cataloging-in-Publication Data
Aviv, Caryn, 1969–
New Jews : the end of the Jewish diaspora /
Caryn Aviv and David Shneer.
p. cm.
Includes bibliographical references and index.
ISBN–13: 978–0–8147–4017–0 (cloth : alk. paper)
ISBN–10: 0–8147–4017–0 (cloth : alk. paper)
ISBN–13: 978–0–8147–4018–7 (pbk. : alk. paper)
ISBN–10: 0–8147–4018–9 (pbk. : alk. paper)
1. Jews—Identity.   2. Jews—Cultural assimilation.
3. Social integration.   4. Jewish diaspora.
5. Israel and the diaspora.
I. Shneer, David, 1972–   II. Title.
DS143.A96   2005
305.892'4—dc22   2005013036

The more I progressed, the more I was forced to abandon the myth of "One People."
I was searching for what I believed in: continuity.
I found only discontinuity.
And the more Jews I met, the less I understood what a Jew looked like. —Frederic Brenner, *Diaspora* (2003)

Home is not a place, but simply an irrevocable condition.
—James Baldwin, *Giovanni's Room* (1956)

Contents

Acknowledgments		ix
Preface		xiii
	Introduction: From Diaspora Jews to New Jews	1
1	Let My People Stay: Moscow's Jews after the Exodus	26
2	Encounters with Ghosts: Youth Tourism and the Diaspora Business	50
3	Temples of American Identity: Jewish Museums in Los Angeles	72
4	Castro, Chelsea, and Tel Aviv: Queer Jews at Home	107
5	Our Kind of Town: New York is a Center of the Jewish Universe	137
	Epilogue: The End of the Jews	172
	Notes	177
	Index	201
	About the Authors	215

Acknowledgments

Most people do not understand what it means to coauthor a book. Usually, collaborating authors divide up the chapters, each writing his or her own section, with the only genuinely cowritten component being the introduction or preface. This book is different in several ways. Throughout each chapter, you will occasionally recognize the individual voices of David, the historian, and Caryn, the sociologist, but, by and large, we wrote all six chapters *collaboratively,* sitting down week after week to produce what you are now reading. We collaborated on research, which meant that Caryn found herself on the streets of Moscow asking about the Jewish Community Center, while David navigated the complex Jewish geography of Brooklyn, where Caryn once lived. In the writing process, collaboration meant that the two of us wrestled together with words, concepts, and ideas, as well as with structure and form. We debated whether we had enough evidence to say what we were saying and whether we were glossing over truths that might be difficult to write for both us as scholars and you, the reader. David cannot thank Caryn, his writing partner, enough for pushing him to take risks in his writing, for challenging his own long-held assumptions about what it means to be Jewish, and for making the process of writing such a joy. Caryn thanks David for encouraging her to think more deeply, to fearlessly question conventional wisdom, and to appreciate the fun of writing and for not taking himself (or her) too seriously. We are already working on our third book, and we both hope there will be more projects in the future.

We received wisdom and sage advice from many people all over the world, from random drinking companions at raucous bars in New York who vetoed bad book titles that we proposed to a sixty-five-year-old Moscow Jewish intellectual who thanked us for asking her about her life. To everyone who told stories, gave advice (both good and bad), helped find materials in archives, gave us interviews, suggested sources, and encouraged us to write, thank you.

Thank you to the Department of Sociology and Anthropology at Loyola University Chicago, and to the Department of History at the University of Denver; thank you also to the Center for Judaic Studies, the Faculty Research Fund, and the Office of Internationalization for supporting our research.

Thanks to the Jewish Studies program at the University of Illinois, especially to Harriet Murav, Bruce Rosenstock, Brett Kaplan, and Matti Bunzl, an amazing group of scholars whose ideas helped us to think about what it means to be at the end of diaspora. Thank you to our colleagues at the University of Denver—especially Pam Eisenbaum, Richard Valantasis, Nancy Reichman, Leah Garrett, Sarah Pessin, Pat Larsen, Jamie Polliard, and Jennifer Reich—whose work also emphasizes the diversity of the Jewish experience and reminds us that we are not working alone. Thank you to many longtime friends and colleagues off whom we've bounced many of these ideas—Matt Hoffman, Yael Chaver, Bonnie Feinberg, Julia Weber, Ellie Knepler, Audrey Sprenger, Shawn Landres, Anna Shternshis, Grace Yoo, Ellen Levine, Debbie Findling, Adaire Klein, Teresa Scherzer, Motya Chlenov, Deborah Yalen, Melodye Feldman, Michael Bar, Naomi Azriel, Andrea Jacobs, Sharmila Rudrappa, and Jamil Khoury. To those who read or critiqued parts of the manuscript—Diane Wolf, Judith Gerson, Debra Kaufman, Lynn Davidman, Judith Wittner, Joanne Kauvar, David Marwell, Yuri Slezkine, Ann Pellegrini, Laura Levitt, Aeyal Gross, Gwynn Kessler, Oren Stier, Dafna Michaelson—thank you. We owe special thanks to David Biale, whose work and teaching have inspired us to see the beauty of Jewish life and to experience its diversity and who has always encouraged us to challenge deeply held beliefs. David wants to thank Yuri Slezkine for making iconoclasm a strength, rather than a liability. He also wants to thank Reginald Zelnik (z"l), whose meticulous reading has made David a better writer and who always passionately fostered the work of others. He is truly missed. Aside from the two of us, the person who has most influenced the book in your hands is our fearless editor, Ilene Kalish. Ilene, we owe you a great debt in your insistence on taking the long view, helping to turn our ideas and raw writing into passionately argued prose. Also thanks to Salwa Jabado and Despina Papazoglou Gimbel for turning our manuscript into this beautiful book.

Finally, thanks to our parents, Jim, Chuck, Diane, and Carol. They are our primary reading audience. If they fall asleep or roll their eyes, we know we need to either jazz up the writing or tone down the jargon. To our siblings and brothers- and sisters-in-law, thanks for feigning interest in our work. And, most important, to Gregg Drinkwater, our most critical editor, traveling companion, researcher, dear friend, and David's husband. Without him, this book would not exist.

Preface

We write this book as "professional Jews," which we define as Jews who make a living from participating in Jewish education, culture, community, and society. Given this profession, we are frequently asked to declare our allegiance to Israel, a place that, although halfway around the world, for many seems to sit at the center of the Jewish universe. On David Shneer's first day on the job as the director of the University of Denver's Center for Judaic Studies, for example, a member of the Board of Directors asked, "What is your commitment to and stance on Israel?" Similarly, Caryn Aviv spent many years shuttling back and forth between Israel and Chicago. When today she recalls these travels, her students and colleagues, both Jewish and non-Jewish, frequently ask, "Weren't you scared to live there?" or "Isn't it dangerous?" More often than not, older Jews declare to her, "We need to support Israel no matter what. If we don't, who will?" Or they ask, "Isn't Israel supposed to be a bulwark against anti-Semitism?"

About Russia, where David travels for research nearly every year, friends and colleagues often ask, "Did you have to stand in line for bread?" or "Are there still Jews there?" or, most often, "It must be dangerous to be a Jew there, with anti-Semitism and the mafia running rampant." Others respond to David's stories about his trips to Moscow by nostalgically reflecting on the 1980s, when American Jewry mobilized to "save Soviet Jews" by protesting at Soviet embassies, writing letters to congressional representatives, smuggling in prayer books, and raising money for Soviet Jewish immigrants.

In America, Jewish communal leaders continue to wring their hands over high rates of interfaith marriage, low levels of Jewish observance among new Jewish immigrants, the lack of a connection to Israel among large numbers of American Jews, the death of Yiddish, and the failure of the younger generation to "keep the faith."

Fears. All of them. Fears that Jewish life is dying around the world. Fears that Israel will be driven into the sea if Jews don't push back in defense. Fears that if American Jews don't stop marrying non-Jews, there won't be any Jews left in fifty years. Fears that if American Jewish leaders do not send Jewish teenagers to Israel and do not build another Holocaust museum, the next generation will not identify as Jews and the memory of the Jewish past will be lost.

In our many years working in Jewish education and in Jewish communities, across the United States, in Russia, and Israel, we rarely hear people exclaim, "Wow! Jews in America are doing a wonderful job of building Jewish culture, educating people, and fostering dynamic visions of a Jewish future." We rarely hear positive comments about the changing relationships to Judaism or the new Jewish ways of raising children being developed by interfaith families across the country.[1] Although many lament the "lack of Jewishness" among recent Russian Jewish immigrants to both the United States and Israel, we seldom hear or read about the new forms of Jewishness these immigrants bring with them. Too few Jews celebrate the renaissance in American Jewish immigrant literature, the like of which has not been seen since the first half of the twentieth century. We rarely hear anyone describe Moscow as a vibrant center of contemporary Jewish life or recognize that Russian is growing in importance as a language of Jewish life, literature, and culture. And hardly ever do we hear people say, "Maybe we're putting too much emphasis on Israel and not enough on our own Jewish communities."

It didn't surprise us, therefore, when, just after the outbreak of the second intifada, in 2000, an editor asked us to write a book about Israel's place in the Jewish world. The editor thought such a book would be "timely," which in the publishing world means that it will sell well. He thought that, "given all of the problems," people would want an authoritative book on Israel. But a quick tour of any local bookstore shows that there is no shortage of "new and important" books about Israel and the crises in the Middle East.

And, further, we weren't at all convinced that Israel was the place to be focusing on in the first place. Rather than write another book that assumes that Israel is the center of the Jewish universe and therefore *the* central crisis in a crisis-ridden Jewish world, we flipped the question on its head. What if we wrote a book, not about fear and crisis, decay and demise, but about the dynamic ways Jews actually live and thrive in many other places around the world? What if we wrote a book that suggested that there might be alternative Jewish universes in which Israel was not the center? What would that book look like, and how might it change the way we commonly think about Jews and Jewish communities?

In doing the research for this book, in places like Los Angeles, Jerusalem, Moscow, New York, Tel Aviv, Warsaw, and Berlin, we often relied on the following facts to help us envision a new map for the Jewish world, one that has multiple homelands, that does not break the Jewish world into a dichotomous relationship between "diaspora" and "Israel," and that suggests a positive vision of the Jewish future:

- Since the nineteenth century, the United States has been the preeminent place in the world to foster significant new forms of Jewish communal religion, such as the Reconstructionist and the Renewal movements.
- In 2003, the year of the most recent migration statistics, more Jews moved *to* Moscow *from* Israel than vice versa.
- There are plenty of Israelis who do not consider themselves Jews, and plenty of Israelis who do not live in Israel.
- New York, not Jerusalem or Tel Aviv, is the home of the international Jewish institutional world and the center of Jewish philanthropy.
- Yiddish is still a spoken language, and the number of people studying Yiddish is growing.

These statements, all of which are examined in this book, throw into question the centrality of Israel as *the* Jewish homeland and as *the* place that will save the Jewish people and Judaism from their supposed "perpetual demise."

Frankly, posing such questions and making such statements public has been a bit scary. Even though Jews are traditionally seen as people who seek knowledge for knowledge's sake and ask more questions to find better answers, in some quarters, questioning the Jewish map is downright heresy. So much of Jewish life, thought, and scholarship revolves around the idea that Israel is, has been, and always will be at the center of the Jewish universe. We are all too aware that this "protectiveness" of Israel is in large part a reaction to rising violence in the Middle East and perceived rising rates of anti-Semitism. Because of these fears, too many questions go unasked. But we believe that answers to these questions are important because, ultimately, they reveal alternative Jewish worlds that are flourishing.

We see a new Jewish map and an end of the Jewish diaspora. We see the emergence of what we have dubbed a new type of Jew—the New Jews. We see this not because all Jews have suddenly moved to Israel or because Jewish life is dead around the world. On the contrary, this book suggests the end of diaspora, because the majority of Jews in the United States, Russia, Germany, and elsewhere no longer see themselves "in diaspora" but instead see themselves at home, not pining for a Promised Land. This new map emerges from the end of the *idea* of diaspora, because Israel is far more complicated than people would like or often make it seem. Jews in Israel do not all feel "at home." Many Israelis, Jews and non-Jews alike, wrestle with the consequences of living in a country marked by a struggling economy and the growing political polarization between religious and secular visions of Israel's future. Many do not feel at home because of Israel's struggle with religious diversity and pluralism *within* the Jewish world. Some Israelis, particularly recent immigrants, do not feel at home because all too often they are stereotyped as prostitutes, housekeepers, or overeducated cab drivers, while others are seen as potential terrorists, security threats, or enemies of the state. And a generation of young, secular Israelis, who live part-time in the United States, travel to India, and have a cellphone glued to their ears, approach the world less as Israeli nationalists and more as global Jews.

The emphasis on "diaspora" and "Israel" has prevented Jews from exploring the diversity of Jewish experience and the ways that Jews craft their identities at home in the places they live. Rather than writing about fears of displacement and violence and the failure of Jews to stand as one, we have written about Jews' *rootedness* in the places they live and about their ability to move around the world because they *choose* to and because they are financially able to. We have written about a new Jewish map populated by New Jews.

Introduction

From Diaspora Jews to New Jews

"Homeland?" He turned the word contemptuously back on the
odious little firebrand.

"I suppose by this you mean some wilderness on the other side of
the globe, on which I have never laid eyes, and which I don't even
know how to picture, but which, from the description, even by
those who profess themselves its eternal lovers, can promise me
nothing.

"And yet, if I am to believe the arguments of people like you, it is
that place, and not here in the Europe of my birth, and of my father's birth, and of my father's father's birth, that I am to think of
as my authentic homeland? . . . I would ask you please not to im-
pose upon me a destiny that I could never experience, but as entirely forced and artificial."

> —Jascha, from Rebecca Goldstein, *Mazel* (1995)

A home is relatives and Jews.

> —"Shai," interview with Naama Sabar

The metaphor of a people longing to go home is compelling. It also
is outdated. —Larry Tye, *Homelands* (2001)

On the first day of a class David teaches on Zionism and nationalism, a student asked him, "Where's the diaspora? And when writing my papers, should I capitalize it or not? Do you say that Jews in the
United States are *in* diaspora or are *the* diaspora?" David explained that
much of the class would be asking those very questions and, when possi-

ble, figuring out some answers. He asked her where she learned the word.

"In Hebrew school and from my parents. We're diaspora Jews."

"*Well, then do you have an answer to the question 'Where is the diaspora?'*"

"Yeah, any place but Israel. . . . Well, at least for Jews."

"*So it must be a place, or a lack of a place. But what about before Israel existed? Was there a diaspora?*"

"Oh, that's a good point."

"*How about Israelis who don't live in Israel? Do they become diaspora Jews?*"

"No, it's about where you're born."

"*So if you move to Israel, you're still really a diaspora Jew?*"

"Well, no, because by moving to Israel and making *aliyah*, you're becoming an Israeli."

In only a few questions, this exchange raises some of the fundamental questions about modern Jewish identity and Jews' understanding of their place in the world. David wanted to respond to her: "If the word 'diaspora' is too amorphous and doesn't really seem to mean anything, why don't you get rid of it?" but decided that would only add to her confusion.

This book is an answer to her questions. We want to uncover the assumptions people make about diaspora. We show how some Jews are rethinking their ideas about Israel and the tensions between exile and home, diaspora and homeland, here and there. Jews are dismantling the very idea of diaspora in the way they live their lives.

Jewish Exile, Diaspora, and Home

Diaspora: 1a: the settling of scattered colonies of Jews outside Palestine after the Babylonian exile. b: the area outside Palestine settled by Jews. c: the Jews living outside Palestine or modern Israel. 2: a dispersion abroad. (Webster's)

Diaspora has become a popular term to describe how ethnic groups live in the world today. As air travel becomes cheaper, as Web phones make virtual visual communication over thousands of miles instantaneous, people are finding new ways of creating communities across time and space. The idea of diaspora assumes that global communities have a center, a place that Africans in the African diaspora, Irish in the Irish diaspora, and Mexicans in the Mexican diaspora can identify with and think about, and perhaps yearn to return to.

The word "diaspora" means dispersion. It originated in the Septuagint, one of the original Greek translations of the Bible: Deuteronomy 28:25: "thou shalt be a diaspora in all kingdoms of the earth." The very word summons up images of Jewish seeds scattered about the earth.[1] The term "diaspora" solidified into European consciousness and the English language only in the modern era. The Oxford English Dictionary cites its first use in English, in 1876. More recently, dozens of collective groups have appropriated the term to explain their geographically scattered communities. Dictionary definitions of the word "diaspora" differ— some refer to actions, others to people, and others to places, depending on how the term is used. However, the word the Greeks translated from the original Hebrew as "dispersion" might, more literally, read, "thou shalt become a *horror* to all the kingdoms of the earth [*ve-hayitah le-za-'avah le-chol mamlechot haarets*]." *Za'avah,* the word in question, means anything from atrocity and outrage to horror and terror, but it does not mean dispersion. That which came to symbolize the Jews' scattering among nations had a much more ominous and threatening tone in the original.

Jews' understanding of their "diaspora" has had a more negative connotation than the rather benign-sounding "dispersion," although the historian Erich Gruen and others have shown that the practices Jews developed to create Jewish diaspora communities were frequently different from the words Jews used to describe the experience of exile. In Hebrew and Yiddish, the term *galut* (*golus*) is a closer equivalent to "diaspora" than *za'avah*. But even in this case, *galut* is an inherently negative term, suggesting spiritual diminishment and exile, rather than just dispersion from a homeland. In Modern Hebrew, the adjective *galuti,* which should simply be translated as "diasporic," in fact is generally translated pejoratively as "ghetto-like, of ghetto nature, exilic, diasporic," suggesting that Jews' relationship to place has changed since the advent of modern Hebrew, Zionism, and the founding of Israel.[2]

Within some Jewish cultures and memories, then, diaspora as *galut* has signified a diminished spiritual and eschatological condition, connected to the negative idea of exile, homelessness, and a yearning for a return to Zion under the guidance of the Messiah. Traditional Jewish texts always figured (and continue to figure) a mythic Zion as the eternal Jewish home, the place to which the Messiah would return Jews. But this was and continues to be a mythic home, a nirvana, a glimpse of the world to come. Many Jews who actually lived in the land we now know as Israel during the two-thousand-year "exile" still conceived of Zion as a mythic place from which they were exiled. Even after the establishment of the state, within and outside Israel, after Jews "forced the hand of history" by doing that which the Messiah had not yet done, there have been religious Jews, namely the ultra-Orthodox groups Reb Arelach and Neturei Kartah, that live in Israel but do not recognize Jewish political sovereignty over the land.[3] In the 1970s, the leader of Lubavitch Hasidism, M. M. Schneerson, declared that Jews who lived in the Holy Land were just as much in exile as those who lived in the diaspora.[4]

Historically, Jews' understanding of home and diaspora was made up of everyday practices and relationships to local communities and to mythic homelands, no matter where one lived. The first theoretician of diaspora, the prophet Jeremiah, who witnessed the destruction of the First Temple in 586 B.C.E. and the subsequent Babylonian Exile, suggested one particular survival strategy. Jews needed to craft a concept of diaspora that would allow them to be at home wherever they were, while still maintaining a memory of place that connected them to Zion. Jeremiah was still too fresh from the real experience of expulsion to move beyond a diaspora/homeland dichotomy, but he told Jews to root themselves in their new communities: "Build houses and live in them, plant gardens and eat their fruit. . . . Multiply there, do not decrease. And seek the welfare of the city to which I have exiled you" (Jeremiah 29:5–7). Although Jews were yearning for their lost homeland when they said the words "If I forget thee, O Jerusalem" (Psalms 137:5), Jeremiah called on Jews to maintain a dynamic tension between movement and rootedness, between being at home and recalling a mythic homeland.

Many Hellenistic Jews in the Second Temple Period (513 B.C.E.–70 C.E.), for example, *chose* to live outside the borders of the Holy Land. While living throughout the Hellenistic empire, they sent money to Jerusalem and conceived of Jerusalem as the *patris*, the homeland, but did not long to return there. In the words of Erich Gruen, "The self-perception of Second Temple Jews projected a tight solidarity between center and diaspora. [But] the images of exile and separation did not haunt them. . . . The respect and awe paid to the Holy Land stood in full harmony with commitment to local community and allegiance to Gentile governance."[5]

While living in exile following the destruction of the Second Temple—what had been the locus of Jewish political and spiritual power and the symbol of Jewish rootedness in Judea—in 70 C.E., Rabbinic Jews crafted a diaspora that allowed them to be home where they were while maintaining cultural differences from the other people with whom they lived. They had to construct senses of home wherever they were in diaspora, because there was no real homeland anymore. In this way, the historic Jewish diaspora differs from many postmodern diasporas, which have an actual political entity, rather than only a symbolic one, that they may call a homeland. If contemporary diasporas create relationships to both a real and a mythic homeland, Jews in Exile only had the mythic, messianic Zion to imagine.

Over the course of several centuries, Jews added varied practices (like Hellenistic Jews' sending of money to the Temple before the Exile) to their repertoire of cultural strategies for remembering the homeland while firmly "rooting" diasporic Jewish cultures in their local places. Jews recited lamenting psalms about exile on fast days and repeated the line "next year in Jerusalem" every Passover, and some made pilgrimages to the Holy Land. Some Jews continued to send money to help support the Jews who remained behind in Zion after the expulsion. And, culturally, many Jews maintained a mythic connection to the Holy Land, a connection celebrated (and sometimes satirized) in liturgy and literature. In S. Y. Abramovitch's classic Yiddish story, *The Brief Travels of Benjamin the Third*, the little town of Tuneyadevka marvels at the arrival of a date from the Holy Land: "You should have seen the town come running to look at it. A Bible was brought to prove that the very same little fruit grew in the Holy Land. The harder the Tuneyadevkans stared at it, the more clearly they saw before their eyes the River Jordan, the Cave of the Patriarchs, the tomb of Mother Rachel, the Wailing Wall. . . . For a moment . . . the whole of Tuneyadevka was in the Land of Israel."[6]

In addition to remembering the mythic Exile from the Holy Land, Jews also had strategies for rooting themselves in places. For example, Jewish communities established cemeteries—a very concrete act of claiming both place and space for themselves that meant acquiring land and investing it with cultural and metaphysical power. Cemeteries are holy ground (and are also impure ground), and no matter how much one culture can wipe away cultural traces of another by destroying buildings, eliminating languages, or killing people, bodies are rooted *in* the ground, not *on* the ground.[7] Jews also established traditional schools (*b'tei midrash*) and ritual bathhouses (*mikva'ot*)—places off-limits to the cultures and peoples around them. These private spaces within the community served as foundations from which to construct community. They are also places that have historically been associated with gender and sexuality, and with the segregation of space and knowledge. These three spaces—cemeteries, bathhouses, and schools—were cornerstones of how Jews practiced home in multiple ways for several centuries, across geographies and cultures.

Although the majority of contemporary Jews no longer use bathhouses and traditional schools as their way of making home, many still perform acts of marking Jewish space by hanging a mezuzah on a doorpost. Ask most American Jews, and they'll say that hanging a mezuzah is one of the most important symbols that visibly and publicly renders a home as "Jewish." Within a mobile modern American culture, the symbol of the mezuzah roots Jews in homes and creates a sense of community. When a Jew moves, she is supposed to leave the mezuzah on the house, rather like Jews leaving bodies in the ground. From the beginning of the mythic diaspora, Jews have created rituals, built structures, and developed relationships to places that simultaneously create a sense of home in the places they live and assert Jews' difference from those around them by remembering Zion.

Jewish Peoples and Jewish Diasporas

Although Jews' relationship to the mythic Zion has always been one of the markers of Jewish difference from the people around them, Jews have always had many diasporas and homelands—from Sephardic Jews who were expelled from medieval Spain in 1492 and longed for a mythic return, to nineteenth- and twentieth-century German Jews, who, before the Holocaust, viewed Germany as their homeland. German Jews made up the bulk of Jewish immigrants to the United States in the nineteenth century. In the years shortly after their primary migration, in the mid-nineteenth century, these Jews maintained strong relationships with Germany by bringing in German rabbis, traveling across the Atlantic, and even importing German forms of Judaism, such as the Reform movement, to America. Similarly, many Jews who left Germany in the 1930s during Nazi rule still thought of Germany as the homeland from which they had been exiled.

At the same time, many Jews were already starting to see themselves as rooted in the places they lived, rather than in diaspora from their former home. German Jews who remained in Germany after it became a country in 1871 increasingly crafted German national identities for themselves. They served in the German army, spoke German, and read German literature. When Eastern European Jews started immigrating to Germany in the 1880s and 1890s, established German Jews often used these new *Ostjuden,* or Eastern Jews, as foils against which they judged their own rootedness in Germany.[8] In the United States, Hebrew Union College, Reform Judaism's American seminary, founded in 1875 in Cincinnati, began to produce the first generation of American-born Reform rabbis. From that point on, German Jews in the United States became deeply invested in seeing America as home by forming organizations, such as the Hebrew Immigrant Aid Society, to expedite the Americanization process for new immigrants coming from less acculturated parts of Europe. Although many American Jews who traced their roots to Germany retained symbolic connections to Germany and to German language and literature, the communal structures they established firmly rooted them in their new homeland.[9]

It wasn't just German Jews who began to see the places they lived as home. Many new Eastern European immigrants felt that America was their true Jewish homeland. The Eastern European Jewish immigrant writer Mary Antin suggested as much when she said, "Not 'may we be next year in Jerusalem,' but 'next year—in America!' So there was our promised land."[10] Today, many Jews living in the American Jewish diaspora, in Phoenix, Atlanta, Denver, and elsewhere, long for a metaphorical "return," or at least a routine pilgrimage, to the American Jewish homeland—New York. A friend of ours who lives in Denver, Colorado, returns to New York six times a year to "recharge her Jewish batteries."

Like American German Jews in the nineteenth century, at the turn of the twentieth century, the new American Jewish immigrants were living in a traditionally conceived diaspora, but not one with its origins in Zion. Most American Jews trace their roots back to the large wave of Jewish migration from Eastern Europe to the United States between 1881 and 1924 and have maintained traditional diasporic connections with family, friends, business connections, and others who "stayed home." Many American Jews retained some connections to Eastern Europe until World War II, speaking the Eastern European Jewish vernacular, sending money back "home," and establishing *landsmanshaftn,* community self-help groups organized around immigrants' hometowns.[11]

The application of the term "diaspora" to early-twentieth-century American Jewry becomes more complicated when discussing the idea of a mythic return. Most American Jews in the first half of the century saw themselves as emigrants from Eastern Europe, immigrants to America, traversing two distinct places and cultures even as those cultures informed each other. Some traveled back and forth; some came to the United States and then returned to Eastern Europe; most stayed permanently in America.[12] They did not see themselves in "diaspora," if by diaspora one presumes a desire to return home. American Jews of Russian and Eastern European descent became very good Americans, embraced the rhetoric of assimilation, and did not generally see tsarist and then Communist Russia as a place of return. They did, however, feel responsible for those "back home" and maintained relationships with their countries of origin. And most American Jews, even most self-professed Zionists, did not think of Israel/Palestine as the yearned-for homeland. Most American Zionists before World War II supported the establishment of Zion as a refuge for persecuted, downtrodden Jews, but not for themselves.

After the Holocaust, and especially after the Cold War, American Jews' notion of placement and roots changed again. In the words of the noted Jewish Studies scholar Deborah Dash Moore, "The destruction of European Jewry shattered the familiar contours of the Jewish world and transformed American Jews into the largest, wealthiest, most stable and secure Jewish community in the diaspora."[13] In a post-Holocaust world, many American Jews came to see Eastern Europe no longer as the real place from which to draw roots but as a mythic home, not one that they want to return to but one that they want to bear witness to. It is a land of Jewish ghosts and of lost cultures. If, for example, Hebrew was once the holy tongue that became the modern Jewish vernacular, Yiddish, the former Jewish vernacular, now has a sense of nostalgic sacredness, of a language and culture now lost. The ways in which Eastern Europe has become a mythic part of the Jewish *past* and not an imagined mythic home in the future is central to understanding how American Jews see themselves at home in America.

More recently, Jews have migrated to the United States from Iran, the former Soviet Union, and even the "promised land" of Israel itself.[14] New York's and Los Angeles's multiple and multiethnic Jewish communities from around the world complicate the notion of diasporic generations and point to the need for mapping the global spaces and communities that Jews inhabit and call home. Researchers have found that many Israelis, avowedly secular residents of the "Jewish" state, develop their first meaningful connections to organized Judaism when living in the United States. Even more interesting is the phenomenon of Israelis who have immigrated to the United States and who later return to Israel as newly minted *American* Jews. They demonstrate their Americanness by participating in the rituals that American Jews have developed around Israel, such as holding a Bar or Bat Mitzvah at the Western Wall in Jerusalem.[15]

Zionism and the End of Exile

Although Jews have always had multiple diasporas and multiple homes, the overarching diaspora in Jewish culture has always been the Exile from Zion. In a world in which the mythic is upstaged by the real Zion, how do Jewish communities reinscribe Zion as the mythic home of Jews, especially as Jews around the world make homes for themselves wherever they are? Why is Zion still so central to the construction of Jewish identity in a global world? How did Jews' ideas of home change once the mythic had become the real, once the ghost of Jewish sovereignty had come "back to life," once Jewish nationalists had established political hegemony over the place that had been a place of memory?

Zionism, the nationalist movement to establish Jewish political independence based on the idea that Jews needed their own territory to be truly safe in the modern world, was predicated on ending the Jews' two-thousand-year exile in other people's homelands. For Jews, Israel evokes particularly resonant, complicated meanings of home. Centuries of migration, history, politics, culture, and religious yearning have layered upon Israel multiple and conflicting meanings of home and homeland. For whom is Israel home, and how so? Has Israel been the "homeland" of Jews since "time immemorial," as some would claim? Is "home" the current state of Israel, with its contested borders, complex struggles for political power, shifting diplomatic alliances, and persistent violence? How should that home be governed, and who should live there as a fully enfranchised citizen? Is Israel a theocratic home where all Jews should live as one nation under God (as interpreted by Orthodox rabbis), or is it a polyglot of cultures and languages, a secular democracy? Is it all of those things? Or none of the above?

The idea of Israel has never been stable. Early debates about Zionism focused on the question of whether Jews should be in search of *a* Jewish homeland or *the* Jewish homeland. The founder of political Zionism, Theodore Herzl, believed that the purpose of a Jewish homeland was to be a place of refuge and thought that any territory governed by Jews would suffice as a Jewish homeland. In the late 1890s and early 1900s, there were plans to establish Jewish homes in such "non-Jewish" places as Uganda and Argentina.[16] But other Zionists emphasized that place and home were not just about territory but also involved memory, myth, and emotion. These Zionists insisted that the Jews' homeland needed to be the historic, mythic Zion, and thus was born the movement to settle Jews in the territory that would eventually become Israel. Once the Zionist movement placed territory in Palestine at the center of Zionism, the next question was, would Jews from around the world move there?

Early Zionists argued that living outside one's historic home was destructive to constituting a stable, modern Jewish identity. Only the establishment of a political place in the Jews' historic homeland would create a fully modern Jew. The reminders and remainders of Exile—language, cultural practices, and religious ideologies—needed to be suppressed or minimized in order to make way for the "new Jews," an identity based on a heroic, explicitly masculine notion of citizenship and belonging.[17]

The founding of a political state was fraught with even more questions about this new Jewish homeland's position in the (Jewish) world. Would it be a European, parliamentary-style democracy in the Middle East that happened to have a lot of Jews? Would the state rely on its nationalist origins and become a Jewish state, possibly compromising some of the ideals of equality, democracy, and universalism? How would the hundreds of thousands of non-Jews who already lived there fit into this vision? In 1950, the Knesset, the Israeli parliament, answered some of these questions when it crafted the "Right of Return," a law that allowed Jews anywhere in the world automatic citizenship in the new country if they moved to Israel. The question of who would fit into this category was and still is one of the most complicated questions for the Israeli government and Israeli society to wrestle with, as demonstrated by recent decisions by the Israeli Supreme court to recognize conversions to Judaism facilitated by non-Orthodox rabbis.[18]

The centrality of the idea of return shows that Zionism, first and foremost, envisioned Israel as the future homeland of *all* Jews, an idea summed up in the phrase that describes Israel's primary function—a place for "the ingathering of the exiles." Even the name of the new state, Israel (the historic word connoting the Jewish people—*am yisrael*), suggests a group of people well beyond the country's borders. But the use of the word "right" in the original law also shows that the Israeli government could not insist on this ingathering. It needed to persuade Jews around the world that they should move to Israel voluntarily and take themselves out of their dispersion. Some did. For most Jews who chose not to physically relocate in Israel, the very least they could do was to recognize and celebrate Israel as the center of Jewish culture and as an emerging and viable source of Jewish identity. And, most important, they could support it financially.

Financial support, in fact, was one of the foundations of the relationship between American Jews and early Zionists in Israel.[19] In 1921, according to the historian Melvin Urofsky, the Twelfth Zionist Congress approved a $6 million budget, 75 percent of which was to come from American Jews. From its inception, the (re)building of the Jewish state would depend on diaspora dollars, most notably American diaspora dollars.[20] The anthropologist Jeffrey Shandler coined the term "impresario culture" to describe the entrepreneurial role American Zionists played in helping to fund the state—primarily as directors and producers—from the safe and relatively removed confines of American Jewish urban enclaves.[21]

The idea that American Jews would participate from a distance, financially and politically, was enshrined in the well-known conversation that took place in 1950 between the first president of Israel, David Ben Gurion, and the then-president of the American Jewish Committee, Jacob Blaustein. Ben Gurion stated unequivocally that "The Jews of the United States . . . have only one political attachment and that is to the United States of America. We should like to see American Jews come and take part in our effort. . . . But the decision as to whether they wish to come . . . rests with the free discretion of each American Jew himself." Blaustein responded, rather curtly: "We must sound a note of caution to Israel and its leaders . . . the matter of good-will between its citizens and those of other countries is a two-way street: that Israel also has a responsibility in this situation—a responsibility in terms of not affecting adversely the sensibilities of Jews who are citizens of other states by what it says or does. In this connection, you are realists and want facts, and I would be less than frank if I did not point out to you that American Jews vigorously repudiate any suggestion or implication that they are in exile. . . . To American Jews, America is home."[22] Israel would be *a* Jewish home, not *the* Jewish home.

Remaking the Diaspora after the Establishment of Israel

After World War II and the establishment of Israeli statehood, the Jews with the most financial and cultural capital were located primarily in North America. Because of this, Zionist discourse sought to reinterpret the hierarchical relationship between "diaspora" and "homeland." Until World War II, "Israel," literally and figuratively, was not on the map of the majority of Jews.[23] Only after the war did Israel and Zionism move to the center of Jewish identity, politics, and overall aspirations for the American Jewish community. After the destruction of the vibrant socialist circles and many religious Jewish communities of Eastern Europe, Zionism became the dominant political ideology.

The discursive and power relationships that shaped global Jewish communities changed dramatically. After the war, the majority of American Jews moved out of the working classes and into the suburbs.[24] They lost their tangible connection to Eastern Europe, where many formerly Jewish towns had been decimated, and in its place began creating the mythic Eastern Europe that haunts American Jews today. As American Jewish identities, practices, and communal affiliations increasingly became options, and as more Jews married non-Jews, Israel became a convenient focal point around which to rally in solidarity.

Jewish communal organizations worldwide have gradually made support for Israel a civic religion around which to build a modern secular Jewish identity. Mainstream American Jewish organizations have used and expanded historical, religious, and cultural tropes in Judaism to cultivate among Jews a sense of connection and belonging to Israel and, through Israel, to one another. These organizations have encouraged "diaspora Jews" to connect to Israel through philanthropy, education, tourism, lobbying, and business ventures. We call these networks of power, finance, and culture that have used Israel to foster diasporic Jewish identities the "diaspora business."

The civic religion of Israel (and the diaspora business that helps build it) evokes resonant meanings and memory. For many Jews, Israel as a physical place remains an emotionally laden, highly effective symbol of Jewish solidarity that often induces powerful feelings of pride, ownership, and belonging. Even in the prestate period, such acts as purchasing wine, oranges, and other food products from Jewish farms in Palestine were championed as acts of Zionism. (These rituals had roots in premodern Jewish rituals about mythic Zion. Recall the town of Tuneyadevka's messianic ecstasy upon the arrival of the date.) The spatial meaning of Zion became something decidedly tangible, a romantic place to which one could send money for trees, daycare centers, and kibbutzim. Many rituals of American Zionism that had been developed in the prestate period became generalized rituals of American Jews. It became traditional for Jewish grandparents to give grandchildren Israeli bonds for a Bar Mitzvah or for a family to plant trees in Israel.[25] Giving money and claiming land became and still are the responsibility of "good" American Jews.

Through music, art, and other forms of creative expression (or forms of kitsch, depending on one's aesthetic taste), Jews have interpreted and imagined Israel as a physical place of meaning, memory, and community. In countless nostalgic songs from the Israeli folkloric tradition, lyricists have waxed poetic about the shores of the Sea of Galilee, the sand dunes that later became the sprawling metropolis of Tel Aviv, and Jerusalem as a city of gold. American Jews purchase paintings, posters, and knick-knacks that symbolize their connection to Israel through images of the Western Wall, the Chagall windows at Hadassah Hospital, the Temple Mount, and the Dead Sea. The body care company Ahava has built its reputation on its romantic connection to the waters and muds of the Dead Sea.[26]

But memory, of course, is always an unpredictable and complex process of construction and myth, particularly in a place as contested as Israel. Yael Zerubavel, in her book *Recovered Roots: Collective Memory and the Making of Israeli National Tradition,* has explored how the Zionist project relied heavily on the selective interpretation of history and traditions to reinvent memories around specific places, such as the fall of Masada and the Temple Mount in Jerusalem. Instead of remembering Masada as a gruesome site of mass suicide, Zionist shapers of memory (including educators, scholars, and military officials) sought to transform Masada into a place that symbolized steadfastness, conviction, and heroism. The physical space of Masada has now become thoroughly touristed and transformed into a national shrine, where American Jewish teenagers now hike the mountain at dawn to see the sun rise over Jordan.[27]

Visions of heroic, powerful Israel became widespread among Jews after the 1967 war, a war laden with emotional rhetoric about an impending second Holocaust. Israel's dramatic victory changed its relationship with global Jewry. For Soviet Jews and other Jews who never left Eastern Europe, Jews who were made invisible by the ghosts haunting global Jewry or were silenced by the Cold War, Zionism was a way to assert Jewishness and was a common way of expressing dissent. Jews in the Soviet Union, and throughout the Eastern bloc, celebrated the 1967 victory and began clamoring for the right to emigrate, especially as anti-Zionist politics became an important facet of Communist political rhetoric. A generation of young American Jews, influenced by the messages of the civil rights movement and the images of heroic Israeli soldiers recapturing the Western Wall, decided to immigrate to Israel and integrate as much as possible into Israeli culture.[28] Many American Jews latched onto Zionism as a source of Jewish pride, even as Israel's occupation of the West Bank, the Gaza Strip, and the Sinai Peninsula became a political liability in the world community.

By the 1970s, everything associated with Israel became important to Jewish communal policymakers, but not for the same reasons as in earlier generations. For American Jewish policymakers, Israel was an important way to sustain and bolster the continuity of American Jewish identities and communities. The Hebrew language was established as part of the curricula in colleges and Jewish high schools in the United States (even the Israeli pronunciation of Hebrew pushed out the once common Eastern European pronunciation taught in American Jewish schools, which is why our parents say "*Yisgadal, ve'yiskadash,*" while we were both trained to say "*Yitgadal, ve'yitkadash*"); Israel came to rival local Jewish charities as the leading recipient of Jewish donations; and a trip to Israel became an important part of a child's Jewish education. In many ways, Zionism reflected a cornerstone of Jewish culture and identity globally. Zionism showed that diaspora discourse was very successful, some say too successful. Israel became the place that would save global Jewry and also preserve an American Jewish identity, or so the policymakers hoped.

Except among leftist and socialist Jews, there was very little debate about Israeli politics and the Israeli government until the 1980s. Immediately after the 1967 War, third-world nationalist movements, socialist governments, and radical movements in the United States began to criticize Israel and Israeli policies toward the Palestinians in the territories, and, by the 1980s, the Zionist idea was no longer immune to criticism within the Jewish world, especially within Israel itself. The 1982 Israeli invasion of Lebanon, and the 1986 Palestinian uprising known as the intifada, turned Jewish victims into "Zionist oppressors" in some parts of the world. Jews in Israel began to engage in open debate and to criticize Israeli militarism for the first time. Communal leaders around the world began questioning whether too much attention was paid to Israel and not enough to "the home front." The British chief rabbi, Jonathan Sacks, pointed out, in 1994, that the dispatch of the greater part of Jewish charitable funds to Israel showed how British Jews had too deeply internalized the idea that they were somehow located on the periphery of Jewish life. He argued that British Jews should spend their Jewish pounds "at home," by which he meant Britain.[29] In Western public opinion, Israel was no longer the sweetheart of the world, the refuge for the oppressed, but was now seen by some as an oppressor in its own right and the object of too much Jewish attention.

Jews beyond Zionism

Some secular and religious Jews have gone so far as to question the certainty of the Zionist idea. Is there a place for a Jewish state in a multicultural, transnational world? Is it ethical to have two tiers of Israeli citizenship based on one's ethnic background, a system in which Jews were given more status than Arabs? By the 1990s, the Jewish voices of criticism, especially within Israel but also around the world, became louder. And thus was born the idea of post-Zionism—an ideology formulated by Israelis who questioned the foundational myths and ideologies of Israel. A whole generation of scholars and intellectuals, known as the "new historians," challenged passionately held beliefs about Israel's founding and about Israel's role in the Jewish world.[30] Did Israel need to be a "Jewish state," or should it become a secular democracy? Did Israel need to deny the messier and unsavory parts of its past in order to make people proud of it as a country? Did Israel still need to demand an in-gathering of all global Jews, or could it develop a healthy partnership *with* global Jews? For some, post-Zionism led to the question of whether a secular Jewish national state was even necessary for Jews to find pride in Jewish culture.[31]

This fear of the disunity of global Jewry has caused some to retrench. The United Jewish Appeal, in its campaigns to increase fund-raising among American Jews, emphasizes Jewish unity and vulnerability to make American Jews feel responsible for their embattled brethren around the world. And, in a grandiose statement of unity, in 1998, members of the Knesset and some leaders of American Jewry signed "A Covenant between the Jewish People of North America and Israel" that reiterated the popular slogan "We are one."

In contrast, as the Jewish Studies scholars Deborah Dash Moore and S. Ilan Troen state, "the intensity and frequency with which such declarations [about unity] are made indicate a growing need to counter a contrary reality."[32] Moore and Troen suggest that the Jewish world is moving toward a reality of greater diversity, toward a multiplicity of identities—"we are many." They are not alone. In the new book *Cultures of the Jews,* David Biale and the many participating authors show that the dynamic tension between unity and diversity has always defined Jews and their cultures from the days of the Bible.[33]

Since the 1980s and 1990s, some Jews have searched for alternatives to Zionism and Israel as the bases of secular Jewish identity and new interest in the diversity of Jewish culture. One place people turned to was the culture that was destroyed in the Holocaust—the Yiddish culture of Eastern Europe. Concerts of traditional folk music from Eastern Europe known as *klezmer* are sold out worldwide, Yiddish Studies courses have spread across college campuses, and publishing houses have begun publishing vast numbers of Yiddish books in English translation. Many of the people who began this search—often progressive, feminist, and queer Jews, but also the *haredim* (ultra-Orthodox) who nostalgically remember pre-Holocaust Eastern European Orthodox culture as the apex of religious Jewish life—felt marginalized by the dominance of Zionism and Israel in American Jewish culture. A second place has been the recovery of Sephardic history—of Jews who derive their roots from medieval Spain —and of Mizrachi cultures of Jews from the Middle East, two centers of Jewish life that historically have been marginalized by the dominance of Ashkenazi elites in the United States and Israel. Witness the rise of the Shas political party and the maintenance of separate North African Jewish communities in Israel, the emergence of IVRI-Nasawi (an association of Sephardic/Mizrachi writers and artists) in the United States, the incorporation of the American Sephardi Federation into New York's Center for Jewish History, the production of Ladino plays and cultural exhibits, and educational projects designed to challenge Ashkenazi hegemony.[34] The seeds of new types of Jewish cultures have begun to flourish, from both the right and the left.

Another direction or place people have turned is to celebrate diaspora. Rootlessness and wandering are valorized, diaspora nationalism is studied, Jews in farflung lands in as many languages as possible are mapped, as the embrace of diaspora becomes the leftist critique of a positivist Jewish history that ends in the establishment of Israel. The historian Howard Wettstein, in the collection *Exiles and Diasporas,* suggests that "exile" and "diaspora," traditionally treated as synonyms, are in fact distinct concepts within Jewish culture and history. Exile, according to Wettstein, presumes expulsion from a home and a sense of things being "not as they should be. Diaspora, on the other hand, although it suggests absence from some center—political or religious or cultural—does not connote anything so hauntingly negative."[35] Lawrence Silberstein, a scholar of Jewish culture, writes that Jewish Studies scholars should embrace the concepts and theories of hybrid and fragmented identities that postcolonial theorists have used to describe South Asian, African, and other historically colonized people.[36] Several popular writers, most of them American, have taken up the task of charting Jewish communities around the globe and have used the traditional idea of Jewish diaspora to capture not Jewish rootlessness but Jewish diversity in the modern world.[37] Finally, the noted scholars Daniel and Jonathan Boyarin argue that the two-thousand-year relationship Jews had with Zion as a mythic and messianic place sublimated the potential for political violence that such nationalistic yearnings for land could have had. "The solution of Zionism—that is, Jewish state hegemony, except insofar as it represented an emergency and temporary rescue operation—seems to us the subversion of Jewish culture and not its culmination. . . . Capturing Judaism in a state transforms entirely the meanings of its social practices."[38] As a mythic notion, Zion helped to maintain cultural continuity, community, and collective identity, without fostering a Jewish nationalism expressed in a desire for political power.

The work of the Boyarins has been instrumental in deconstructing static notions of Jewish identity by theorizing an anti-Zionist politics without negating the importance of Jews' connection to a place called Zion. The Boyarins turn to diaspora as a solution. "We propose Diaspora as a theoretical and historical model to replace national self-determination."[39] The Boyarins see a future of permanent and celebrated diaspora, not just for Jews but for all people. The Jews' two-thousand-year history of living apart from, and as part of, others' societies is a model for future interaction of various groups. For the Boyarins, such a conception "allows a formulation of Jewish identity not as a proud resting place (hence not as a form of integrism or nativism) but as a perpetual, creative diasporic tension."[40] This conception of diaspora allows Jews, like many indigenous peoples of the world, to have a connection to a land without having dominion over that land, a memory of place without power over place. Some contemporary European Jewish intellectuals, such as Richard Marienstras, call for a revival of diaspora Judaism through secular Hebrew and Yiddish culture, which he calls a "cultural politics of the Diaspora."[41] And scholars and writers have heeded this call by filling Jewish bookshelves with books about the Jewish diaspora.

We question whether the rise of diaspora as the concept that best articulates this kind of group and individual identity in the modern world has discounted or overshadowed the extent to which people—as individuals and as groups—are creating new forms of home in a more mobile world. Many scholars of other diasporas have shown the problems of presuming that "imagined communities"—groups that identify as a collective without each person knowing every member of the group— have centers and peripheries. And, as James Clifford points out, global people do not live "in diaspora," because global people do not live either "at home" or "in exile." For global people, home is constantly shifting.[42]

While Clifford and other scholars are interested in movement, mobility, frontiers, borders, and fluidity—ideas central to the body of theory known as transnationalism—we are interested in how people construct something called "home" and root themselves to those homes. The literary scholar Leah Garrett suggests that observers have seen the "Jewish condition" in one of two ways: "Critics often see Jews as having 'legs,' not 'roots.' If they are merely walking over the land, rather than rooted in it, their placement must always, and necessarily, be in relation to the lands that they traverse ('their' lands). The other choice becomes Zionist nationalism, where 'we' are at home on our land." Garrett argues that Yiddish literature offers a third alternative "of understanding how Jews on the cusp of modernism envisioned the world beyond 'Diaspora' and 'Zionism' . . . the third possibility is what we see in the literature of travel: the use of literature to revise the world and to envision the 'here and now' of Eastern Europe as our here and now. Jewish writers, then, were re-envisioning the Jewish map, reconceiving the relationship between here and there, as part of modernization." For these writers, Zion could be right where they were.[43]

The following chapters explore the ways in which Jews today craft identities, not as diasporic, homeless, or exilic subjects but as people rooted in and tied to particular places. These roots shape how new Jews identify themselves and view the world and how new Jews also traverse many places as part of the process of communal identity formation.

Methodologically, we approach these questions as an historian and a sociologist, and this book reflects our interdisciplinary approach. We interweave historical analysis, literary readings, interview data, and ethnographic research in each of these chapters to show the many ways Jews are thinking about the end of diaspora.[44] We interrupt the narrative flow of the text to include stories and notes from our research trips as a way to show how we ourselves are implicated in these processes, since our own lives are evidence of Jewry going global. We are both scholars and activists who have traveled to many places to do research, visit families, and go on holiday, while approaching each of these places as American Jews raised in the suburbs in the 1970s. Caryn has visited Israel numerous times and also lived there to write her dissertation during the Oslo peace process of the 1990s, while David lived in Moscow during the same period.

Politically, we want to question the centrality of Israel in Jewish geography, culture, and memory. And intellectually, we want to move beyond the term "diaspora" as a mode of explaining postmodern collective identity, since such a conceptualization reinforces notions of centers and peripheries and emphasizes motion and rootlessness, often at the expense of home and rootedness.

Rather than refer to Jews as "in Israel" or "in (the) diaspora," we refer to new Jews as "global" and break down the inherent dichotomy that the Israel/diaspora metaphor maintains. In this post-Zionist, post-Soviet, post-American-melting-pot moment, we show that looking at Jews as global rather than diasporic/Israeli serves several purposes.

First, we wonder why people still break down Jewish identity and Jewish geography into two metacategories—Israel and everyone else commonly referred to as "the diaspora." Such labeling has the homogenizing effect of suggesting that everyone not in Israel has something in common and that all those in Israel share a common experience. In this way, we question the place of privilege of Jews who live in Israel within the Israel/diaspora dichotomy.

Second, we question the very notion of a unified Jewish people who live within these two categories of Israel and diaspora. We argue that a collective unified whole, "the Jewish people," does not describe how Jewish identities and communities operate and instead use the idea of Jewish peoples. The idea of unity is often mobilized to create a semblance of collective solidarity in response to historical persecution or in order to make Jews feel responsible for people with whom they may have very little in common.[45] As Jews, especially in America, feel more secure socially and economically and have power over place and space, they are beginning to examine internal differences. The question of Jewish difference has become all the more pressing with the mass migration of Jews from the former Soviet Union to Israel, Germany, and the United States. These groups of Jews speak different languages from the Jews in their new host countries, maintain different senses of Jewish identity, and often maintain separate communal institutions. By examining how Jews feel rooted in different places, such as Los Angeles, Moscow, and Jerusalem, and how Jews experience places and their Jewishness differently, we emphasize Jewish diversity. What does, in fact, an upper-middle-class professional, secular Jew in Los Angeles have in common with a working-class Israeli Sephardic religious Jew in Bnei Brak except the fact that each one calls herself a Jew?

Third, by deemphasizing "diaspora," which connotes powerlessness, and "homeland," which connotes power, we suggest that power within the Jewish world—cultural, political, economic—flows in many directions and to and from diverse places.

Jews Dismantling Diaspora

We believe that the valorization of diaspora has been useful, not just for Jews but for all groups of people who live in multiple places, for deconstructing notions of permanence and of the assumed confluence of space, place, and culture. But the rise of diaspora—the celebration of displacement, rootlessness, exile, and hybridity—has overshadowed the ways in which many Jews are remaking their sense of home and establishing new kinds of roots, not just to particular pieces of land but also to concepts, ideas, stories, and spaces. To understand Jewish cultural and identity formations in the contemporary world, we believe that, as Barbara Kirschenblatt-Gimblett put it, "we need to theorize how space is being reterritorialized in the contemporary world."[46] Kirschenblatt-Gimblett also suggests that the ability of people, money, and culture to move around the world easily and rapidly "not only divides and disperses people and activities that once occupied a contiguous space—and not only or necessarily by means of violence—but also collapses spaces of dispersal by abbreviating the time it takes to get from here to there."[47] She encourages us to consider the "uncoupling of displacement, dispersion, and diaspora." Zvi Gitelman agrees that "we are moving to a global shtetl; Jewish people have been drawn into closer and more frequent contact with each other by contemporary communications, by increased travel due to technology and affluence, by a sense of mutual responsibility stimulated by the Holocaust as evinced in the campaigns for Soviet, Syrian, and Ethiopian Jewry, by greater access to the former Soviet Union and Eastern Europe, and by the centrality of Israel as a common denominator for world Jewry."[48] Maybe people who have some kind of collective identity, or who make up an imagined community, can be dispersed without the experience of displacement.

But why rely on diaspora at all? The term has become a catch-all phrase to describe complex spatial and identity formations in a fragmented world. Since all imagined communities live in multiple places, one could easily argue that all groups could fit under the rubric "diaspora." If anyone can consider himself or herself a part of a diaspora, then the word loses its meaning. Another problem with the term "diaspora" is that it still presumes that there is a single center of a given community, an idea that the example of contemporary Jewry shows is simply not true. As Kirschenblatt-Gimblett states, "New spaces of dispersal are produced —traversed and compressed by technologies of connection and telepresence. Physical locations can be experienced as accidents of proximity, while common interest, rather than common location, can become the basis of social life in a medium where location is defined not by geographical coordinates but by the topic of conversation."[49] Among those who study Jews, according to Biale, "the categories of Israel and Diaspora no longer occupy the central place in scholarly agendas they once held."[50]

Young Jews understand this. *Kol Dor* (Voice of a Generation), an international network of twenty- and thirty-something Jewish leaders from twelve countries, including Israel, met for its first conference in May 2004. One of the group's first resolutions stated that participants refuse to use any kind of "Israel-Diaspora" discourse and instead would speak in terms of a "global Jewish discourse."[51] Some young Jews from around the world, then, are abandoning diaspora because it envisions the Jewish world hierarchically with Israel on top, "the diaspora" on bottom. Young American Jews are also questioning the links between Israeli Jews and those in other parts of the world. In the recent National Jewish Population Survey, only 20 percent of Jewish college students felt "very emotionally attached to Israel."[52]

We suggest that a global politics that recognizes the tensions between rootedness and movement and the realness of both should guide our thinking about identities and spaces. In this book, we explore ways Jews are making home in a global, not diasporic, world. We examine how Jews use travel, money, memory, organizations, and power to constitute new identities and to create new relationships to real and mythic homelands, and we show that often the real and the mythic are the same place. We also show how the ability to be rooted, to live in a postdiasporic moment, is a sign of affluence, power, and privilege as Jews have "made it" in many of the societies in which they live.

Chapter 1, about Jews in Moscow, describes the activities of Jews who resist the notion that they somehow do not live at home where they are and should live in Israel or the United States. Moscow's Jews are the ones who spurned the Exodus narrative that Israeli and American Jews created for them during the Cold War. By seeing how today's Jews in Moscow struggle to assert their own forms of identity and community, we want to emphasize diversity within global Jewry and to expose the financial, cultural, and social power dynamics that shape Jewish identities and communities. In chapter 2, we use the experiences of American Jews who travel to and live in Eastern Europe and Israel to introduce the idea of the "diaspora business" and to question what it means to be an Israeli or an American Jew. We examine March of the Living and taglit birthright israel, two teen/young adult Jewish identity travel programs, to show how diaspora discourse is taught, spread, and contested.[53] We ask why Jews in America feel that they need to send their children to Israel in order for them to feel Jewish and how Jews create a new Jewish map by imagining Eastern Europe (where more than 1.5 million Jews still live) to be a graveyard, while Israel is envisioned as the land of triumph. Chapter 3 explores two Jewish museums in Los Angeles and asks what it means to be a Jew in America. We compare the Museum of Tolerance, one of the first Holocaust museums in the United States, with the Skirball Cultural Center to show how different Jewish communities and generations present America as a homeland for Jews. Chapter 4, about lesbian, gay, bisexual, and transgender Jews in Israel and North America, explores the multiple identities of Jews who traverse many global communities. We explore how national cultures and roots to those cultures affect individual and communal identities.

Our final chapter shows that New York is the place around which the global Jewish world pivots. We show how New York is the center of the diaspora business, home of the largest Russian-speaking Jewish community in the world, ahead of Moscow,[54] home to the most important Jewish art museum and one of the most innovative Jewish historical museums in the world, the site of the only queer Jewish synagogue in the world with two full-time rabbis and several rabbinic interns, and also the home of multiple and multiethnic Jewish communities.

In all of these chapters, we examine the national, symbolic, and intimate processes of homemaking by showing Jews exerting power over space and place, and over one another, across different geopolitical boundaries, and through various media and cultural practices. To call a place home is a statement of power (Zionists know this best). By arguing that a place is home, Jews express a sense of entitlement, control, and familiarity. Home is a place where people practice identity and intimacy. We examine both the ways that Jewish discourses reinscribe diaspora into the language of global Jews and at the same time how global Jews encounter these discourses, sometimes actively resisting, others times passively ignoring the idea of diaspora.

If the Boyarins lament the founding of a political state as that which undermined the traditional, benign relationship of Jews to a mythic Zion, Palestinians lament the founding of a political state as that which made Palestinians into a diaspora. Jews in the United States, Russia, Germany, and elsewhere are, in many ways, privileged, because they can choose where to live and can visit family members and friends in multiple places around the world. Palestinians do not have such a choice. The Right of Return is a privilege that allows Jews to construct new kinds of relationships to their mythic and real homes, and the presence of a diaspora business allows Jews to root themselves in, and route themselves to, many places. If (or, more likely, when) a Palestinian state comes to exist, Palestinians around the world will, we hope, have the opportunity to decide where to live and will have the privilege and choice of asking, "Where is home?" as Jews have. We recognize that this discussion implies power over place, both discursive power and military power, and we also recognize that discourse and guns are not the same thing. Our attempt to unravel the power dynamics that shape Jewish communities and identities in a global world is meant to expose both the diversity and the privilege of global Jewish experience.

That Jews are privileged may feel ironic precisely because many global Jews feel embattled, vulnerable, and under siege. The research for this project took place both before and after September 11, 2001, before and after the decline of the Israeli economy, the start of the second intifada, the American occupation of Iraq, and the recent rise in criticism of Israeli policies that at times elides into criticism of global Jewry. Ironically, it is the very idea that Israel is the Jewish homeland and, therefore, that all Jews are tied to this political entity that has also blurred the boundaries between criticism of Israeli politics and criticism of Jews writ large. If Jews have trouble drawing a line between global Jewry and the State of Israel, it is no wonder that others do, too.

In this climate, we recognize that some Jews do not feel privileged, some Jews do not feel safe, and some Jews no longer feel rooted. Most Jews we talk to these days feel a heightened sense of precariousness about their identities as Jews in this historical period of uncertainty. Jews in Europe feel threatened by an increase in anti-Semitic acts. Some of the Americans in Israel described in chapter 2 have left Israel and returned to the United States as violence has increased and the opportunities for employment have vanished. Taglit/birthright israel has at times struggled to recruit American Jewish students to take advantage of its free trips to Israel. Parents of teenagers on the March of the Living have been afraid for the children's safety, not in Poland but in Israel.[55] As American rabbis tell their congregants to stop traveling to "anti-Semitic" Europe and go "support the Jewish state" with their tourist dollars, many Israelis are simultaneously leaving Israel for calmer waters in the United States. And, late in 2004, two key figures on the Israeli political scene resurrected the Zionist imperative to move to Israel. Ariel Sharon called on French Jewry to abandon the land of Jewish emancipation and the French Revolution, a place he referred to as the home of the "wildest anti-Semitism," for safer ground in the Holy Land. Not surprisingly, some French Jewish organizations took offense at the notion that they were somehow not at home in France.[56] More disturbingly, the former chief rabbi of Israel, Rabbi Israel Meir Lau, declared that Jews should all leave Europe: "I'm telling you there is no future for European Jewry."[57]

No home is permanent, no group is ever permanently rooted or permanently diasporic, and power over places, communities, and identities can be gained or lost. As Jews feel threatened and as criticism of Israeli policies mounts, many cling to ideas of safety and refuge and reassert the unity of the Jewish people. But perhaps it is precisely in times of turmoil, when home feels unsafe, when others are clamoring for power, that Jews should not see power as a zero-sum game but should recognize their privileged position in the world as a people with internal diversities and multiple homes and should engage the world not out of fear but out of the power of rootedness.

1

Let My People Stay
Moscow's Jews after the Exodus

A Russian joke: "You know that the Soviet Union had fifteen re-
publics. But do you know which one became the sixteenth?" "Israel."

Jews feel much freer in Russia, and can now decide for themselves
whether or not to stay or leave.
> —Rabbi Berel Lazar, Chabad rabbi (one of two chief rabbis
> of Russia, and a close associate of Vladimir Putin)

To be a Jew in Russia means to return to your roots.
> —Rabbi Adolf Shayevich, traditional Orthodox rabbi (the other
> chief rabbi of Russia, and *not* a close associate of Putin)

    In the summer of 2004, Caryn joined David on one of his an-
nual research trips to Moscow. The two of us went in order to examine
together how Moscow Jews define themselves in an era when the state is
no longer intimately involved in shaping identity, as had been the case in
the Soviet Union for seventy years. We chose to focus on Moscow because
it is the home of a wide range of local and international Jewish organizations and is by far the largest urban center in the former Soviet Union (the
city of Moscow is home to nearly ten million people, with several million
more living in the surrounding region). Moscow became a Jewish city in
the twentieth century only after the Communists lifted restrictions on
Jewish residence. In the 1920s, hundreds of thousands of Jews migrated
to Moscow from the smaller cities of Ukraine and Belorussia, quickly
transforming the city into one of the world's largest Jewish population
centers.[1] Although Moscow lost tens of thousands of Jews during World
War II and the Holocaust, the city's Jewish population was not deci-

mated, as was the case in so many other Eastern European and Russian cities, because the Nazis never occupied the city. Moscow, therefore, maintained a continuous and always growing Jewish population throughout the twentieth century.[2] Finally, we chose to study Moscow, because demographically Moscow's Jews look very much like Jews in other major metropolitan areas worldwide—integrated, relatively wealthy, and secular.

Have Moscow's post-Soviet Jews set up synagogues, Jewish schools, and summer camps the way their American coreligionists did throughout the twentieth century? Are today's Moscow Jews interested in being Jewish at all after living without Jewish community for so long? Most observers of Jewish life in Russia, along with the primarily American- and Israeli-based international Jewish organizations that have funded rescue efforts to "save them" during both the Soviet and the post-Soviet eras, use words like "crisis," "decline," or, in a fit of hyperbole, "end" to describe Moscow Jewish life.[3] But this language and these dire predictions echo the concerns and fears that drive American Jews to "save their children" from intermarriage and assimilation by sending them to Israel and Auschwitz. Did Moscow's Jews see the same problems and feel the same anxiety about their future? How could one of the largest Jewish communities in the world be dying?[4]

From David's field notes, June 2002:

It's been nearly three years since I was last in Moscow in 1999. In my first twenty-four hours during this current research visit, I was immediately struck by the fact that Jews seemed to be everywhere . . . at least traces of Jews. At the Russian Conservatory, "the Julliard School" of Russia, I saw an advertisement for a concert of "Jewish national and contemporary Israeli music" sponsored by the Union of Jewish Religious Organizations of Russia. While walking by music kiosks in Moscow's subway stations, I had already glimpsed CDs of Jewish folk music. I saw a Hasidic Jew walking down the street. I even saw a huge banner in the Moscow subway from the Jewish Agency, Israel's emigration agency, advertising study abroad programs in Israel. Okay, so maybe I'm a bit oversensitive to "spotting the Jew," but there were certainly more traces of Jews in Moscow than I had witnessed in the past.

At the same time, I also had my first experience (first for this trip, anyway) with the pervasive and shockingly normative anti-Semitism of Russian culture and society. While dealing with visa issues at a travel agency whose offices are located in the former Union of Soviet Writers' building, I checked out a book kiosk located in the lobby of the building. The kiosk had a banner over it suggesting that it was an official book seller of the current Union of Russian Writers, but its affiliation was not clear. Among titles from Pushkin, books about Russian Orthodoxy, and other literary and religious texts, I found the following titles: *The Protocols of the Elders of Zion, The Zionist Factor,* and the ever popular *Jewish Fascism.* I almost didn't notice these "classic" anti-Semitic titles, but a woman browsing next to me pointed them out to me. Without batting an eyelash, she asked the salesman, "Do you have *The Protocols?*"

"Of course," as he pointed out the beaten up display copy sitting on the table that had clearly been examined by many customers before her. She looked at it, put it down, and I then picked it up.

"Is this a good book?" I asked her.

"Certainly."

"Why?"

"It tells you how the world runs."

After desperately searching for another copy, the salesman returned to tell the distraught woman that unfortunately they only had the tattered display copy of the *Protocols* left. Might she be interested in *Jewish Fascism?*

As I stood there, not expecting to be "doing research" while waiting to fix my visa, I realized that I needed to rethink my research agenda. I had come to Moscow to observe, take part in, and try to understand the growth and development of Jewish life in Moscow. I wanted to understand how Moscow's Jews resist what most Jews outside the former Soviet Union see as this community's future: anti-Semitism, emigration to Israel and the West, and the simultaneous slow death of Jewish life in Moscow. I also assumed that the overwhelming emphasis on Russian anti-Semitism and Russian Jewish intermarriage on the part of American and Israeli Jewish organizations might be a bit overstated.

And here I was, being taught about the importance of the *Protocols of the Elders of Zion* in the building of the former Union of Soviet Writers. Was I wrong? Was the emigration narrative still the most obvious response Jews could have to life in Moscow? Were there ways to fight against anti-Semitism? Was anti-Semitism really as central to crafting Jewish identity in Moscow as non-Soviet Jews think it is? What should I have said to this woman? I told her I was Jewish. At that moment, she had two options: apologize for offending me and go about her business or recoil in shock that she had spoken to the enemy. She chose the second option, turned, and left.

David's brief conversation with this woman reminded him that as much as he was searching for ways in which Jews are settled in Moscow, how the idea of diaspora, of not feeling at home while longing for some other "home," namely Zion, might not best describe the way many Jews view the world, perhaps it did describe life for Moscow's Jews. At least that was his gut reaction as an American outsider in Russia.

Moscow's Jews do not respond to this kind of experience as viscerally as David did. He told several Moscow Jewish contacts, friends, and informants about the encounter, and the general response was: "David, she was a stupid peasant woman. What's the big deal?" They took a certain level of social anti-Semitism for granted. Indeed, the historian Bernard Wasserstein argues that post-Soviet Jews live in a constant state of fear of anti-Semitism, and he thinks that this is what makes all post-Soviet Jews into potential emigrants.[5] But what David's informants were saying was that, yes, they lived with social anti-Semitism, but they did not live with fear.

As David spoke with integrated, urban, secular Jews, it was clear that for most of them, anti-Semitism did not shake their sense of feeling settled in Moscow. But the incident forced David, as an American, to ask how Jews can feel settled here even when other Russians continue to treat them as foreigners.

Winston Churchill once described Russia as "a riddle wrapped in a mystery inside an enigma." To many contemporary observers, it seems that Moscow's Jews are, as well. On the one hand, since the Soviet Union opened a tiny crack in its borders in the 1970s, emigration from the "land of state-sponsored anti-Semitism" has been the dominant lens through which everyone has seen Jewish life in Russia. "Get the Jews out of the land of oppression," demanded Jewish organizations in the United States, Israel, and Western Europe. "To where?" was another question. But with the Soviet Union gone, the black-and-white world of the free liberal West and the evil, repressive anti-Semitic Soviet Union no longer exists, and now locals and global Jewish organizations are deeply involved in shaping Russia's Jewish present and future.

Because of the mass emigration of Soviet Jewry, most Moscow Jews have family in Israel, the United States, Europe, or Australia. The presence of Russian Jews around the world allows Moscow to function as "home" for this Russian "diaspora" community. Moscow is now at the center of a Jewish universe, one that is Russian speaking but often equally at home in Hebrew and English.

For example, Mikhail, one of the people we interviewed for this book, is a powerful media mogul living in Moscow.[6] He is Jewish and has immediate family that lives in Israel and relatives in the United States. His Jewish family network is global, but Mikhail is settled in Moscow. He has no desire to move anywhere else . . . and why would he? He has a great job, access to power, and a deep social network—of Jews and non-Jews. Despite being at home as a Jew in Moscow, he does not participate in anything Jewish and has no connection to the city's Jewish community.

It is Mikhail's lack of Jewish communal connection that causes alarm for Jewish leaders around the world, the same alarm that prompts American Jews to fund tours like taglit/birthright israel and March of the Living. But Mikhail does not see that there is a problem. He does not worry about the fact that Jews and non-Jews marry, nor is he as interested in anti-Semitism as Americans and Israelis are. For post-Soviet Jews, intermarriage and anti-Semitism are facts of life, not problems to worry about and solve. But as global Jewish organizations become more influential in local Jewish affairs, Mikhail may soon be preoccupied with these questions.

As emigration from Russia declines and Moscow's Jews feel settled, we show how Moscow is becoming integrated into the global Jewish order by examining the people, institutions, and financing that help build home in Moscow. From the establishment of two competing Jewish community centers to the very public struggles between rabbis who represent different versions of Jewish authenticity, the debates about being a Jew at home in Moscow reflect the tension between local and global Jewish identities. If the history of Jews in Moscow is so different from other Jewish histories, why does Jewish communal development in Moscow now look so similar?

The Cold War, The "Exodus," and Russian Jewish Identities

In the years shortly after the Bolshevik Revolution, in 1917, Jews became one of the most vibrant social and cultural groups within Soviet society. The new government professed socialism and atheism and oversaw the massive urbanization of Soviet citizens, notable among them Jews. Most Jews therefore developed secular identities that had little to do with the religion and traditions of the small towns, known as *shtetls* in Yiddish, that many of their parents and grandparents had come from. Starting in 1932, the state became directly involved in shaping Jewish identity through the use of internal passports, which had a section identifying each Soviet citizen by his or her "nationality." In the Soviet Union, Jews constituted a separate nationality, and their lives and senses of self were shaped by what was printed in their passports.

Through the 1930s, the state even supported the attempts of socialist Jewish intellectuals to organize and promote Soviet Jewish national identity and culture through Yiddish newspapers, films, publishing houses, and schools.[7] But, with World War II, the Holocaust, and the inauguration of Stalin's official anti-Semitism in the 1940s, Jews' connection to even a secular or cultural Jewish identity became tenuous at best. The same Soviet Yiddish culture that had been developed in the 1920s with state support was suppressed by the state, and in the late 1940s, many Jewish intellectuals were arrested and murdered on charges of "nationalism," "Zionism," and "cosmopolitanism," words that were splashed on Soviet newspapers in the years before Stalin's death in 1953. Even after Stalin's death, Soviet Jews feared the label "Jew," the word printed in their passports, as it sometimes prevented them from being accepted into institutions of higher education or from being awarded particular government posts. Jewish cultural and social organizations that flourished in the interwar period disappeared, and, with them, so too did a public Jewish culture. During the general liberalization in Soviet society in the 1960s, Jews began to respond to state-sponsored anti-Semitism by joining movements aimed at reforming the government.

In some cases, in response to state anti-Semitism, Jews developed their own forms of Jewish identity and community.[8] One Soviet-era underground publication (*samizdat*), called *I Am a Jew,* proposed some ways Jews self-identified as Jews.[9] Writers in the collection argued that what distinguished Jews from other people was a passion for education and their social position, both of and apart from Soviet society. After the 1967 Six-Day War in Israel and the subsequent rise of Soviet anti-Zionism, learning Hebrew and becoming a Zionist were two of the most common ways Jews simultaneously expressed a Jewish self-identity and an anti-Soviet politics.

In the 1970s, the Soviet Union began granting exit visas in a gesture of détente, and some Soviet Jews spoke with their feet by leaving the Soviet Union, primarily for Israel or the United States.[10] The American Jewish drive to help Soviet Jews emigrate followed directly on the heels of the civil rights movement. For some American Jews in the New Left, the émigré campaign became a new form of activism as the 1960s movement splintered into more specific ethnic, gender, and racial groups. Jews lobbied their congressional representatives, protested at Soviet embassies, established letter-writing campaigns, and, in one case, even resorted to terrorism.[11] On the issue of Soviet Jews, American Jewish liberal politics calling for civil rights dovetailed with Cold War anti-Communism, which was looking for anything at all to create an atmosphere of anti-Sovietism. What better cause than the persecuted Jews in the Soviet Union?[12] In fact, despite Jewish integration into early Soviet society, Western Jews have long protested "Jewish persecution" in the Soviet Union as a way to express anti-Communist sentiments. As early as 1930, the American Jewish Congress called a conference to protest the persecution of rabbis in the Soviet Union and succeeded in obtaining release for several rabbis who had been imprisoned for illegally leading Jewish congregations.[13]

In the 1970s, similar lobbying efforts were so successful that the U.S. Congress passed the Jackson-Vanik Amendment, in 1974, which linked the granting of most-favored-nation trading status to recognition of human rights in a given country. In this case, the human rights problem was the inability of Soviet Jews to emigrate. The United States designated Soviet émigrés as political refugees, allowing those who did leave to easily come to America. In the 1970s, with Zionist sentiment increasing in popularity among American Jews, especially after the 1967 and 1973 wars in Israel, the voices calling for the freedom for Jews to emigrate overwhelmed those voices calling for the freedom to practice Judaism wherever Jews wanted. It was the Exodus story all over again, and books began appearing with titles like *Let My People Go*.[14]

While American politicians adopted the cause of Jewish emigration as a new tool in their anti-Soviet campaign, Israelis pointed to continuing Soviet anti-Semitism to remind the world why Israel, which saw itself as the place of refuge for world Jewry, was necessary in the first place. Since its founding, in 1948, Israel had courted Jewish emigrants from around the world to help build and populate the "Jewish state." The Law of Return, Israel's special Jewish immigration law, gives the right of citizenship to every Jew and to his or her family members in two descending generations. Israeli immigration law uses the Jewish legal (*halachic*) definition to answer the question "Who is a Jew?" But the desire to import more potential Israeli citizens was so strong that, in 1971, Israel expanded the Law of Return to include Soviet Jews' non-Jewish relatives in two descending generations. Although in Israel non-Jewish spouses of Soviet Jews were and are considered non-Jews, in Russian society anyone—regardless of passport, self-identity, or religious affiliation—who has the right to immigrate to Israel is seen as a Jew.

With this new law, early Soviet émigrés followed the Zionist path to Israel. Emigration and, more specifically, immigration to Israel (*aliyah*) was the primary route envisioned by global Jews for Soviet Jewry, a route funded by the diaspora business and by Israel's Jewish Agency as a way to increase the Jewish population of Israel.[15] American organizations and the Israeli political electorate made the leaders of this Exodus, like Ida Nudel and Natan Sharansky, into popular figures and heroes.[16]

The Soviet Union's oppressive policies and its destruction of Jewish culture, however, were only part of the reason that American and Israeli Jews thought Soviet Jews needed to leave. In addition, the American and Israeli post-Holocaust perception of Eastern Europe as dead Jewish space—a vision reflected through trips like March of the Living—only added weight to the idea that a living Jewish future could not happen in Russia.[17]

With the gradual and sporadic lifting of emigration restrictions under Brezhnev and then Gorbachev, Jews began applying en masse for exit visas. The diaspora business focused on the question of exit, leaving the question of where to immigrate up to the migrants. But Israelis intended for Soviet, and then post-Soviet, Jews to come specifically to Israel, even if that was not the first choice of migrants themselves. The route for Russian Jews would be, as the title of several books suggested, "from Moscow to Jerusalem." In the words of Bernard Wasserstein, "an unholy alliance developed between Moscow and Jerusalem, each of which for its own reasons wished to prevent emigration to countries other than Israel."[18]

Emigration fever decimated Soviet Jewry demographically and culturally. Between 1968 and 1989, 240,000 Jews (or 11 percent of the Jewish population, according to the 1970 Soviet Census) left the Soviet Union.[19] In the beginning, most Jews went to Israel, but by 1978, more than 50 percent of Soviet Jewish émigrés headed to the United States. In fact, most Russian Jews originally had left the Soviet Union for socioeconomic, rather than religious or Zionist, reasons.[20] And, given the harsh anti-Israel propaganda in the Soviet media and the less-than-flattering reports some new immigrants to Israel were giving about life there, it is not surprising that the United States seemed a more appealing destination. Most Russian émigrés saw the United States as the land of opportunity, while Israel was the land of last resort or a way station to somewhere better, since any Jew, and even non-Jewish family members, could get a visa there.

The twenty-year period of Jewish emigration from the Soviet Union was marked by ups and downs in the rate of emigration. After the Soviet invasion of Afghanistan in 1980, U.S. grain embargoes, and the end of U.S.-Soviet détente, the Soviet Union no longer felt compelled by Jackson-Vanik, and Jewish emigration was cut off. From 1980 to 1985, few Soviet Jews left the country, and it is in these years that the "refusenik" movement developed, complete with rituals and symbols intended to cultivate solidarity among American Jews. American Jews held door-to-door fund-raising drives, protested, and held "twinning" Bar and Bat Mitzvah ceremonies for the "silent" Soviet Jews who could no longer leave their land of oppression. (David had a twin-in-absentia at his Bar Mitzvah, in 1985, Igor Vaisman, from Kishinev. Whether or not Igor would have appreciated the gesture or found it another example of American presumption about other people's identity work is a question he has not been able to answer.)

The early 1980s clampdown on emigration after the 1970s exodus also forced Soviet Jews to envision a domestic Jewish community and a Russian Jewish religious identity, distinct from the secular identities held by most Jews since the Bolshevik Revolution.[21] In 1983, Zinovy Kogan started a progressive Jewish prayer group, known as a *minyan,* in his kitchen. In Minsk, activists formed a Zionist group and in 1988 constituted a Hebrew teachers' association. Minsk Jews also established *ulpanim,* intensive Hebrew classes, for prospective emigrants to Israel. By the late 1980s, as a result of *glasnost,* Moscow's Jews and Jews throughout the Soviet Union began finding new ways of self-identifying as ethnic and religious Jews. By 1991, fifty-five different Jewish newspapers, magazines, and other publications circulated in the nearly defunct Soviet Union.[22] In the years that followed, Moscow alone saw the establishment of several schools, institutes of higher education, cultural groups, social groups, and several religious congregations. By mid-1994, there were four *yeshivas,* four Jewish teachers' seminaries, and four religious day schools in Moscow. Despite the lament of many Jewish leaders that most

Russian Jews do not participate in Jewish organizations, institutions, or communities, since 1994, the number of Jewish institutions, publications, and other markers of community in Moscow has continued to increase.

Simultaneously, throughout the 1990s, Jews continued to leave. In 1989, Gorbachev opened up emigration, and a precipitous drop in the Jewish population of the Soviet Union began. But, given this liberalization, the United States stopped marking Soviet Jews as refugees. As the Cold War ended, and the borders to the United States became less porous, immigration to Israel increased dramatically.[23] From 1990 to 1993, 578,029 Russian Jews emigrated, most going to Israel. In December 1990 alone, more than 34,000 immigrants arrived in Israel, the highest number in one month in Israeli history.[24] By 1994, Jewish emigration had permanently altered the character and composition of the Jewish state, almost immediately influencing the political discourse and party system in the *Knesset* (Israeli parliament). Between 1989 and 2003, more than 930,000 Jews and their non-Jewish relatives from the former Soviet Union settled in Israel, about 378,000 emigrated to the United States, and roughly 200,000 went to Germany.[25] Zvi Gitelman, one of the foremost observers of contemporary Russian Jewish demographics and identity, laments that "the Jewish population of the former Russian Empire and Soviet Union had shrunk to a little over 10% of what it had been at the beginning of [the twentieth] century, from 5.2 million to about 600,000."[26] Others give much higher statistics for the number of Jews remaining in the former Soviet Union. One Russian source suggests a number of 1.5 million.[27] Although emigration fever subsided in the early 1990s, Jews continued to emigrate in large numbers.

Most observers presume that there is a direct link between these high rates of emigration and anti-Semitism. But, at the very moment emigration peaked in the late 1980s and early 1990s, the Soviet Union officially abandoned anti-Semitism. Since then, Russian leaders have decried acts of anti-Semitism and have constantly reminded Jews that they should feel at home in Russia. In 1996, the Russian state abandoned its effort to police national identity by eliminating the line in passports that asked citizens to declare their nationality. The state no longer defines Jews.

The First Ones In: Global Jews Come to Moscow

As Israeli and American organizations and governments were organizing an exodus, and as Russian Jewish émigrés were setting up homes and communities in New York, Tel Aviv, Düsseldorf, and Berlin, Moscow Jews were simultaneously reestablishing Russian Jewish culture in Moscow. They did so with the help of global Jewish organizations that understood Jewish life in two ways—as a religion and as a collective identity. These organizations had a difficult time understanding and grappling with the legacies of how the Soviet state defined Jews and how Moscow Jews defined themselves.

Enter Chabad-Lubavitch, an outreach branch of Hasidic Judaism focused on helping Jews strengthen their ties to Judaism. Chabad prides itself on fostering Jewish life wherever Jews are, even under difficult conditions. The movement claims that throughout the Soviet era, rather than supporting initiatives to get Soviet Jews out, it was secretly fostering Jewish life by bringing in Jewish books and arranging exchanges between Soviet Jews and undercover Chabad emissaries.[28] With the advent of *perestroika,* and then the collapse of Communism, Chabad wasted no time in establishing a presence in Russia, seeing an opportunity to make "lapsed Jews," like the secular Mikhail, into better Jews. Chabad very quickly became the dominant and most politically connected Jewish organization in Russia, and, in 1999, in a sign of political and institutional independence, it separated from other national Jewish groups to form its own Federation of Jewish Communities of Russia (FJCR).[29]

By early 2005, Chabad boasted of an institutional presence in nearly forty cities in Russia alone, and its network continues to expand.[30] In Moscow, Chabad sponsors dozens of different organizations, including schools, ritual bathhouses (*mikvehs*), a burial society (*chevrah kadisha*), a bookstore, a kosher food store, and four different congregations.[31] When observant Jews visit Moscow, they invariably end up at a Chabad-sponsored institution—either for kosher meat, religious services, or local Jewish news. According to its own statistics, the Chabad Russian-language monthly magazine, *Lekhaim,* has a national circulation of fifty thousand even though the number of Chabad-affiliated Jews in Russia is only ten thousand to fifteen thousand.[32] In other words, most consumers of Chabad's publications and programs are not Hasidic Jews. Chabad's mission is to be public and proactive about helping former Soviet Jews "rediscover" their Judaism.[33]

The head Chabad rabbi of Russia is Berel Lazar, who is based in Moscow but spends much of his time touring throughout the former Soviet Union. He is a native of Milan, Italy, and spent ten years in the United States training to be a rabbi before moving to Russia in the early 1990s. He first became interested in the Soviet Union in the 1980s when he was sent there on an official cultural exchange. He encountered "the difficult living conditions in Russia" and at the same time was moved by "the underground activists who not only saved the structure of Jewish life but also tried to spread knowledge about it."[34] In 2000, the Chabad organization of Russia named him "chief rabbi of Russia," a title that other media sources and even the Russian president began applying to him. In October 2000, Rabbi Lazar appeared with Vladimir Putin for the opening of a Jewish community center in Moscow, showing that the president was giving de facto consent to Lazar's new title. In March 2002, U.S. president George W. Bush made the first visit by an American president to a Russian synagogue in St. Petersburg and had a meeting with Lazar.

It is perhaps odd that a Russian-speaking, Italian Hasidic Jew trained in the United States has been named chief rabbi of Russia, a country where most Jews eat pork and do not know the names of the five books of the Torah. The screaming divide between the nontraditional Jewish identities of Jews in Moscow and Rabbi Lazar's appearance and observance is even more obvious than the fact that he is not Russian. Chabad forces Moscow Jews to ask a question that might not have occurred to them otherwise: "Who is an authentic Jew?"

The fact that a Lubavitch rabbi functions as the symbolic head of Russian Jewry demonstrates that Chabad's goals of expanding the Jewish population in Russia, its tight connections with sources of political and economic power, and its aggressive outreach and fund-raising have been successful. Chabad's success also demonstrates the power of proaction and of "being first," even though Chabad by no means represents the majority of contemporary Russian Jews. Since Chabad was one of the largest international Jewish organizations *not* investing most of its energy in getting Jews out of the Soviet Union in the 1980s and early 1990s (its mission is, after all, to encourage lapsed Jews to become more observant), it has been rewarded by being the organization most successful at rooting Jews in Moscow.

In 1999, when David was living in Moscow, he saw Chabad claiming public space firsthand. From David's field notes:

For years, Chabad has been holding very garish Hanukkah celebrations in downtown Moscow, passing out free candles and menorahs (*chanukiyot*), and making Moscow's Jews feel like it was "okay" to be Jewish (and to "look Jewish") on the streets of Moscow. In 1999, the Hanukkah lighting festivities lasted eight days and eight nights, although the big party was reserved for the first night. As I approached the celebration, which was just blocks from my apartment, I noticed that Chabad was handing out free menorahs and candles (something they do throughout the world on Hanukkah to make sure wayward Jews have the proper paraphernalia), a rock band played cheesy klezmeresque music, and people danced, lots of people, more than I expected to see. A giant gleaming menorah stood watch over Moscow's main boulevard, Tverskaia Street, as young and old, families and singles, even some young adults danced the horah. And even though this was a Chabad-sponsored event, there was a hardly a Chabadnik in sight.

Not only is Chabad spearheading a religious revival, it has also taken a lead in reestablishing nonreligious Jewish culture and society in Russia by sponsoring seemingly secular book readings, art festivals, and other cultural and social events. And, not surprisingly, it has done so with the help of the federal government.[35] Mikhail Gluz, the president of Chabad's Federation of Jewish Communities of Russia (FJCR), has stressed that "changes in recent years have created unique conditions for the development of Jewish culture, which is now supported by the state." In order to build Jewish culture, Gluz suggests that Russia's Jewish community "has formed a very close partner relationship with the federal government and the authorities in a number of the country's regions."[36] The relationship with the state is so close that, in November 2001, at the annual Congress of the FJCR, Sergei Abramov, the deputy head of the presidential administration, read a message of greeting from President Putin: "The congress is inspired by the idea of restoring ethnic and religious traditions." The Russian Minister of Culture, Mikhail Shvydkoi, also delivered a welcoming address emphasizing that the Ministry of Culture is prepared to back the FJCR's initiatives to revive Jewish culture.[37] In many ways, Chabad's version of Judaism is becoming the state-recognized version of Russian Jewish life.

A Tale of Two Rabbis

Not everyone appreciates Chabad's impact on Jewish life in Moscow or Chabad's cozy relationship with the federal government. The Russian Jewish Congress, a competing national Jewish organization funded by several wealthy, non-Chabad Russian Jews, and Mikhail Chlenov's organization, the Congress of Jewish Religious Organizations and Communities of Russia (CJROCR), an Orthodox umbrella organization, have argued publicly that Chabad's relationship with the Ministry of Culture has helped it become the primary representative of Russian Jewry.[38] These organizations, in fact, claim that another man is the chief rabbi of Russia. Adolf Shayevich, religious head of the CJROCR, has been the rabbi at the Moscow Choral Synagogue since 1980. In many ways, he is the opposite of Rabbi Lazar and a quintessential product of the Soviet Union's relationship to its Jewish population. He is a native Russian Jew, born in Birobidzhan, the autonomous Jewish republic established by Stalin in the Russian Far East before the turn to overt anti-Semitism. Shayevich had a secular, Communist upbringing as a member of the Communist youth league. Only when he moved to Moscow, in 1972, did he become interested in Judaism. Shayevich trained in the one-and-only rabbinic seminary in the former Communist bloc, in Hungary; he returned to Moscow in 1980 and has been there ever since.[39] Although he wears a *kippah*, Shayevich does not have a long beard and does not wear the black suits and coats associated with Chabad. He has the support of the non-Hasidic organized establishment, ranging from progressive religious Jewish organizations to more secular, socially oriented groups like the Russian Jewish Congress, in addition to the support of the non-Hasidic diaspora business. The competition between these groups reflects a struggle for cultural power and who defines Jewish authenticity in Russia. This struggle raises a key question: Are the more internationally recognized forms of Jewish identity, as represented by Chabad and other religious groups, more "authentic" than the more locally inspired forms of Jewish identity that tend to have little to do with religion?

The battles over Jewish identities and communities involve not only present-day representations but also symbols and spaces of the Jewish past. In the heyday of its campaign to make the Soviet Union an atheist nation, the Soviet state engaged in an antireligious campaign, and socialist Jewish intellectuals actively brought this campaign to Jewish spaces, as well. Throughout the 1920s and 1930s, socialist Jews invested with state power coopted synagogues and turned them into clubs, museums, storage facilities, and other kinds of spaces deemed more useful for the project of building socialism.

In post-Soviet Russia, Jewish groups are now competing to gain control over these empty synagogues throughout the former Soviet Union. A supporter of Shayevich has suggested that Lazar-supported factions have already expelled Shayevich-supported factions from local synagogues in the cities of Rostov-on-Don, Smolensk, and Kostroma. This Reform rabbi predicted that governors and mayors may end up having to choose sides in these disputes according to "who has the most money."[40] The drive to claim empty synagogues is as much symbolic as it is economic. These groups are fighting over the historical legacy of Russian Jewry, with the possible hope of repopulating these empty spaces with real, live Jews.

The fact that the two rabbis who open this chapter are competing for the title of chief rabbi and for the government's attention, and that the government is indeed funding Jewish communal life, is one sign that Jews are reclaiming symbolic and political space in Moscow. They were each interviewed for a special 2002 issue of the Russian magazine *Rodina* (Motherland), which was dedicated to Russian Jewry.[41] Each rabbi talked about assimilation, in terms of both religious and national identity. In Shayevich's interview, "Be Russians by Remaining Jews," he emphasized the commonalities of Jewish and Russian culture, especially the post-Soviet search for roots. Shayevich approaches questions of Jewish identity as indigenous to Russian culture and argues that Jews are more influenced by Russian culture than by traditional (or global) Jewish culture. Berel Lazar, from his nonnative, multicultural vantage point, talks about how he "became Russian" as part of his mission to Judaize the Jews of Moscow with the help of Chabad, a global Jewish organization with its headquarters on Eastern Parkway, in the Crown Heights section of Brooklyn. The tale of these two rabbis reflects the tension between local and global Jewish understandings of identity.

As part of this project, we are also interested in the images of Jews that pervade Russian culture. If you ask people in Russia, no matter what their religious or ethnic traditions, they believe they can tell who is a Jew by her or his physiognomy. David once asked someone how the person knew he was a Jew, and the response was, "You look like a Jew . . . dark hair, dark eyes, but you're smart." The last comment differentiated him from other "dark" people in Russian society, namely those from the Caucasus, who are the preeminent "other" in contemporary Russia. These reified, and racist, images of Jews pervade all discourse in Russia.

From David's field notes, 2002:

> The special issue of *Rodina* (Motherland) on Russian Jewry caught my eye in the way it presented authentic Jewishness. The cover is made up of two paintings by Vladimir Liubarov called "Yosef" (1998) and "Adam and Eve" (2000). Joseph (Yosef) is the centerpiece of the cover. He is represented as a Hasid with an enormous nose, black hat, side-locks (*peis*), and a small prayer book in hand. Adam and Eve are, rather ahistorically, also represented as Hasidic, fully clothed and reclining in what could be the Garden of Eden. The fact that the editors of this edition of *Rodina*, including some active Jewish communal leaders, chose quintessential stereotypical images of Eastern European Jewry, and also those images that look the most "un-Russian," suggests that the question of Russianness and rootedness, of sameness and difference, of Jew-ishness as both religion and ethnicity, is still hotly contested. Moreover, the opening photoessay shows Hasidic Jews making a pilgrimage to the city of Uman, in Ukraine, to visit the grave of Rabbi Nachman of Brat-slav. Big beards and black hats prevail—in print, in photography, and in Russian Jewish cultural politics.

The Emergence of a Russian Reform Judaism

In late September 1999, Interfax, the Russian news wire service, sent a brief report that a new synagogue had been opened in Moscow where "men and women could sit together." The item referred to the official opening of Moscow's first Reform synagogue, Congregation *Hineini*.

From David's field notes, 2002:

> On my way to Friday night services at *Hineni*: Walking down the small lane where the Reform synagogue is located, I hunted desperately for some visible sign of a synagogue. In fact, unlike Chabad's synagogues, which have Jewish stars and "mitzvah-mobiles" as part of the façade, there are no markers from the outside that 2 Vsevolozhsky Lane, a turn-of-the-century building with a 1990s contemporary interior, is the head-quarters of progressive Jewry in Russia. After finding the correct en-

trance, my partner and I entered the building, encountered one person who ignored our presence, and, after a few minutes of searching, I found the small sanctuary. After waiting a while, the rabbi and cantor, both male, unlike our previous visits in 1999 when all the service leaders were women, arrived. They began leading the congregation, a group of about thirty people ranging in age from seventeen to seventy-five, in a few *niggunim* [melodies] to "warm up." The two then led the congregation in a very standard Reform movement Friday night service with guitar and upbeat melodies imported directly from the Union of American Hebrew Congregations in the United States,[42] the umbrella organization of American Reform Jewish congregations.

Since Reform Judaism believes that religion should be accessible to the congregants in their native language, most of the service was in Russian. This suggested that Reform Judaism is perhaps the most "rooted" form of Judaism on Moscow's Jewish landscape. Although Reform Judaism is global, Reform Jews themselves adapt their worship and identities to the local cultures that they call home. In Orthodox synagogues, the services take place almost entirely in Hebrew and thus are by nature international, rather than particularly Russian. Other than my partner and me, I never saw another nonnative Russian at *Hineni*. *Hineni* was the only place where I felt like foreign Jews were not especially welcome. My native Russian-language skills were my pass to belonging, but they were tenuous, since I clearly dressed differently. At the Choral Synagogue—the traditional Orthodox, but not Chabad, synagogue—as I approached the building, a seemingly impoverished Moscow Jew approached me, "*Zdravtsvuyte! Shalom!*" I ignored him, as my experiences with synagogue "greeters" is that they are looking for money from foreign tourists. The Choral Synagogue was clearly accustomed to accommodating visiting Jews from Israel or the United States. *Hineni* had no such feel. It was by and for Russian Jews. I was the visitor.

In the United States, the Reform movement is the dominant form of Judaism, and together with the Conservative movement, non-Orthodox Jews account for the vast majority of practicing Jews in the United States. Although the possibility of non-Orthodox religious life is taken for granted in the United States and some Western European countries, in Russia the public face of Judaism, as represented by the competing chief rabbis, is strictly Orthodox.

By 2005, the movement for Progressive Judaism had grown to include nearly thirty congregations in Russia and more than seventy throughout the former Soviet Union, all of which participate in the Union of Religious Communities of Modern Judaism in Russia (URCMJR).[43] In that same year, the World Congress of Progressive Judaism held its international conference in Moscow, emphasizing Russia as a center of progressive Judaism. On a 1999 research trip, David met with Rabbi Chaim Ben-Yakov, at the time the only progressive rabbi in Russia. Ben-Yakov, a native Russian trained at the Reform movement rabbinic seminary in Jerusalem, came to Moscow in 1997 to serve as the spiritual leader of Moscow's and Russia's progressive Jewish community.

Ben-Yakov recognizes the complex reality of Jewish life in Moscow. Like his American and European rabbinic counterparts, he realizes that most Moscow Jews are secular. In Ben-Yakov's words, "In our community, men and women are absolutely equal, and we understand that Jews are searching for ways to integrate Jewish and modern life. Jews should go to the theater and to the synagogue."[44] The congregation caters to a young Jewish audience, what one might call the post-Soviet generation of Jews, which, according to Ben-Yakov, "has been searching for spirituality, but has not found it in any existing orthodox congregations. After sixty years of no organized Jewish life in the Soviet Union, Russian Jews are looking for a place where their intellectual questions will be answered and where there are various answers to their religious questions."

Despite these dramatic acts of establishing a native Reform Judaism, Moscow's Reform Jews still operate within the discourses of diaspora and the paths of emigration and still assume that Jewish identity must revolve around religious practice. According to Ben-Yakov, "Right now, if a Russian Jew wants to be a rabbi, he first has to learn English," by which he means that a Russian Jew would have to be trained in the United States or, more often, England or Israel if he or she were to become a leader of Russia's nascent progressive Jewish movement. All leaders I spoke with at *Hineni* recognized that for Moscow's and Russia's Reform Jewish communities to thrive and expand, they needed an institutional infrastructure to develop a Russian-language rabbinic and administrative leadership. Such an institutional infrastructure is already being put into place with the establishment of the *Machon* para-rabbinic training program in Moscow that serves as a postgraduate training program for potential rabbis.[45] Students from around Russia come to Moscow for two years of intensive study in Jewish history, culture, texts, and Jewish communal work.

Nelly Shulman, the first female rabbi of Russia and a product of the *Machon* program, is a perfect example of how Russian Reform Judaism is enmeshed in diasporic relations with other Jewish centers and is also developing its own forms of Jewish rootedness in Russia. Born in 1972, Shulman trained to be a rabbi at Leo Baeck College, in London. In 1998, she moved to Minsk, Belarus, and has served as the chief Reform rabbi of this capital city, a daunting task for a newly minted rabbi in a country run by an authoritarian leader, and in a place that has not seen much organized Jewish development. Ironically, Shulman thinks that being a woman benefits her in her attempt to get young Belorussian Jews excited about Judaism. "In other countries you go to a psychologist for advice, but people don't do that here. A lot of women in provincial places talk to me about issues like abortion, sexual harassment in the workplace, their families."[46] Shulman shows that as Russia develops its own rabbis, it will also develop its own definition of the rabbinate, in her case two parts therapist, one part legal adviser, one part Jewish leader.

The Story of Two Jewish Community Centers

One thing that all Jewish parties can agree upon is the need to expand communal infrastructure beyond the walls of the synagogue. Not surprisingly, Chabad met that challenge first by establishing Moscow's first Jewish community center, in 2000.

Field Trip #1: The Chabad Jewish Community Center in Marina Roshcha, December 2003

From David's field notes:

After a twenty-minute walk from the closest metro station, I arrived at the seven-story, enormous newly constructed complex that calls itself the Jewish Community Center of Moscow. Founded next door to one of the two primary Chabad Lubavitch synagogues in Moscow, the Marina Roshcha Jewish Community Center is an impressive site. There are barricades protecting the front entrance from potential car bombs and several guards observing everyone coming and going. Strict security makes sense in a place that has seen several bombings and other hate crimes in the past few years. Upon entrance, I found myself in a very typical, and very beautiful, Jewish community center. An older Russian Jewish woman took my coat, as is routine in all buildings in Moscow in the winter. I approached the information desk, collected flyers, inquired about the library, and was politely sent up to the seventh floor to investigate the book holdings. The library contained an outstanding collection of contemporary Russian-language Judaica, newspapers, academic journals, and banks of computers with high-speed Internet access.

Since this was a Chabad institution, I kept expecting to see men in black hats and women in long skirts. Instead, I saw a diverse group of people, presumably Jewish, and only an occasional black hat. But there were more subtle signs of Chabad everywhere. At the information desk, there was a box of *kippot* for men to wear upon entrance into the building, and perhaps even to take home with them. The café was strictly glatt kosher, and there were flyers for religious celebrations.

After descending, I entered the kosher café, looked around, impressed by the amount of money that went into the construction of this very large complex, and left after about an hour-long visit. Marble floors, fast elevators, relatively polite staff, easily accessible information, open spaces in the lobby and café areas, and all-new construction made the Marina Roshcha JCC a very pleasant place to spend some time. It felt like many other public Jewish cultural centers around the world—lots of money, lots of programming, and lots of people.[47]

Field Trip #2: The Jewish Community Center on Bol'shaia Nikitskaia, December 2003

In 2001, the Nikitskaia Jewish Community Center opened in the center of Moscow in a classic turn-of-the-century building. Unlike Chabad's Marina Roshcha JCC, which was funded primarily by wealthy Russian Jewish donors, the Nikitskaia JCC was built with international funding primarily from the American Joint Distribution Committee, an international Jewish philanthropy that has funded Jewish projects in Russia and the Soviet Union since the nineteenth century.

From David's field notes:

Finding the Nikitskaia JCC was much more difficult than finding the Marina Roshcha JCC and, in retrospect, was one of the most unwelcoming Jewish spaces I visited in all of Moscow. The relatively small sign marking the building as Jewish was off to the side, and a schedule of events was posted next to the locked, unmarked door with a call button.

Conversation in Russian with the security guard:

"Hello, I'd like to come into the Jewish Community Center."

"Why?"

"To see the inside."

"What do you want to see?"

"I don't know. I haven't been inside yet to know exactly what I want to see."

"Can you be more specific?"

"Fine. I want to see your bookstore."

With that, I was buzzed in by the surly guard expecting to be patted down and sent on my way. The place was completely empty. I was again questioned about my motives for attending. There were, after all, no programs at the moment. What could I possibly want? I asked again about the books and was sent up to the library.

The Nikitskaia JCC houses one of the most impressive Jewish institutions in Moscow, the Jewish Book Store (*Dom evreiskoi knigi*), which was founded in 2001 and had published fourteen books by November 2003. I spoke with the assistant director, who proudly talked about the ten-thousand-volume library collection, the fourteen publications, and the large number of periodicals that the library subscribed to. I noticed the Yiddish book collection as well, but she said, not surprisingly, that hardly anyone uses the Yiddish books.

Unlike the library at Marina Roshcha, the Nikitskaia library was up two flights of stairs and behind an unmarked door. There were only two people using it, even though it has one of the best current Judaica collections in the country. What in fact did this JCC offer? It didn't seem to have a kosher café (it may have, but it was not labeled and was not open), no information desk, and no flyers to take. Who was the intended audience of this JCC, and what was its purpose?

The Chabad JCC, which used global—and especially American—models of community building, was much more open, comfortable, and popular than the Nikitskaia JCC, which was closed, cold, and inaccessible. It is clear that Chabad leadership—Berel Lazar from Italy and the staff at the headquarters in New York—knows better than native Russian Jews how to bring people in the door, if that is the goal. The Marina Roshcha JCC invited both young and old to wear a *kippah*, eat a kosher meal, and read a Jewish book in nonthreatening ways. And they also successfully raised money to build the place. But how?

How Are Russian Jewish Communities Financed?

Lev Levaiev, a Russian-born diamond tycoon who now lives in Israel, is one of Chabad's largest donors in the entire world, and nearly all of his fortune is devoted to resurrecting Jewish life in Moscow and throughout Russia.[48] In 1993, he founded the Or Avner Chabad Lubavitch Fund, based in Moscow, which, as of 2002, supported seventy schools throughout the former Soviet Union. Levaiev and others like him helped build the Marina Roshcha JCC.[49] Although not a practicing Chabadnik himself, Levaiev maintains an emotional connection to the institution that he funds so generously. In an interview with the Israeli daily newspaper *Maariv*, which was immediately published in a Russian-language Jewish journal, he invoked the deceased Chabad rebbe, Menachem Mendel Schneerson, as one of his inspirations and spiritual mentors: "If I have to evaluate a particularly important situation, I imagine the Lubavitch Rebbe and my father."[50] By positioning itself as the arbiter of Jewish authenticity and the bearer of Jewish tradition in Russia, Chabad successfully focuses Russian Jews' desires to reinvigorate Jewish life through a specific religious lens.

Ben-Yakov's Reform congregation receives most of its financial support not from wealthy Russian Jewish tycoons but from the World Union for Progressive Judaism, which has its headquarters in Jerusalem and regional offices in London, New York, and Moscow. The mission of the World Union is "to preserve Jewish integrity wherever Jews live; to encourage integration without assimilation; to respond to modernity while perpetuating the Jewish experience; to pursue social justice and equal rights for all." It is no accident that the bulk of *Hineni*'s funding comes from this diaspora business organization. According to Ben-Yakov, "Soviet Jews do not have a tradition of giving money to religious organizations. First on the list would be cultural activities, theater groups and choirs, and only last would be giving money to a congregation."

Although they have little in common, both Ben-Yakov and Lazar stress religious practice as the way to rebuild Jewish life in Moscow. But what about nonreligious Jewish identity, which has been the primary way Jews have identified since the Russian Revolution? The funding of most other Russian Jewish organizations comes from secular global Jewish organizations. Two of the most important are the New York–based Joint Distribution Committee (JDC) and Israel's Jewish Agency in Russia. The JDC, an arm of the North American Jewish Federation, focuses its attention on social and educational services. The JDC's mission is to "address the needs of Jews in distress wherever such international assistance is required." Unlike Chabad, which responds to "opportunities" to reinvigorate Jewish life, the JDC responds to "problems" and "crises".[51] The other large funding operation is the Jewish Agency, a branch of the Israeli government, whose ultimate aim is to increase immigration to Israel. The Jewish Agency also sees the state of Moscow Jewry as a crisis and, therefore, Moscow Jews as potential immigrants. For this reason, most of the social and cultural work done by the Agency has a connection to Israel.

Unlike the Jewish Agency, the Jewish Community Development Fund (JCDF) emphasizes that Moscow is a Jewish home with its slogan "They aren't stuck there. They live there." The JCDF provides grants to Jewish cultural and social organizations throughout the former Soviet Union in order to "support the efforts of Soviet Jews themselves. . . . . The JCDF has concentrated its efforts on the needs of emerging Jewish communities as articulated by the communities themselves. Empowerment has been at the heart of our philosophy."[52] This emphasis on development and local independence is reflected in the overall philosophy of JCDF's parent organization, American Jewish World Service. The JCDF is, in philanthropy-speak, constituency driven rather than donor driven, in order to let primarily secular Jews create the kinds of organizations they want, rather than the kinds of institutions that Chabad or global Reform institutions think Moscow's Jews should have.

Both through local and global initiatives, Moscow is now home to two JCCs, a Holocaust museum, two Jewish publishing houses, several kosher restaurants, many Jewish schools, and several synagogues. Despite the fact that a woman tried to sell David *The Protocols,* that Mikhail has never been and never intends to go to either JCC, and that Lev Levaiev lives in Israel, it is simply not possible to argue that Jewish life in Moscow is dying. All signs show that Jewish life in the city is growing. Moscow Jews are settled. Jews are so settled in Moscow, and in all of

Russia, that, for the first time in history, more Russian Jews now migrate *to* Russia from Israel than the other way around. According to a report released by the Federation of Jewish Communities of Russia, about fifty thousand Jewish former emigrants to Israel have returned to Russia since 2001. Over the same period, only about thirty thousand Russian Jews have left for Israel.[53] With state anti-Semitism officially ended and an economic climate more promising than Israel's, Moscow is becoming a place where Jews want to live.

2

Encounters with Ghosts
Youth Tourism and the Diaspora Business

Don't just be a tourist, make a difference.
—From the Web site of Livnot U'Lehibanot
(To Build and Be Built) Programs in Israel

In 1999, Caryn attended an Ascent weekend, a program for English-speaking tourists and students in Israel offered by Livnot U'lehibanot, a Chabad Lubavitch Hasidic program that conducts outreach among unaffiliated Jews. The following is excerpted from her field notes:

On Friday evening, our group of twelve young women walked into the dark, cramped, and tiny women's section of the Beit Knesset Kosov in Tzfat (a town in northern Israel, famous for its history of Jewish mystics). The women's section was bounded by a dark wooden trellis *mechitzah* (partition to separate women from men) covered with thick white lace doilies. It was difficult to see what was happening in the men's section. A row of young girls sat in the front of the section, swaying and praying intently. The women seemed to range in age from their early thirties to their seventies, and everyone wore modest, high-neck dresses with long sleeves and skirts that almost touched the floor. Some women (presumably married) wore headscarves that fully covered their hair, or fancy, stiff-looking hats with their hair carefully tucked and concealed underneath, in accordance with the laws of *tsniut* (modesty). I found a prayer book, written entirely in Hebrew, and managed to locate the beginning of the Friday night service, while an older man in the men's section with an incredibly deep, croaking voice began to sing a plaintive melody in a minor key.

The melodies, which were inflected with Yiddish pronunciation, were different from the tunes I was familiar with from my Conservative movement upbringing. The men's section was extremely vocal. Individual men's voices cried out as if in pain, some murmured along with the prayer leader, others occasionally shouted while everyone prayed along in unison. Then the prayer leader began singing a *niggun* (wordless melody), with the repeated ending "*Shabbes Koy-desh*" (Holy Sabbath), as he closed his eyes and began to bang his hand rhythmically on the lectern. Soon the men caught on and began singing with gusto, clapping in time, their voices rising in volume and intensity. After minutes of fervent singing, all the men pushed their chairs to either side of the *shul* [Yiddish for synagogue], and began to dance ecstatically in circles to the melody. Their singing got louder and louder as they danced more frenetically, holding onto their huge fur *shtreimel* hats, throwing their hands up in the air to the ceiling, and yelling the words "*Shabbes Koy-desh*!" at the top of their lungs.

It was quite an exhilarating spectacle to witness.

Was this a gospel revival or a vaguely remembered scene from *Fiddler on the Roof*? For a moment, I secretly wished that I could pass as a young boy by wearing Orthodox drag to get over on the other side of the *mechitzah*, because I wanted to participate and observe more directly. I had had *Yentl* moments like this before, where I felt my gender constricting what I could see and the kind of field work I could do in Orthodox settings.

Meanwhile, the women just sat patiently, softly singing the words. Deborah and Ariella, the young American Chabad staffers, grabbed our hands and enlisted us into a cramped little circle dance, swaying back and forth and moving toward the center of the circle and back while singing ecstatically with their eyes closed and big smiles on their faces. The service concluded quickly afterward, and people filed out of the *shul* onto the small cobblestone square. As we waited outside for the rest of the group, Deborah walked over to me with a beatific smile on her face and gushed, "I so love this *shul*! I can't get enough of the energy here; it's so amazing and holy! What did you think?" I told her truthfully that it was unlike anything I had ever seen before.

Many young American Jews have been on organized tours to Eastern Europe or Israel. These pilgrimages are designed to encourage a strong sense of Jewish identity for the rest of one's lifetime. There are now hundreds of programs that send Jews of all ages to Israel to dig for archeological treasures, pray in synagogues, fire guns, excavate bones, learn a little Hebrew, pick olives and oranges, and scuba dive, among other pastimes. Most trips to Eastern Europe, like March of the Living, use the Holocaust as their source of identity tourism, although, increasingly, Jewish organizations organize Jewish culture tours to places like Krakow, Prague, and Vilnius. These tours and trips often attempt to reinforce traditional notions of diaspora and homeland by situating America as an exilic place of weakening Jewish identity, positing Israel as the center of Jewish life and Eastern Europe as the center of Jewish death. In this sense, Israel and Eastern Europe are used as a theatrical backdrop on which to construct and strengthen Jewish identities for Jews in America and around the world. This kind of tourism and identity travel is part of what we call the diaspora business.

The diaspora business is a broad institutional and organizational terrain that complicates the differences between home and abroad, centers and peripheries, in a shifting, increasingly compressed global world of capital, people, ideas, and national borders.[1] This business's chief aim is to shore up the perceived diminishing religious, ethnic, and cultural identities of individual established Jewish communities around the world, while simultaneously benefiting Israel, the United States, and now Eastern Europe, through finance, tourism, cultural exchanges, product import/export, and employment.[2] Organizations like Chabad Lubavitch, a branch of Hasidic Judaism, are among the most visible and successful organizations in this business. The broader Jewish travel industry is less about sustaining already existing connections and memories between individuals and communities than it is about inventing new relationships between American Jews and other Jewish places. These educational and historical tours of Israel and Eastern Europe include intense group experiences within particular religious worlds, such as Orthodox schools, known as *yeshivas,* and volunteer work opportunities for Jewish teens and young adults, as a way to strengthen the allegiances and solidarity among Jews from different countries and to create a sense of global nationhood, often with Israel at the center of that tourist universe.

Similar forms of travel exist for other ethnic groups[3] and even for Israeli Jews of immigrant origins,[4] but, within the Jewish world, this form of diaspora business is the *foundation* of global Jewish tourism, and, as such, it garners both intense scrutiny and serious communal investment. Imagine if every South Asian teen in America were expected to spend a summer during his or her high school years living in Bangalore or Mumbai with the goal not of meeting a spouse in India but of connecting with Indian soil? Or imagine if the NAACP spent a large portion of its resources sending African American kids to West Africa on a tour of the key sites in the slave trade and to learn about Yoruba culture in order to instill pride in their African (American) heritage. Jewish parents and communal leaders send children around the world, especially to Israel, to shore up a Jewish future. But, increasingly, leaders imagine the future of Jewish youth not in Israel but "at home."

A History of Jewish Youth Travel

Prior to the 1980s, few trips existed to bring Jews to Communist Eastern Europe, and most trips to Israel focused on developing and deepening Jews' commitment to Zionism and Israel, rather than on using Israel as a means to strengthen identity. The collective efforts of Jewish communal organizations to view Israel and Eastern Europe as important places to create or solidify rooted, global Jewish identities is relatively new.

Palestine, and then later Israel, was initially a place in which American Jews could remake themselves into full-fledged Zionists and potentially become citizens of a new Jewish state. The Zionist kibbutz and youth movements The Young Guard (*Ha'shomer Hatza'ir*) and Young Judaea provided the initial infrastructure and ideological foundation for travel to Palestine and Israel from the 1930s through the 1950s.[5] Kibbutz members began to solicit volunteers from abroad to work as cheap laborers and in exchange offered the promise of an appealing, romantic image of an idyllic, pastoral life and extolled the virtues of "Hebrew" agricultural labor. These programs explicitly touted resettlement to Israel as the highest virtue and expression of commitment to the nascent Jewish nation-state. This ideological position also dovetailed with the emerging Israeli educational establishment's positioning of the Bible as a key text and ancient Jewish history as a master narrative in which to introduce recent and potential immigrants (i.e., tourists and temporary kibbutz residents) to *yediat ha'aretz*—knowledge and love of the land of Israel as a key mechanism for creating loyalty to the nation.[6]

The postwar economic expansion of the 1950s proved to be a golden era, both in the wider American Jewish world and in the establishment of the diaspora business infrastructure. While American Jews were busy moving to the suburbs and building large synagogues, the type of programs that offered youth-oriented travel to Israel changed and expanded.[7] Young Judaea and the American Jewish denominational movements established summer Israel programs in the 1950s that were attended by young Jews who later assumed key leadership and policy-making positions in these movements' communal organizations.[8] Rabbis, Jewish educators, and other community leaders staffed early programs as unpaid workers in exchange for the trip to Israel. Meanwhile, the World Zionist Organization and local "outposts" of American denominations recruited Israelis to serve as cultural and ideological liaisons with American Jews. As global travel increased through expanded commercial airline services in the 1960s, the *Histadrut* (Labor Zionist trade union) steadily developed and devoted resources to create an Israeli tourism infrastructure. This organizational structure also served as a pipeline for young Americans interested in casual employment and became an important pathway for many people engaged in gradual migration via extended visits, temporary employment, and other semipermanent relationships to Israel.[9] For many upper-middle-class Americans with a passport and a plane ticket, shuttling between America and Israel through gradual migration has been the process, rather than the outcome, by which some of them came to call a new place "home."

Gradual migration and the burgeoning diaspora business accomplished several important objectives. Not only did they increasingly link American Jews to specific people and places within Israel through organized programs, but they also funneled critical dollars to the emerging state. As in the prestate period, American Jews continued to support Zionism with financial resources, but not necessarily by becoming citizens. This support translated into opportunities for Zionist "impresarios," both at home and in Israel, who could market campaigns for Israel Bonds, plan cultural exchanges with Israeli dance troupes, and coordinate travel.[10] The development of tourism also created a physical infrastructure for the growing presence in Israel of American Jewish communal and religious organizations, something foreign to the very secular Zionist establishment. Finally, tourism provided employment to Israelis and, in some cases, to American immigrants who had chosen to move there.

In 1955, Hebrew University began offering one-year study-abroad programs for foreign students, and, in 1971, it opened its foreign studies school, now called the Rothberg School for Overseas Students, initially to create an institutional infrastructure for potential immigrants.[11] Similar programs opened at Tel Aviv and Haifa universities a few years later. By the 1980s, spending an academic year in Israel had become a rite of passage for many American Jewish university students.

But if, in 1955, American students in Israel were seen as potential immigrants and as a source of labor for flourishing kibbutzim, now both students and universities generally view a year in Israel as a study-abroad program to learn about what it means to be an American Jew, rather than as an immersion in Zionism and a potential route to *aliyah*. In the past thirty years, the promotion of *aliyah* has diminished as a centerpiece of American Zionism in response to the increasing rootedness of Jewish communities in the United States, Latin America, and Europe. Other contributing factors have been the ebb and flow of political conflict in the Middle East; and the accumulation of material wealth in Europe and North America (and, for some, even in Eastern Europe), in contrast to the historically hardscrabble, difficult economic climate of Israel. Recognizing that Jews have become increasingly rooted in the United States and have reaped the financial and social rewards of assimilation, global Jewish organizations have shifted their goals and begun to use Israel as a backdrop for different purposes. The sociologist Shaul Kelner writes: "The classical European Zionist argument that acculturation and assimilation were inevitable in open societies, and that communal boundaries and cultural integrity could be maintained only by physical resettlement in a self-determining Jewish state, was so far from communal consensus that no serious plan for promoting mass emigration was ever put forward in the central organs of American Jewry."[12]

In the 1970s and early 1980s, several key diaspora business organizations were founded to provide the logistical and educational support structure for emerging relationships between global Jewish organizations. But now these organizations made Israel a tourist site and the international Jewish homeland, rather than the place to which American Jewish youth should move. *Melitz:* The Center for Jewish-Zionist Education was established in 1973, and the Kibbutz Program Center was created in New York in the late 1970s. American denominational programs, especially for the Reform and Conservative movements, became more sophisticated in their efforts to keep a steady stream of young people and capital flowing between Israel and North American Jewish communities as part of the larger project of youth education, including *Otzma, Nativ,* United Synagogue Youth, and Camp Ramah.

The hallmark of these identity trips was, and continues to be, their shared emphasis on pilgrimage and the building of Jewish identity through carefully planned educational programs, rather than simply touring for pleasure. From its humble beginnings as a vehicle for kibbutz labor to its more recent incarnation as a conduit for postmodern forms of mass tourism, the diaspora business has consistently focused its efforts on designing, promoting, and implementing programs with specific educational objectives based on the different ideologies and goals of organizational sponsors.

Making Jews More Jewish

In 1990, the National Jewish Population Survey, conducted by the Council of Jewish Federations, released data that suggested decreasing levels of Jewish communal affiliation, increasing intimate relationships and marriage between Jews and non-Jews, declining group cohesion, and an overall "waning of Jewish identity." With the publication of this study, fear gripped the Jewish communal and policy establishment, sparking a wide-ranging debate about a "crisis of continuity" as a defining threat to Jewish life. The enormous impact of this study on the Jewish community cannot be overstated and resulted in deep reflection, anxiety, and a shift in organizational priorities. In particular, the study sparked a newfound enthusiasm among Jewish communal professionals for the role Israel could play in shoring up American Jewish identities.

If in the 1990s American Jews were suddenly gripped with anxiety about the future, then Israel, as the symbolic and emotional "center" or "home" of global Jewry, could provide a solution, even though the majority of Jews around the world choose *not* to live there. Despite the idea of Israel as center, most of the programs, organizations, and companies engaged in diaspora business work are wholly transnational, with offices in several countries, a satellite in Israel, Web sites with multiple languages that can be accessed from anywhere in the world, and daily e-mail communication. In true global fashion, this constellation of relationships and organizations, moving freely across international boundaries, often blurs the lines between private enterprise, Israeli state funding, the nonprofit world, and philanthropy. For instance, the Jewish Agency sends *shlichim* (messengers or cultural attachés) to Jewish communities around the world with the task of raising money for Israel.[13]

Where is the global, and where is the local? In many cases, the answer is both, simultaneously.

Using tropes of history and biblical inheritance, diaspora business organizations offer an emotional promise to visitors to renew their spirituality, their Jewish identity, and their sense of place in a hostile world. For example, Caryn's ethnographic fieldwork with Livnot U'lehibanot (To Build and Be Built) promised to show her "some of the most beautiful parts of the country as well as the beauty of Judaism, challenging you from a physical, intellectual, and spiritual standpoint, and by doing so, help create strong feelings of accomplishment, self growth, and connection."[14] The programs provide carefully marketed and tailored experiences for their participants, and they offer an opportunity to dive into a particular ideological perspective, a set of practices and behaviors, and a specific emotional vocabulary in which participants can construct, interpret, and authenticate meaning and changing notions of selfhood.[15] These experiences induce powerful emotions, such as pride, religious awe, anger at historical persecution of Jews, camaraderie, a sense of entitlement toward the "land of Israel," nostalgia, and longing for a "return to Zion." Participants who experience emotional and identity transformations through these organizations are encouraged to translate those feelings into action. For young American Jews, this involves several possibilities: dating and marrying other Jews, joining Jewish organizations, becoming a Jewish professional, becoming involved with the Jewish political establishment, donating money, or simply creating a social circle of other like-minded Jews.

"Saving the Jews in Six Weeks or Less"

The diaspora business focus on travel reflects the emergent consensus among Jewish communities around the world that educational travel to Jewish sites and spaces are key ways to construct, maintain, and ensure the reproduction of Jews. If Jews participate in travel to Jewish sites, so the logic goes, then they will come home with a reinvigorated or newly minted sense of passion and excitement for what it means to be Jewish and will want to somehow translate that enthusiasm into tangible practices connected to specific Jewish communities *at home*. This can range from lighting candles on Friday night to usher in *Shabbat* to stepping into a Hillel house, the international network of university Jewish student associations, for the first time in a college career, to taking a Jewish studies course, to deciding to keep kosher.

These programs run the gamut of religious practices and political affiliations, from thoroughly secular to Hasidic and charedi.[16] They tailor "Israel experiences" for different groups on the basis of age, class, sexuality, family arrangements, and level of institutional involvement.[17] Programs range from intensive *yeshiva* study run by Orthodox Torah seminaries to informal secular summer tours that put American kids on a bus and zigzag across the country. Some even meld *yeshiva* study and participation on a kibbutz. In modern Orthodox circles, it is possible for young men to spend a year combining *yeshiva* study with a short course of basic training in the Israeli Army (called *hesder yeshivot*). At the other end of the Jewish ideological spectrum, the United Jewish Communities, the umbrella organization of Jewish federations in North America, offers a work-study program, called Otzma, to recent college graduates, which emphasizes the principles of *tikkun olam* (repairing the world), secular Zionism, and egalitarian, religiously pluralist Jewish study.

Taglit/Birthright Israel

In 1999, several philanthropists offered a multimillion-dollar challenge to the Jewish community to organize free trips to Israel for young people as a way to counteract the alarming trends outlined in the National Jewish Population Survey of 1990. These American Jewish philanthropists initiated birthright israel with the expectation of receiving matching funds from Israel's Ministry of Education and the United Jewish Communities, the American network of Jewish federations. By late 2003, taglit/birthright israel had sent more than forty thousand Jewish young adults to Israel.[18] The essential element of birthright is a ten-day tour for Jews ages 18–26, stopping at all the major secular and religious tourist destinations in Israel, including Masada and the Western Wall, and allowing for leisure time in resort areas like Eilat. In true global fashion, participants hail from the United States, Australia, South Africa, Russia, Eastern Europe, and South America.

Birthright's actual programming is subcontracted to thirty different organizations that range in ideology, denomination, mission, and type (these include for-profit travel agencies and nonprofit Jewish communal agencies). To routinize the process and avoid duplication of efforts, birthright provides logistical coordination and support and also maintains basic curricular requirements for all organizations. The itineraries are standardized and based on established logistical considerations and constraints. The trips include visits to holy sites, nature hikes, managed encounters with Israelis (known as *mifgashim*), visits to places of historical and contemporary significance (such as the Israeli Parliament), and some socializing. Since the program's inception, but especially since the second intifada began in 2000, all tours avoid visiting sites in the West Bank and in the Gaza Strip. This sidesteps potential danger but also avoids confronting a central fact of Israel's contemporary condition: conflict, occupation, and militarism as key elements of everyday life.

In addition to leisure activities and days of shopping, the program organizes structured group discussions at each tourist site visited. Participants are encouraged to tell their life stories as individuals, but also as links to grander narratives about Jewish peoplehood and politics. Michelle, a twenty-year-old college student, described her experience as follows:

> The goal of birthright is to just get them to go, and a lot of the people who go aren't really Jewish, they don't go to services, and aren't into the religious aspect. . . . The other intent was to get us in touch with our Jewish roots. There was one huge conversation about whether our roots mattered to us and it was overwhelming how many people felt like our roots were irrelevant to contemporary Judaism and identity. That's one of the problems with birthright—everything was discussed to death, and people just wanted to have a vacation.

Michelle's experience points to the tension between the organizer's goals and the participants' desires. Birthright provides the opportunity for participants to have fun while revising their personal and "the Jewish people's" history. But what the students do with this opportunity is ultimately up to them. Apparently, some philanthropists feared that birthright students weren't doing as much as they could and recently instituted the "Charlie Awards" (a cash award of several thousand dollars, named after one participating philanthropist) as an incentive to parlay their tourism experience into Jewish communal service at home.[19]

The Ever-Present Past: March of the Living and Tourism to Eastern Europe

David went to Eastern Europe in high school, to the Soviet Union to be precise. He went as an American high school student on a "friendship exchange" with teenagers from "behind the iron curtain." It was the era of Sting wondering whether the Russians loved their children, of Reagan and the Evil Empire. It was the 1980s at the height of *perestroika* and *glasnost*, and he wanted to see what was "over there." He wanted to go to see busts of Lenin and the Kremlin but had virtually no interest in going to Eastern Europe to encounter his Jewish past. His parents let him go, but there was definitely a sense of strangeness if not trepidation at the prospect of sending a suburban Jewish teenager to the Soviet Union (and not to Israel). David still remembers the reaction of his grandfather, Charlie Shneer (z"l), to the news that David was venturing back to the place from which he himself had come. "Why would you want to go to that horrible place that I fled from?" David's grandfather wasn't a Zionist, so he didn't push David to go to Israel, although learning more Hebrew wouldn't have been so terrible. Until that moment it hadn't occurred to David that visiting the Soviet Union was in some ways a return home for his family. In fact, since David's first trip to the Soviet Union, David's parents, aunt, and uncle have all made trips to Russia and Ukraine, coming to visit him while he was living there, each of them envisioning the trip both as a visit to the former Communist country with which he had become intimate and as a depressing return to their Jewish homes. None of them has ever been back again.

Fast-forward fifteen years. David is now a professor of Eastern European Jewish history, teaches classes on the Holocaust and Jewish culture, and has students, mostly but not exclusively Jewish, begging him to take them on a study trip to visit "Jewish Eastern Europe."

"What do you want to see?" David asks.

"All the places my grandparents came from and all the cool old Communist places."

"If you want to see Jewish Eastern Europe, do you want to go to the Hillel[20] in Moscow or the small Reform synagogue in Kiev?"

"Not really. I want to see the old stuff."

"Is there anything you want to see of today's Jewish Eastern Europe?"

"What do you mean?"

The irony is usually lost on them.

. . .

Eastern Europe became a popular site for Jewish heritage travel over the past twenty years, first on a small scale in response to the opening provided by Poland's Solidarity movement, and Gorbachev's *glasnost* (openness) and *perestroika* (restructuring), and then at a significantly increased rate following the demise of the Soviet Union, the reunification of Germany, and the democratization process that swept through the region in the 1990s. In this short time, however, this place haunted by the Holocaust has become a central focus of Jewish heritage travel, second only to Israel. Driven by memory and nostalgia for a lost or imagined past, this new tourism is also a symbol of an increasingly globalized tourism industry in which travel to formerly forbidden, exotic, and unfamiliar places has become de rigueur. Eastern Europe represents the romanticized birthplace of American Jewish folklore as imagined through *Fiddler on the Roof,* kitchen Yiddish, and tales of *shtetl* life while simultaneously evoking fears of persecution and the geographic center of genocidal anti-Semitism.[21] A trip to Eastern Europe for American Jews of Eastern European background is becoming a central rite of Jewish passage for adult children of Holocaust survivors, affluent baby-boomer American Jews, and their children, although for different reasons.[22]

In the context of fading direct memories of the Holocaust, the tourist organizations that are part of the diaspora business take young adults to witness the ashes, crematoria, cemeteries, and somber memorials to the dead Jewish communities of Europe. The burden of remembering the genocidal horrors of the Holocaust has assumed new urgency as survivors —the narrative storytellers who implore us to remember—age and pass away. Debbie Findling, a San Francisco–based Jewish communal professional who has studied Jewish tourism to Eastern Europe, writes: "A paradox exists for the generation that survived the Holocaust. In the immediate aftermath, many survivors simply wanted to forget and move on with their lives, while imploring the next generation to remember."[23] This imperative to remember has motivated and mobilized Jews around the world to devote millions of dollars and countless hours of creative energy toward documenting and rendering visible—in the form of monuments, memorials, museums, books, films, archives, and Web sites—these ghosts.[24] It also led to the creation of March of the Living, which introduces young Jews to the ghosts of the past through direct, experiential engagement with the physical structures that stand as witnesses and legacies of Eastern European Jewry's destruction.

March of the Living (MOTL) was established in 1988 by the Israeli Ministry of Education to use the Holocaust and the founding of the State of Israel as two axes around which to mark Jewish time—the Holocaust as the Jewish past and Israel as the Jewish future. According to Findling, the March of the Living "is clearly a symbolic journey whose message is one of rising out of the metaphoric and literal ashes of Poland to life and future in Israel."[25] The anthropologist Jack Kugelmass concurs, suggesting that "the death camps in Poland act as condensation symbols for the entire Jewish past, while Israel, the end point of the journey, is schematized as the Jewish future."[26]

Every year, March of the Living brings thousands of teenagers and young adults from more than fifty countries to Poland and Israel[27] to explore the enormity of the Holocaust. Its mission is "to create memories, leading to a revitalized commitment to Judaism, Israel and the Jewish People. It will allow Marchers to educate their peers about the Holocaust and to fight those who would deny its history, while forging a dynamic link with Israel, with many returning to strengthen that connection."[28] Perhaps most important, Jewish communal professionals hope that March of the Living, like all other identity travel for Jewish youth, will prevent assimilation and intermarriage in the North American Jewish community.[29]

In a carefully scripted, unfolding emotional drama, March of the Living offers a compelling, stark contrast: between the living and the dead, grief and elation, mourning and celebration, destruction and renewal, past and future. According to Dafna Michaelson, a March of the Living participant and former director of MOTL for the New York region:

> [March of the Living] is our opportunity to reaffirm that there are Jews all around the world, that we're a strong people, that we'll continue to go on and make great changes in terms of hate and intolerance and bettering this world. Hitler, you did not win.

After being part of and leading thousands of Jews from around the world on marches through the Polish countryside, Michaelson argues that MOTL reaffirms communal solidarity through memory, sadness, and fear. Young Jews go to Israel and Poland to discover and make meaningful their own sense of what it means to be rooted and Jewish in a global world. Their parents, though, travel to Eastern Europe for other reasons. Their interest in the Holocaust more likely leads them to visit Holocaust museums, while a trip to Eastern Europe allows them to explore roots and lost pasts. It's a trip driven by nostalgia, more than identity building.

Although preparation for the March begins months before the plane touches down in Poland, the actual March of the Living itinerary begins in Warsaw with visits to the Jewish Museum, the Noczyk Synagogue, the Jewish Cultural Center, the Warsaw Jewish cemetery, and a memorial ceremony at the Rappaport Memorial in the former Warsaw ghetto.[30] Students experience powerful emotions of solidarity and sadness during the key component of the Poland itinerary, the literal "March of the Living," a one-mile, somber, silent walk between the extermination camps at Auschwitz and Birkenau (also known as Auschwitz II). Students then travel to Treblinka and Majdanek and conclude their tour of Poland in "Jewish Krakow," visiting the Ramo synagogue, Schindler's factory, Plaszow, and several empty synagogues before flying to Israel.

Participants retrace and reenact grisly scenes of suffering to avenge the memory of victims. From the organization's Web site:

> As one of the Marchers . . . you will experience Jewish history where it was made. This time, however, there will be a difference. It will be a March of the Living with thousands of Jewish youth, like yourself, marching shoulder to shoulder. You will participate in a memorial service at one of the gas chambers/crematoria in Birkenau, which will conclude with the singing of *Hatikvah* [the Israeli national anthem], reaffirming "Am Yisrael Chai—The Jewish People Live."

At Auschwitz, participants view mountains of stolen luggage and victims' shoes. They stand in the courtyard next to the wall where thousands of Jews were shot at close range. They wander silently through gas chambers, their mouths open in shock, horror, and disgust that the very ground upon which they stand was the site of so much death. For the participants of MOTL, walking through the quiet, placid, almost eerie physical structures of genocide shatters the conventional distinctions between here and there, memory and reality. As the Holocaust scholar James Young points out, a visit to the site of a Polish extermination camp is not simply a visit to a memory site, like visiting a memorial or a Holocaust museum, because the events of the past happened there. Visitors can picture the violence that took place in the spaces that they now occupy.[31]

Organizers prepare students to see Poland as dead, frozen, and fearful, despite the nation's booming economy, its 2004 entry into the European Union, and its increasingly vibrant Jewish and philo-Semitic cultural scene. If Poland and Eastern Europe are seen as dead, they cannot function as real places from which Jews are in diaspora. They cannot serve as a "home" with the possibility of return for the Jewish youth who participate in MOTL, most of whom are of Ashkenazic or Eastern European descent. In a global world, "home" comes to be the places where these students live and the Jews' "eternal home," Israel, even if most of the participants trace their roots to Russia and Eastern Europe.

After students have been emotionally drained by their encounters in Poland, they fly to Israel. The sociologist Jackie Feldman writes: "After the gray deprivation, vulnerability and death of Poland, Israel is constructed as the land of milk and honey, sexy soldiers, military force, sun, beach, and abundant falafel and chocolate. Israel is an idealized 'future-of-the-Jewish-people' world."[32] Findling speculates that the trip is scheduled in spring, not just because it coincides with the modern Jewish mourning holidays of Yom Ha-Shoah and Israeli Memorial Day, Yom Ha-Zikaron, but also because it is the time of year when Poland is often gray, while Israel is verdant and warm.[33]

Upon arrival at Ben Gurion airport, the visitors are immediately whisked off to the Golan Heights. They then visit a few synagogues in the area and have a cruise on the Sea of Galilee. The next day, students visit a military base and tour the north of the country. On Yom Ha-Zikaron, students visit Tsfat and Acco and stay overnight in Nahariya. On Yom Ha-Atzma'ut, Israeli Independence Day, organizers link the Israeli present and future to the dead European past. The day begins with a visit to Kibbutz Lochamei Getaot (Ghetto Fighters Kibbutz), whose name symbolizes the Israeli memory of the Holocaust as a moment of heroism rather than of existential tragedy. Students then tour Atlit, the British detention center near Haifa that held illegal Jewish immigrants attempting to flee the destruction of Europe during and after World War II, with the goal of reminding students of the injustices done to Holocaust victims by the British. On their final two days, students plant trees, have organized meetings with Israeli teens in Tel Aviv, spend *Shabbat* in Israeli homes, and tour Jerusalem's Old City before boarding a plane to go home.

March of the Living teaches global Jews a Zionist narrative of history that moves from European death in the past to Israeli life in the future. At the same time, the trip aims to instill in participants a sense of global Jewish unity, using fear of anti-Semitism as its main tactic. Sarah, a young Orthodox woman who first participated in March of the Living in 1990 and then became a staff member, said:

> There's no experience like walking through Auschwitz to learn about the Holocaust. . . . Our goal for [the students] . . . is that . . . we need to work *together* as a global community, not against each other.

Perhaps most important, March of the Living uses both Poland and Israel as a backdrop for instilling a new form of Jewish identity, rooted in the places from which these students come. The Jewish Studies scholar Oren Stier argues that the March fosters a sense of sacredness around the Holocaust and Israel and that it is a key component in fostering American Jewish civic religion.[34] According to a sociological study about the effects of the March, Jews return home, wherever that may be, with a stronger sense of Jewish identity, more positive attitudes toward Israel, and a more developed sense of social responsibility. If the March shows American Jewish teenagers that the past is Poland and the present is Israel, then it also hopes to show them that their future is simply at home.

Is Aliyah *Still on the Agenda?*
Religious Nationalism and Identity Travel

For a few organizations, the transformation of self in relation to one's Jewish community and Israel (as place and nation) still translates directly into the hope of making *aliyah* (immigration to Israel). However, unlike fifty years ago, when *aliyah* meant making a commitment to building the secular Jewish nation, today moving to Israel is an aspect of personal transformation that marks both deep religious commitment and a public declaration of one's emotional and national allegiances.[35] For example, while conducting research in Israel in 1999, Caryn interviewed Emily, a thirty-year-old American from the West Coast, who described her experience attending Chabad's *Livnot U'Lehibanot*:

> It was like a warm Jewish womb that I didn't ever want to leave. It was the first time I felt really loved, like I belonged to something larger than

myself and was part of a community. I felt like the power of Judaism had so much to offer that I couldn't turn it down and I couldn't not live here. So I came back.

Unable to find and recreate that rich sense of community in California after her religious transformation, Emily changed her name to Zohar, grew increasingly observant, and returned to Israel for further study with no immediate plans to return to the United States.

That encouragement of transformation and the potential promise of *aliyah* is often coupled with a stinging critique of pluralistic denominations in American Judaism and of modernity and American popular culture more generally. On another Orthodox weekend program Caryn attended in Israel, Ya'acov, the patriarch of the American family who hosted a *Shabbat* lunch, proclaimed that "no Jews have any business living in *golus* [the diaspora] anymore." According to him, the diaspora has been a disastrous experiment in moral corruption and assimilation. Ya'acov had lived for many years in Los Angeles prior to his move to Israel, and Caryn gathered from talking with him that afternoon that his religious observance was of relatively recent origin. When she asked him what he meant, he replied,

The way Judaism is practiced in America today is a *shonda* [Yiddish for an embarrassment]. It's not really Judaism, and anyone who tells you otherwise doesn't know what he's talking about. I think it's bizarre that anyone who wants to make *aliyah* today is considered crazy, when, in fact, that Jew is actually doing what *Hashem* [God] wants all of us to do, what we should do if we knew what was good for us! You see, most Americans don't even know they're still enslaved in *Mitzrayim* [Egypt]. What with all the lust for material things and money, with all that garbage on television, it's hard to know what *Hashem* really wants us from us. It's hard to keep the *mitzvos* [obligations and commandments] and be true to Torah in *golus*. Believe me [he points toward all of us], I know what I'm talking about.

What *Hashem* really wants is for us to be true to Torah and live here [he points his finger down on the table to emphasize his thought]. *Ba'aretz* [in the land of Israel], it's easy to see why *Hashem* gave us *torah b'sinai* [the Torah at Mt. Sinai]. The beauty of *mitzvos*, the joy that we get from doing what *Hashem* wants us to do, it's easy to live by the *halacha* [law] *ba'aretz*. That's why I'm here with my family. [He leans back in his chair, folds his hands over his stomach, and smiles at the group of young Americans assembled around his table.] That's why all of you should be here, too.

In the case of Ya'acov, identity travel was about strengthening religious observance and furthering a form of religious Zionism that was a minor voice in Israel fifty years ago but that now plays a major role in Israeli politics. By traveling to Israel and seeing "true Jewish religiosity" in action, Ya'acov argued, young Americans would realize the spiritual poverty of American culture and materialism and transform themselves into more religiously observant and fervently Zionist Jews.

A common strategy for encouraging and facilitating this transformation combines Jewish education programs with structured emotional, financial, and logistical support for those who choose this path. In other words, some programs blur the line between fostering tourism and subsidizing gradual migration.[36] For example, *Mercaz Hamagshimim* is the Reform movement's "soft landing," the institutional infrastructure that makes being (and potentially settling) in Israel as painfree as possible for liberal English speakers in Jerusalem. It provides courses, job listings, social networks, and social programs to make being in Jerusalem less stressful. Orthodox schools, known as *yeshivot,* provide another popular route for offering both the promise of transformation and the practicalities of support. For example, in Jerusalem, Caryn met Yonatan, a *ba'al tshuvah* (newly religious Jew) from Baltimore at a *Shabbat* dinner in 1998. Over chicken and *challah,* Yonatan (originally Jon) told her about how his lack of religious education as a kid had left a spiritual void inside him as an adult. After meeting a rabbi/chaplain at the hospital where he worked, in Baltimore, Yonatan became increasingly interested in Jewish textual study and religious observance. His rabbi encouraged him to pursue further study in Israel. So Yonatan came to Jerusalem to study at a very popular Zionist *yeshiva* with only four hundred dollars in his pocket. After an intensive four-month immersion in the religious and communal life of the *yeshiva,* Yonatan felt convinced that his future belonged in Israel, despite his having very little idea of how he might earn a living once the program ended.

The Intifada and Costs of Continuing Violence

> We appreciate the difficulties of travel during these trying days, especially to Israel, but we cannot give in to our fears. If we do not continue to visit and link our destiny with Jews everywhere, we will lose the next generation of Jews and let terrorism win. We will show you first-hand how Jews around the globe cope and flourish as they look toward a better future, in a way that will make you prouder and more inspired by Reform Judaism than ever before.
> —ARZA/World Union of Progressive Judaism travel brochure, 2003

> As I stood next to the Kotel with my hand upon its wall, I listened, absorbed, imagined, remembered, and prayed. Standing there, a flood of warmth and comfort filled my body. I was in Israel. I was safe.
> —Sarah Marlin, San Antonio, Texas, MOTL participant

March of the Living participants like Sarah often contrast the fear they felt in Poland with the safety they experienced in Israel. Since the second intifada began in 2000, the definition of safety has shifted. Parents began pulling their children out of MOTL, not because of Polish anti-Semitism but because of bus bombs in Israel. But the truth, for Sarah and all Jewish travel organizers, is that no one is safe at the Western Wall—neither Jews, who constantly worry about suicide bombers, nor Palestinians, who fear Israeli police repression. The desires of MOTL to show students a fearful Europe and a safe Israel now conflict with the reality of a wealthy, relatively peaceful Europe and an embattled Israel, and this led to declining participation. Students and parents now often choose to do more identity work "at home."

Violence impacted other forms of identity travel to Israel, as well. Since the second intifada began, many American universities took an even bolder step and stopped sending their students to Israel.[37]

Describing her experience with birthright 2002, Michelle explains:

> Security was so tight—for our own good, and it was hard to do anything on our own. We went out to a club one night and didn't have a lot of alone time. During the trip, I felt like it was ridiculous. But then there was a suicide bombing in Tel Aviv while we were there. And one of the students got on the microphone and started translating, so students got on their cell phones to call family and were really affected. I think it

made people feel connected to the land even more. One of the boys got taken off the bus during our trip (he was Israeli), because he got called up for duty.

Political violence profoundly impacted birthright israel in multiple ways. First and foremost, participation rates among American Jewish young people dropped, prompting detailed explanations of security measures by organizers to assuage parents' fears and anxieties about their children's safety and well-being. Second, trip itineraries changed to avoid potentially dangerous areas. Time spent in large crowded areas, such as Jerusalem's downtown pedestrian mall, the open-air market, and the Western Wall, was curtailed, and visits were closely monitored. Finally, birthright israel organizers made a concerted effort to conduct outreach to potential participants in other regions of the world, such as South America, Russia, and Eastern Europe, as a way to compensate for declining rates of American participation.

The complete disintegration of the Middle East peace process, the September 11 terror attacks, and the second intifada devastated the tourism industry within Israel. In 2001, Israeli tourism advertising used the slogan "Now, more than ever, we need you here in solidarity," in an effort to staunch severe economic losses. In the same year, Israel's Ministry of Tourism announced a joint effort with some American Jewish groups to sponsor emergency "solidarity missions" to shore up flagging morale. These campaigns appealed to global Jews' sense of collective responsibility to support the beleaguered Jewish state. They also attempted to allay fears by emphasizing heightened "security measures" to ensure tourists' safety at a time when the death toll among Palestinians and Israelis was mounting daily.

However, these emotional appeals to loyalty and obligation were not sufficient enough to convince the American Jewish public. Israeli government officials reacted with rage when, in 2001, the Reform movement decided to cancel all its summer youth tours due to security concerns and parents' fears.[38] Organizations then enlisted more aggressive marketing and recruitment strategies. Some in the diaspora business encouraged major donors to underwrite and subsidize the cost of trips to Israel as an incentive. Still, enrollment for most programs decreased considerably, causing serious economic strain for many involved in Jewish identity tourism. And birthright israel's future was thrown into question when the financially strapped Israeli Ministry of Education pulled its funding late in 2003.[39] At the same time, the United Jewish Communities also failed to commit further funding to the project.[40]

For most of the 1980s and 1990s, Jewish identity travel constructed Eastern Europe as a site of historical danger, destruction, and death, while Israel was essentialized as the Promised Land of refuge for diaspora Jews.[41] But with the persistent violence of the second intifada, the way Jews relate to these historical places has changed dramatically. Jewish organizations' emotional appeals to loyalty and obligation have not convinced the American Jewish public that Israel remains a safe place for travel. During the intifada, summer identity tours that would have taken Jewish youth to Israel were rerouted to "safer" parts of the globe (Argentina, for example), and some were canceled altogether.[42] Despite domestic terror alerts from the U.S. Department of Homeland Security, most Americans see America as a safer place than Israel.

These changes suggest that using Israel as a backdrop for developing American Jewish identities at home was useful at a particular historical moment. In the 1990s, a semblance of peace defined Israeli-Palestinian relations, and Eastern Europe opened its doors to Holocaust tourists for the first time. In such an environment, youth identity tourism to Israel and Holocaust sites in Eastern Europe made sense. But with the second intifada, that moment of optimism in the Middle East passed. And, as an economically vibrant Eastern Europe joins the European Union and becomes home to new Jewish cultures, Jewish identity travel and the diaspora business have changed.[43]

More students are rediscovering and studying the rich Jewish histories of the United States and Eastern Europe, of Yiddish and *klezmer,* as viable routes to constructing Jewish identity.[44] And with renewed hopes for Middle East peace following Yassir Arafat's death late in 2004, tourism to Israel is picking up. Jewish youth—and the diaspora business that shuttles them around—now have choices about where to travel and what aspects of Jewish culture to explore.

We imagine that ten years from now, diaspora business organizations will spend as much money sending young Jews to Vilnius to study Yiddish or to Prague to study Jewish art and architecture as they do sending young Jews to Israel. While many will still choose to climb Masada at dawn or volunteer for six weeks in the Israeli army, we imagine new Jewish youth traveling to New York to study in *yeshivas,* visit Jewish museums, conduct family history research at Jewish archives, learn Russian in

Jewish immigrant neighborhoods, and eat their way through Jewish New York as culinary tourists.

Travel is still integral to the new Jewish map, and Israel will always be an important part of that map, but in our "March of the Living," travel will no longer focus on Jews' encounter with ghosts and death but will be about new Jews' encounters with one another. Rather than seeing a Jew's "birthright" as a nationalistic claim to land, we see it as a claim to culture, history, and heritage, whether that happens to be in New York, Moscow, Buenos Aires, Berlin, or Jerusalem.

3

Temples of American Identity
Jewish Museums in Los Angeles

Beverly Hills felt like it was [all Jewish]. . . . All of my Jewish
friends ate rye bread with mustard and there was one non-Jewish
boy in the group that I went around with and he . . . used mayon-
naise on white bread.   —Dean Kaye, 1977

To American Jews, America is home. There exist their thriving
roots; there is the country which they have helped to build; and
there they share its fruits and its destiny.
                          —Jacob Blaustein, president of the American
                                  Jewish Committee, 1949–1954

The Skirball Cultural Center is dedicated to exploring the connections between the age-old Jewish heritage and American democracy.
                          —Skirball Cultural Center Web site

The Museum of Tolerance is a high tech, hands-on experiential museum that focuses on two central themes through unique interactive
exhibits: the dynamics of racism and prejudice in America and the
history of the Holocaust—the ultimate example of man's inhumanity to man.   —Museum of Tolerance Web site

Over the past thirty to forty years, museums have become central places where American Jews constitute their identity and publicly display themselves to broad audiences. One critic has suggested that "museums are becoming synagogues," in that they serve not just as a place to
display artifacts as they once might have but also as cultural, culinary,
and community centers, children's day care providers, and concert halls.

The religion professor Deborah Dash Moore argues that "Jews seem to be fascinated with looking at representations of themselves and their culture."[1] Synagogues used to be the places in which Jews constituted their communal Jewish identities. But the spate of museums, and the vast quantities of money spent on them, suggests that, in the future, these institutions and the numerous community programs they spawn might be the preeminent Jewish communal places of the future. Today, anyone can visit major cultural institutions, such as the Jewish Museum, in New York, the U.S. Holocaust Memorial Museum, in Washington, D.C., the Skirball Center, in Los Angeles, the Spertus Museum, in Chicago, and smaller but locally important Jewish cultural venues throughout the country, to learn about American Jewish history and heritage.[2] The stories of, on the one hand, immigration, adaptation, and integration into American culture and, on the other, genocidal destruction are depicted through exhibitions, Web sites, and programs designed to celebrate the quintessential "American-ness" of the Jewish experience in the United States over the past two centuries and the diversity of Jewish life around the world. But these celebrations are also haunted by the ghosts of twentieth-century war and remind viewers of the evanescence of such immigrant success.

For American Jews in particular, museums are one of the primary sites where they craft their identities as Americans and as Jews. Museums are places to learn origin stories, to see family and communal histories, and to congregate out of cultural, not religious impulses. In this chapter, we examine the Skirball Cultural Center and the Simon Wiesenthal Museum of Tolerance–Bet Ha-Shoah, the two largest and best-funded Jewish museums and cultural institutions in Los Angeles, in order to examine how Jews use museums to understand themselves as Jewish Americans. We explore how new Jews engage in identity construction, among themselves and to a wider non-Jewish public, within broader conversations about race, public space, and the contested meaning of belonging in America.

Origins of the Jewish Museum

Jewish museums are a relatively new phenomenon, born at the end of the nineteenth century in Europe. According to Richard Cohen, "The turning point in the collection and exhibition of Judaica was that juncture in the history of European Jewry when the process of leaving the 'ghetto' was fully matured and the bulk of western and central European Jewish society had achieved emancipation."[3] One of the earliest exhibits of Judaica, the Anglo-Jewish Exhibition at London's Royal Albert Hall, in 1887, involved some of the same questions of identity, sameness, and difference that contemporary American Jewish museums wrestle with today. For both, the Jewish museum and public displays of Jewishness have been about social positioning. A prominent ethnographer in Victorian England said that the Anglo-Jewish Exhibition was a confirmation of his view that Jews "were men, not merely theologians," and it emphasized their "'human aspect,' in the manner of their jargons, names, and customs."[4] The exhibition revealed an assimilationist strain in Jewish self-presentation that continued well into the twentieth century.

The *Jewish Chronicle*, Britain's preeminent Jewish newspaper, devoted much attention to the exhibition and stressed the Jewish-Gentile relations implicit in it:

> England has to be proud of her treatment of Jews, and Jews have to be grateful to a great country that has held up the beacon of tolerance thru [*sic*] so many years of misrepresentation and ill-will. From this point of view the Exhibition is truly Anglo-Jewish, and in the best sense of the word, national.[5]

The exhibition also strove to display and promote a Judaism that was cultured, respectable, and elegant: concerts with Jewish music were performed during the exhibition and distinguished scholars gave lectures. As we will soon see, the Skirball Cultural Center in Los Angeles, as the English exhibition did for England, shows how America's historic openness has made it possible for Jews to be Americans, especially through the lens of class and social standing. The Museum of Tolerance employs a similar message of tolerance, or lack thereof, to remind Jews of an ugly recent past and the potential for violence to happen again in the present.

More than London, central Europe—namely Vienna and Prague—was the birthplace of Jewish museums. This was a product of the broader Jewish intellectual cultures that developed in Central Europe following Jews' emancipation in Europe in the eighteenth and nineteenth centuries. In both cities, the museums were part of assimilated Jews' drive toward maintaining historical consciousness of their Jewish past as they culturally assimilated into the dominant cultures around them. Vienna's museum was established in the 1890s, and, like Los Angeles museum curators today, its founders were driven by a sense of responsibility for presenting a particular image of the Jewish past and, implicitly, the Jewish present. The organizers were responding to the embrace of modernity and the waning interest in "things Jewish" among Prague's and Vienna's Jewish communities. All of the early Jewish museums and exhibitions were founded by Jews who themselves were distanced from the nonassimilated Jewish past they were trying to present. Salomon Hugo Lieben, the guiding force behind Prague's Jewish museum, received a German education and viewed the gradual transformation of Bohemian Jewry into "Czechs" quite favorably.[6] He and the others who supported his efforts were intimately connected with Czech society and received severe criticism from certain Jewish groups because of their assimilatory stance. Lieben made special effort to collect and preserve Jewish artifacts that had originated either in Prague or Bohemia.[7] The museum was meant to bear witness to the deep-seated connection of Jews to their particular place of settlement and to their historic presence in a given country, an impulse at work behind the major exhibitions of contemporary Jewish museums in the twenty-first century.

The example of the Skirball Cultural Center, founded by Reform Jews in the United States, shows that the impetus to establish a Jewish museum has not changed much from that behind the exhibitions in Vienna, Prague, and London. The Skirball's permanent collection and exhibition of Jewish cultural and religious objects and artwork depicts Jews' engagement with modernity and popular culture and celebrates Jewish American history as a quintessential immigration and successful adaptation narrative. In all cases, Jewish museums were founded by acculturated Jews looking to root themselves in their landscapes both as Jews and as cosmopolitan citizens of the place in which they lived. They taught acculturated Jews about Jewish religion by exhibiting Judaica and other Jewish artifacts. They displayed for their acculturated communities a celebratory and triumphant interpretation of the Jewish past, present, and future.

The Emergence of the Holocaust Museum

The first public Holocaust commemoration in America took place on December 2, 1942, when 500,000 New York Jews stopped work for ten minutes, both to mourn those already killed and to call attention to the ongoing massacre.[8] However, museums dedicated to the Holocaust did not start appearing until the late 1970s.[9] By 2000, there were Holocaust museums or learning centers in such diverse places as El Paso, Texas; Augusta, Maine; St. Petersburg, Florida; Richmond, Virginia; Detroit, Michigan; Los Angeles, California; and other major cities, as well. Some of these museums deal exclusively with the Holocaust and double as memorials to the victims of the Holocaust. Others, like the Museum of Tolerance–Bet Ha-Shoah, expand their mission to include educational exhibits about other genocides, human rights, and cultural diversity.[10]

Like Jewish cultural and art museums, Holocaust museums, which are usually spearheaded by local Jewish organizations, negotiate the tension between sameness and differences, uniqueness and universality. By calling for a Holocaust museum, as opposed to a museum on the Native American genocide, slavery, or any other atrocity, Jews emphatically make the claim that the mass murder of European Jewry was a unique event in history and should be marked as such. At the same time, these museums wrestle with the presence of other victims of Nazi Germany (as represented by the debate between six million Jewish victims of the Holocaust or eleven million victims more generally) and with the obvious examples of other genocides in twentieth-century history. If the Holocaust is unique, then how can (or should) it be used as a lesson about tolerance in general? If the Holocaust is not unique, then how do (and should) Jews get to claim a special victim status? And, in the American context, when a Holocaust museum talks about tolerance, one must ask tolerance of what, and for what purpose? Should some forms of diversity be celebrated but not others?

In the United States, where questions of identity and victimization have become so politically contested, the place of a Holocaust museum in the American landscape illuminates many of these tensions. Michael Berenbaum, the former director of the U.S. Holocaust Memorial Museum, in Washington, D.C., suggests that the use of the Holocaust in the United States is different from that in Israel or other places in the world. "If Israelis turn to the Holocaust as proof that the whole world is against them, American Jews reinforce their commitment to pluralism by recalling the atrocities that sprang from intolerance."[11] This model of tolerance as the framing concept for Holocaust museums in America demonstrates just how fully rooted American Jews are in the cultural landscape.

The Museum of Tolerance–Bet Ha-Shoah, in Los Angeles, one of the oldest Holocaust museums in the country, is also a site in which these tensions are played out, however with a very different timbre and tone. One of the most interesting aspects of this museum is that, unlike Jewish culture and history museums, which have generally been spearheaded by acculturated Jews looking to root themselves in a national landscape, the Museum of Tolerance was founded and is currently run by Orthodox Jews—those for whom tolerance of difference in America, rather than aspirations of sameness, is paramount. The fact that Orthodox Jews in the United States constantly navigate their existence as different in relation to everyone else around them (including non-Orthodox Jews) makes the idea of celebrating diversity and tolerance as a founding value for a museum that much more compelling and imperative. Indirectly, the subtext of such a museum's goal of tolerance also serves as a political tool to stave off the potential of future harm to those considered "different." The Museum of Tolerance shows that Berenbaum's distinction between the "Israeli" nationalistic use of the Holocaust and the American "pluralistic" use actually coexist in one place, in which Jews move between and operate within both paradigms simultaneously.

Los Angeles: The Newest Home of American Jews

Home to both the Museum of Tolerance and the Skirball Museum, Los Angeles is one of the newest Jewish cities in the world. Jews have lived in L.A. since its founding in the nineteenth century; a Jew served on the first city council, in 1850. Los Angeles did not become a part of Jewish geography, however, until early-twentieth-century Eastern European Jewish immigrants bought land and built companies that later became the Hollywood studio system in the 1920s and 1930s.[12] After World War II, a massive influx of migrants fled the Midwest and the East Coast for the land of Hollywood, beaches, and a booming postwar economy.[13] As a result of economic shifts and white flight, the Westside and the San Fernando Valley quickly replaced the prewar Los Angeles Jewish neighborhood in Boyle Heights as the homes of L.A. Jewry.[14] In 1946, observers estimated that each month sixteen thousand newcomers were arriving in Los Angeles; more than two thousand of those were Jews, well above the 3.5 percent of Angelenos who were Jewish that year and above the 8 percent of the U.S. urban population that was Jewish.[15] By the end of the 1950s, 18 percent of the Los Angeles population was Jewish, making it the second largest Jewish community in the country; by 1969, there were more than half a million Jews in Los Angeles, making it the third largest Jewish community in the world, behind New York and Tel Aviv.

Migrants to Los Angeles in the 1950s established their own form of self-help organizations, along the lines of the Eastern European immigrants' *landsmanshaftn*—the mutual aid organizations Jewish immigrants established in the New World on the basis of geographic, political, and social divisions from the Old World—but without the cultural and religious distinctiveness of the earlier generation's organizations. These L.A. organizations were centers of secular ethnic sociability, anchoring their members in unfamiliar urban territory through nostalgic evocations of the well-known world that had been abandoned, the worlds of Chicago and New York.[16] In its postwar incarnation, Los Angeles became home to Jewish communities and identities not linked to communal forms inherited from traditional Judaism and not inherited from immigrant relatives. Postwar Los Angeles was a tabula rasa on which Jews sought to create new forms of Jewish communal expression without the legacies of European oppression and East Coast Anglo-Saxon exclusion of Jews. Charles Brown, head of the L.A. Jewish Community Council, said, in 1952, "[In Los Angeles] there are no vested interests, here there are no sacred cows, here there is no cold hand of the past. There is an opportunity to develop new forms of Jewish communal living geared in a realistic fashion to the actual needs of the Jewish community and creating through the democratic process of people participating in shaping their own destiny."[17] Although some discriminatory housing and hiring policies still existed in some places, in many ways, as Deborah Dash Moore has argued, Jewish migrants to Los Angeles saw themselves as white Americans who had left behind families, neighborhoods, and institutions associated with their past and who were now free to craft new identities and communities accordingly.[18]

In the 1950s, Los Angeles was becoming a frontier Jewish culture. Major New York Jewish organizations established Los Angeles branches by soliciting Hollywood's support. Rabbinic seminaries in New York began establishing West Coast seminaries. But, as with other processes of migration and globalization, the question remained: Would Los Angeles Jewish culture simply be an import of New York's culture, with all of its entrenched political and denominational divisiveness? And what would it mean to be an L.A. Jew? Los Angeles and its atmosphere of freedom and lack of East Coast–influenced social norms made many Jewish leaders think that the city would be the home of innovative forms of Jewish communities, identities, and cultures.

Simon Greenberg, the first president of the University of Judaism, the Conservative movement's Los Angeles seminary, founded in 1947, reflected on these tensions: "We had to overcome the feeling on the West Coast that this was a new community. Why did it have to import the [denominational] divisions of the East Coast? Why can't we have one school for the Jews of the West Coast?"[19] In fact, students agree that studying at the L.A. branch of a rabbinic seminary *is* different from studying at the New York branch precisely because of its "L.A. outlook."

Los Angeles, known for Hollywood, beaches, muscles, and blond hair, does not strike most observers as a natural home for the elite world of museum culture and the display of historical imagination. But, because of the lack of traditional Jewish geography and the presence of money, creativity, and a desire to innovate, in the 1970s and 1980s, Los Angeles became the West Coast anchor of American Jewish museum culture.

Precisely because Los Angeles has developed its own kind of rooted Jewish communities, identities, and institutions, Jewish immigrants from abroad increasingly look to Los Angeles as an alternative to the historic New York as the American Jewish "melting pot." Although New York has the largest Russian-speaking Jewish population in the world, Los Angeles is in the top five. L.A. is also home to the largest Persian Jewish population in the world,[20] a large Israeli population,[21] and a smaller Ethiopian community. Like earlier waves of migrants from Chicago, New York, and Tel Aviv, these more recent arrivals have formed their own distinctive subcultures and communal institutions, sometimes to the consternation of Ashkenazi Jewish professionals who seek to encourage newer immigrants to join existing organizations.[22] Like the tensions that existed in New York between established German Jews and immigrant "greenhorns" from Eastern Europe at the turn of the twentieth century, Los Angeles now has its conflicts between the established Jews who have lived there for many years and more recent, global Jewish immigrants.

Museum of Tolerance–Bet Ha-Shoah

In 1977, Rabbi Martin Hier, an Orthodox rabbi from Vancouver, Canada, moved to Los Angeles and launched the idea of a Holocaust museum. Although Elie Wiesel's books about the Holocaust had been circulating in English for more than fifteen years, the television program *Holo-*

caust, which many scholars cite as a pivotal moment in the populariza-
tion of Holocaust awareness, had not yet been aired, and President Jimmy
Carter had not yet made public his idea for a national museum to the
Holocaust in Washington, D.C.

From the beginning, museum founders agreed that this Holocaust museum would not aim for just a Jewish audience. They wanted a museum
in which the development of identity around a tragic event, which most
Holocaust museums and memorials organize as their centerpiece, would
take a back seat to the more universal didactic messages of the Holocaust.
The English part of the name of the museum, Museum of Tolerance, suggested a broader mission that resonated with the prevailing American
ethos of tolerance, acceptance, and integration in the years following the
heyday of civil rights activism and echoed academic discussions of "race
relations" theory at the time.[23] Today, on the way to the Museum of Tolerance, one can walk (or, more likely, drive) down Pico Boulevard in West
Los Angeles, an urban retail stretch with a dense concentration of Jewish-
owned establishments, and see signs in Farsi, Hebrew, and Russian. In the
stores themselves, you're just as likely to hear those languages, as well as
New York–, Philadelphia–, and South African–accented English.

But it is not so much L.A.'s Jewish diversity that made the Museum of
Tolerance a perfect fit for Los Angeles as its broader ethnic diversity, notably including African Americans, Asian Americans, and Latinos. The
Museum's Director of Education, Adaire Klein, said, "This museum has
to be in Los Angeles, the most diverse city in the country. This is the kind
of place that needs to talk about appreciating difference."[24] After the L.A.
Watts riots of 1965, and given the broader history of racial tensions and
power struggles, most recently in the 1990s, with the media spectacles
that surrounded Rodney King and O. J. Simpson, a museum of tolerance
in the heart of Los Angeles made perfect sense, a sort of civic paean to the
virtue and value of pluralism in an ethnically diverse, fragmented urban
landscape.

In 1977, Hier and a few other Orthodox Jews of Los Angeles, with
financial backing from the Belzberg family, in Canada, bought a small
building in the heart of Orthodox Jewish Los Angeles on Pico Boulevard.[25] The initial purchase of the building had a grander purpose than
the housing of a small Holocaust museum. Hier and the West Coast Orthodox establishment also used the building as the foundation for an Orthodox *yeshiva* that became the West Coast branch of Yeshiva University
(YULA), the Orthodox university in New York. In other words, the mem-

ory of the Holocaust and the flourishing of Orthodox Jewish education emerged simultaneously next to each other, living on the same turf in a city whose Jews are more likely to be involved in Hollywood than they are in *yeshiva* culture.

The initial museum was a very small affair, according to Klein, its first director of libraries and education. She described the museum complex as a series of small rooms that led into the small archival and library holdings, which in turn led into the office of the institute. Around back was the *yeshiva*. They rearranged the exhibit so that the museum could have its own area and opened it up to the public in 1977. "From the beginning, the main audience for the museum was school children." This Holocaust museum conveyed its civic goals as soon as it opened its doors, and the museum took its charge to be an educational institution seriously. "The exhibits in the original museum were 'old style,' with artifacts behind glass, small captions. It wasn't exciting," Klein commented. Some critics have had a different reading of the original Simon Wiesenthal Museum. "This low-tech affair was fashioned by and for Jews holding nothing against the Gentiles back—an outsized portrait of [the Holocaust-era pope] Pius XII was given a prominent place among pictures of those who 'didn't care.' The message was that Jews have enemies, murderous enemies, and should look out."[26] These two messages—victimization through indifference or deliberate aggression and the need to tolerate differences—also informed the second, more grandiose and sophisticated incarnation of the museum when it opened in 1993.

The building of the new Museum of Tolerance cost $50 million, and much of that money was raised among people in Los Angeles. The Hollywood film industry provided the museum with financial and political sustenance, marketing ideas, and the tools for presenting much of its material. The list of major donors includes Sherry Lansing, Ron Meyer, Gerald Levin, Jeffrey Katzenberg, and Paramount executive Jonathan Dolgen.[27] If, in 1977, the Simon Wiesenthal Center was financially and administratively an Orthodox Jewish affair, the construction of the new complex drew from many non-Jewish and liberal, secular Hollywood players.

The New Museum—Bigger and Better

The new Museum of Tolerance is housed in a large, squat, brown brick building in the heart of the Pico-Robertson neighborhood. Every day, throngs of students from various ethnic backgrounds mill around awaiting admission; the guided museum tours are carefully timed to prevent overcrowding. Security guards stand at both the initial entrance to the museum and just past the ticket center to pat down visitors, perhaps because of the perceived need for increased security after the events of September 11, 2001, or perhaps as an indication of how the museum's staff feel about the subject matter and potential vulnerability of its assets and exhibits. As an odd side note, this museum dedicated to promoting racial and ethnic tolerance houses a Judaica shop, replete with all sorts of gift items. It strikes us as strange that the museum sells Judaica—menorahs, seder plates, dreidels, and mezuzahs—as, after all, this is a museum dedicated to tolerance, not Jewish culture.

Much of what makes the Museum of Tolerance unique is its very Los Angeles/Hollywood-style presentation. The museum uses technology in every aspect of its educational mission, from interactive displays to colorful neon lights to large trick doors that won't open (reminiscent of the Haunted House at Disneyland) to games that are meant to make the museum interesting to its primary audience—students. In the words of one commentator, "The Simon Wiesenthal Center has created an experiential exhibit where emotions and images, not objects, become the driving and powerful artifacts."[28] This experience-centered approach is one of the aspects that differentiates the Museum of Tolerance from the U.S. Holocaust Memorial Museum, which uses the opposite approach by making artifacts the center of the permanent exhibition. The Holocaust scholar Oren Stier says about the U.S. Holocaust Memorial Museum, "Americans could 'touch' the reality of the Holocaust through a museum whose use of artifacts would shrink the geographical distance between Poland and America and make permeable the boundaries between Holocaust and American space."[29] In his study of the semiotics of the Museum of Tolerance, Stier argues that, in good Hollywood fashion, simulation is the mode through which the museum teaches its lessons. It makes people "participate" by asking them questions, forcing them to make choices, and, in the most extreme example, assigning each visitor the identity of a Holocaust victim.[30]

The museum continues to rely on the film expertise of Hollywood to produce many of its educational videos, and Rabbi Hier even coproduced a documentary on racism and intolerance about the L.A. race riots and another on genocide that won Oscars. Some critics have suggested that the museum is too much Hollywood, not enough history. There are, for example, virtually no artifacts in the museum. Museum staffers say that this is its strength—only through technology can it reach its target audience; only through experiential education can people be made to "feel" intolerance. The museum uses emotion rather than reason to affect its guests; feelings, not artifacts, are what people remember long after their visit. This is the underlying message of the museum itself: Intolerance is, after all, about emotion over reason. And, with enough education, so the story goes, people will "lose" their intolerance, and the world will be a safer, less violent place. Whether visitors embrace real-life "diverse" people whose cultures are explored in the educational exhibits remains an open question.

On our most recent visit, the second floor of the museum housed a temporary exhibit on diversity entitled "Peaceful Warriors," which strikes us as an odd title for an exhibit on nonviolence.[31] The exhibition focused mostly on race and racism, the most politically mainstream civil rights movement, without mentioning other important and still-contested struggles such as feminism, queer rights, and the environmental movement. Photographs, paraphernalia, and paintings of Martin Luther King, Jr., Sojourner Truth, and Cesar Chavez adorned the walls along one side of the exhibit, along with small posters describing the likes of Nelson Mandela, the Dalai Lama, Gandhi, Jane Addams, Chief Seattle, and Desmond Tutu. These historical and political figures were lionized in the posters, which presented brief descriptions of their work and particular struggles, written in simple language that was clearly intended for school-age children. Along another wall was a display that depicted the iconography of tolerance that the museum applauds, with more photographs of Gandhi, King, and Lech Walesa. There were no women in this second iconographic representation, and almost no discussion of what these people did or why we should care; the wall simply provided an artistic space that functioned somewhere between a somber memorial and a kitschy homage. The underlying message of this exhibit remained unclear. What do visitors learn substantively about what these famous figures accomplished within a broader political context?

The temporary exhibit space transitioned into a multimedia learning center that focuses on the Holocaust and that hums with activity. Hollywood and Silicon Valley emerge in full force, and it's obvious to even the most naïve visitor that the museum relies on toys, graphics, and sound to attract its visitors.

Computer stations are set up every ten feet to attract and encourage kids to explore the Holocaust. Video screening rooms with plush seating are spaced every twenty feet around the perimeter of the circular walkway in which the exhibit is arranged. There are no guides or glass cases housing artifacts here, just high-tech workstations that allow users to browse digitized archives, scroll through complex historical diagrams, and choose which idea or topic they want to focus on after looking at menu screens. The method used to appeal to museum participants is interactive and distancing simultaneously. People walking through can either choose to explore as much as they want in several media or opt out entirely and learn nothing at all, instead choosing to snooze in one of the comfy chairs in the viewing rooms. As we wandered through the area, we also wondered why a student needed to come to the museum to participate in these virtual activities, when the museum could easily provide access via the Web and therefore make information available to anyone.

This unscripted, democratic section of the museum is liberating for users but also threatens to undermine the curators' intent, since people can engage as little or as much as they want. Whereas in traditional museums visitors are guided through a maze of carefully curated exhibits and artifacts, this self-guided multimedia approach requires the students to take the initiative to learn on their own, if they so choose, rather than patiently listen or read canned text. The museum curators have, in essence, democratized and relinquished control over the interpretative process, allowing viewers to find their own pathways to learn what they desire.

After spending time in the multimedia center waiting for their tour, visitors descended into the main exhibit by walking in a spiral circle down to the basement, where, on this day, a Jewish woman in her seventies greeted the throngs of students and introduced herself as the guide for our tour. In reality, the woman served as a shepherd, telling the students when to move forward, while the exhibit itself was narrated by disembodied voiceovers. The main exhibit differs profoundly in pedagogical approach from the multimedia center, in that it uses traditional, somewhat archaic-looking textual and artifact-based methods to convey its message, which focuses on race and anti-Semitism as the cornerstones of hatred in the United States. At the main entrance of the exhibit, visitors are confronted with two doors with the words "Prejudiced" and "Unprejudiced"[32] and are asked by the overhead narration to choose which door they want to walk through. But it's a trick question, as the "Unprejudiced" door is actually locked, forcing everyone to walk through the "Prejudiced" door as a means to make visitors start thinking about classification and discrimination. All visitors then enter the "Tolerancenter."

The Tolerancenter opens with the history of slavery, civil rights, and the experience of African Americans. As we experienced in the temporary exhibit, race is the guiding form of "difference" in the museum. By connecting racial (in)tolerance to the Holocaust, the museum suggests that historical experiences of discrimination—whether African American or Jewish—are linked in certain ways. From the treatment of slaves in the eighteenth century to Martin Luther King, Jr., in the 1960s to the Los Angeles race riots in 1991, the museum's Tolerancenter makes tolerance of physical difference its primary lens. However, even though the museum focuses intently on racial tolerance and difference, the center does not mention the key historical and social patterns that contribute to racism and intolerance, such as persistent residential segregation, bank redlining, racial profiling, and economic inequality.

Perhaps most striking about this section of the museum is the use of film as an ideological and emotional tool that ended up confusing us as viewers about the purpose of the visit. After a presentation on the history of discrimination against African Americans, a ten-minute film, *It Is Called Genocide*, briefly documents three twentieth-century genocides— the Armenian genocide, the Cambodian genocide, and the massacre and starvation of millions throughout Latin America, which the film labels "genocide." Viewers witness gruesome footage of atrocities, including pictures of children scarred by their recruitment into armies, but are provided little historical and political context to help them understand how and why these events occurred.

There is no mention of the Holocaust. That is preserved as a unique event in history with its own section of the exhibit. Thus, the lessons of the Holocaust are visually and cognitively separated from those of the Tolerancenter. The Holocaust was not about diffuse intolerance; it was about the targeted and rabid hatred of Jews. At the end of the film on genocide, images of World War II show mutilated bodies, refugees marching, and the carnage of war. Then scenes from the assassination of Israeli prime minister Yitzhak Rabin provide an explicitly Jewish reference to the issue of genocide as a hint of what's to come in the next section of the museum, which explores the Holocaust. Were the results of intolerance the real message of the film? What was the purpose of displaying "necro-pornography"—using images of violence and death to fascinate—with disturbing images that undoubtedly cause serious anxiety and distress in adults, let alone the many children wandering in and out of the viewing theater?

The links between the Holocaust and the message of tolerance feel disconnected after one has witnessed such grisly footage. The Holocaust happened to Jews and happened a long time ago. Bosnia, Rwanda, and race riots are what we have to think about, because they're happening now, in our own lives. Some scholars push further and question whether the Holocaust is useful as a tool to teach tolerance at all. Peter Novick, in his book *The Holocaust in American Life,* questions the usefulness of the Holocaust as didactic lesson. Novick argues that showing this evil behavior as a moral extreme, rather than showing that all people can participate in intolerance that can lead to violence, conditions the viewer to think, "Wow, I would never do that, so I'm not that bad."[33] From its inception, the Museum of Tolerance preempted such criticisms by "remind[ing] future generations of the disastrous consequences of intolerance run amok, using the Nazi Holocaust as the ultimate example of man's inhumanity to man. It serves as a vivid warning that intolerance, when given full reign, can lead to mass murder in the worst degree."[34] The Museum of Tolerance was on the cutting edge of making the Holocaust the moral lesson for all Americans, but maybe Novick was right. The unnatural linking of the two pieces of the museum shows vividly the tension that coexists in the museum—as a museum dedicated to Jewish particularity even as it tries to teach universal messages about tolerance and hatred.

Connecting Tolerance to the Holocaust

As a stark contrast to the necropornography of the Tolerancenter, the Holocaust section of the main exhibit opens with yet another film, this one entitled *Echoes That Remain.* Unlike the genocide film, this one shows footage of *shtetls* and synagogues, a romantic depiction of the richness of pre-Shoah Jewish communities, and almost exclusively shows "exotic," observant, rural Jews, rather than secular, assimilated, and cosmopolitan Jews living in large cities. The film culminates with an ominous foreshadowing of the horrors that await these unsuspecting Jews across Europe by introducing the evil intentions of the Nazi regime.

The curators of the Museum of Tolerance flirt dangerously with the tendency toward the "Disneyfication" of history by partitioning and reducing history into three acts in classic Hollywood fashion so that visitors with limited attention spans will remain riveted to the story. The first act, for which the film *Echoes* sets the stage, glorifies a lost past and romanticizes prewar Jewish life as the golden years. Nowhere in this narrative are conflicts within Jewish communities implied, nor are social problems of European society more generally (such as poverty or gender inequality) ever mentioned. The last scene of the first act ends with storm clouds looming on the horizon and ominous music playing as the Nazi Party ascends to power and begins to restrict the rights and movements of Jews in Germany.

The second act explores in ugly, stark detail the global conflict generated by the Third Reich and the unbelievable suffering, persecution, and death that descended upon Europe during the war. The exhibit in Act 2 begins to resemble a "genocide fun house" in which the curators use experiential and spatial strategies to induce specific emotions in visitors, such as identification with the victims (by giving fake ID cards of actual Holocaust victims or survivors), fear (herding people through faux replicas of gas chambers), and sorrow (black displays of candles, tombstones, somber music).

After a while, all the necroporn and images of death seem to numb or alienate the students shuffling through the exhibit; during our fieldwork, we saw several students literally tune out by putting on headphones and closing their eyes as we stopped in front of dioramas of gas chambers.

As the narrative structure of March of the Living moves from Poland to Israel, as a reward for having vicariously survived the grisly, exhausting scenes of Act 2, museum visitors see the beginning of redemption in Act 3 with the establishment of the State of Israel as a haven for oppressed Jews who survived the war and a brief homage to "righteous Gentiles" who attempted to save, smuggle, or hide Jews, sometimes at the expense of their own lives. But this Hollywood production does not tout the happy ending it could have. Letting visitors leave with an upbeat message of hope and redemption and the possibility of tolerant understanding might dilute the seriousness of the museum's mission to instill fear that such atrocities might and, indeed, still do happen. To end with a rousing celebration of the State of Israel might lessen the emotional and ideological impact of the museum's didactic intentions. And, on a deeper level, instilling hope also detracts from the power of the phrase *"never again."* If the Tolerancenter's goal is to educate visitors about the universalism of genocide, then the Holocaust exhibit clearly demonstrates the idea of moral vigilance as an institutional and individual bulwark against the possibility of future genocide. This exhibit aims to instill in future Jewish and non-Jewish generations some semblance of empathy for the historical persecution of Jews.

Is the Museum a Jewish Museum?

The Simon Wiesenthal Center, which is the organizational director, owner, and operator of the museum, is a Jewish institution, whose primary mission is to combat anti-Semitism around the world. The dual tasks of raising the specter of anti-Semitism while preaching tolerance create tensions in the Museum of Tolerance–Bet Ha-Shoah, reflecting the ambivalence some American Jews feel as Americans and as Jews. Its mission is to teach the hundreds of thousands of school children who visit the museum that tolerance is fragile and that Jews were the worst victims of intolerance in history. Like March of the Living, the museum's other task is to remind Jews that anti-Semitism can rear its ugly head anytime, anyplace, and to instill a sense of vigilance, and perhaps anxiety, among comfortable, bourgeois American Jews who have made it in the United States. The institution relies on Jews' guilt over being secure in their status as American Jews, on Jews' sense of responsibility for *am yisrael,* the people of Israel, and on Jews' wealth to make it one of the best-funded Jewish institutions in the country.

This Janus-faced representation of American Jews shows up in the mission of the institution and in the construction of the museum, with its Tolerancenter and its Holocaust section. The name of the museum even suggests this—Museum of Tolerance–Bet Ha-Shoah. The Holocaust section represented in the Hebrew phrase "Bet Ha-Shoah," which literally means House of Catastrophe does not even use words like "tolerance" as part of its "lessons about the Holocaust." The lesson of the Holocaust section is that Jews are victims in history. What seems an even bigger omission is the fact that the story of the Holocaust as presented by the museum is about only Jews. Unlike the U.S. Holocaust Memorial Museum, in Washington, which goes to great lengths to include all victims of the Holocaust, the Museum of Tolerance does not talk about other victims. In this way, Bet Ha-Shoah is a Jewish museum and attempts to maintain the uniqueness of the Holocaust as a Jewish event. Because of its ability to be Janus-faced, to be both a tolerance center preaching universal messages of diversity and acceptance and an old-fashioned Holocaust museum emphasizing the uniqueness of the Jewish experience of persecution, the institution convinced public agencies to grant it $5 million for developing its educational material.

Cynics see the tolerance aspect of the museum as a front, a way to raise funds for an institution whose primary job is to stoke the fires of fear among American Jews and to promote right-wing and pro-Zionist Jewish politics. This view envisions a world in which Jews are the primary victims of intolerance, one in which Jews are hated worldwide, and one in which Jews have both a right and a duty to be tribal, insular, and particularistic, to defend themselves in an intolerant world. "Tolerance" is a nonthreatening way to give the museum a high profile in order to compete with the proliferation of other cultural institutions in a racially diverse Los Angeles. The tolerance frame also increases fund-raising opportunities among non-Jews. It allows the museum to get funding from local, state, and federal governments, and it separates it from the rest of the institutional Jewish community in Los Angeles. In 1985, the ACLU filed a lawsuit to stop the state of California from giving the museum a matching grant, arguing that the museum's founder was a clergyman and that the Center was really a front for Yeshiva University Los Angeles. The case settled out of court.[35] And there are quite a few cynics. Many people point to the strategies Rabbi Hier used to raise the $50 million for the new museum—how he manipulated language in the House hearings on funding the educational part of the museum to ensure that the funding came through.

But after visiting the museum and meeting some of the people who run it, we find that the cynical approach does not adequately explain why the group of Orthodox Jews that makes up the leadership and board of this institution would found such a museum. There is too much investment and involvement in the tolerance part of the message to dismiss it as a front for right-wing Orthodox politics. In fact, the museum is planning an expansion that will create a new section on tolerance, even further shrinking the physical presence of the Holocaust in the museum's narrative. This raises an interesting question: Are the persuasiveness and the emotional power of the Holocaust waning in the face of other, more potentially compelling narratives? The Simon Wiesenthal Center's Bet Ha-Shoah—Museum of Tolerance brilliantly articulates the paradoxes of American Jewish identities and the ways some factions of American Jews create a place for themselves as American Jews.

Going Global

The Museum of Tolerance has established or is breaking ground on several new satellites around the world—one in New York, one in Paris, and the largest in Jerusalem. The New York campus, which opened in 2003, educates public service employees, including police officers, librarians, and other "frontline professionals," on issues of hate and tolerance.[36] And New York, like Los Angeles, can tap into its own diversity to generate a municipal-specific narrative (the conflict between African Americans and Orthodox Jews in Crown Heights, Brooklyn, rather than the L.A. race riots, for example).

The plan for the "European Museum of Mutual Respect" was announced in May 2002 by the French multimedia mogul Jean-Marie Messier, then the chairman and CEO of Vivendi Universal. In many ways, the museum is a reaction to the general rise of right-wing politics in France and Europe and reflects the new importance of the museum as an educational site. In Messier's words, "Never before in our recent history has there been such a need for a place such as this, a place of reflection, a place to remind us of the importance of mutual respect, as we face an uprising of the extreme right in Europe, of racism and xenophobia everywhere." Messier claims that he will personally lead the five-year project.[37] The difference in words between the American "tolerance" and the more refined "mutual respect" shows that the Simon Wiesenthal Center tailors its mission to specific cultural and political landscapes.

More interesting is the expansion of the Wiesenthal Center to Israel. The $200 million project for the museum and conference center, both designed by the famed architect Frank Gehry, will further complicate the issues of identity and place at stake in the museum.[38] The center will be named the Winnick Institute Jerusalem in honor of the project's main donor, Gary Winnick, a Los Angeles dot-com billionaire who gave $40 million to the Wiesenthal. In May 2004, none other than Arnold

Schwarzenegger, as governor of California, laid the cornerstone of the new museum, which is scheduled to open in 2007. The Jerusalem municipality has leased three acres of land on French Hill at the foot of Mount Scopus for the project, which has received vocal support from Israeli and American leaders across the political spectrum. The museum will be interactive and experiential, geared "toward the Internet generation." As for content, Israeli educators will determine what and how the museum presents its message. Museum leaders state that the exhibits will be in Hebrew, English, and Arabic.

The museum's leaders have promised the Israeli government that it will be a "museum of tolerance" and will not compete with the state-sponsored *Yad va-Shem* Holocaust museum and research center in Jerusalem. But what does a museum of tolerance look like on the Israeli landscape? According to Hier, the museum will focus on promoting civility and tolerance among Jews, and between Jews and non-Jews. In the words of its mission statement, the museum will be a "world center to heighten consciousness and a catalyst to enhance sensitivity on issues of human dignity and responsibility. It will seek to promote civility and respect among Jews, and between people of all faiths and creeds."[39] Gehry sees the museum as "the kind of place the pope would visit if he came to Jerusalem," suggesting that it will be a place of universal, possibly religious, values and a site where visiting dignitaries can pay respect to Jewish suffering. (Currently, visiting dignitaries go to *Yad va-Shem*.) It is unclear who the intended audience is. Israelis? Palestinians? American Jewish tourists? Will the museum spend time talking about suicide bombings, or will it address issues of racism in Israeli society, the historical treatment of Sephardic and Mizrahi Jews, the dual-class citizenship that separates Jews and Arabs in Israel? In a 1997 interview, Hier suggested that the museum will focus on intra-Jewish issues. The first main section will deal with the past one hundred years of Jewish history in Israel and the Diaspora, and the second will focus on contemporary flash points of tension and strife among different segments of the Jewish world.[40] But Winnick says that the institution will not be seen as a Jewish museum: "This is a secular new institution. It's for the Arab, it's for the Jew, it's for the Christian. It's for anyone who lives in oppression, anyone who lives in prejudice."[41] Some critics, including Abraham Foxman, national director of the Anti-Defamation League, have questioned whether a museum is the most effective way to deal with intolerance in Israel.[42]

Opening a tolerance museum on French Hill, at the very edge of the West Bank, has a certain amount of irony built into it. Can this museum talk about domestic Israeli tolerance and anti-Semitism at the same time that it talks about race and racism and Israeli relations with Palestinians? Can the museum effectively tackle the deep split between the religious and the secular in Israel and avoid talking about the separate Arab and Jewish societies that coexist uneasily in Israel? These are the challenges of bringing a particularly American Holocaust museum to Israel.

The Skirball Museum: The Quintessential American Jewish Cultural Landmark

Jewish life in America has been abundant and there is much to celebrate. The Skirball Cultural Center stands as a creative national treasure.
—Jane Alexander, former chair of the National Endowment for the Arts

The most understated story in Jewish history is the American-Jewish experience. It may indeed be the most glorious of stories, but it is untold. Perhaps we are not "good news" people.
—Uri Herscher, founder and CEO, Skirball
Cultural Center–Hebrew Union College[43]

On reflecting on the Skirball Museum's contribution to the Los Angeles cultural landscape, one critic replied, "The Skirball has a good shot at reversing L.A.'s cultural amnesia."[44] Another suggested that the placement of the Skirball on a sagebrush-covered hillside nestled atop one of the busiest freeways in the world, and its design by one of Israel's top architects, serves as a nice metaphor of the tension between the location in postmodern Los Angeles and the subject, the "eternal" Jews. "Even if the Skirball had not been designed by an Israeli," Herbert Muschamp, the architecture critic for the *New York Times,* commented, "its surroundings would recall the terrain of Israel. In Los Angeles terms, of course, the pass is brilliantly urban: the freeway represents urbanity here more than buildings do. As the cars stream by, they seem more deeply rooted than the Skirball. Not in space, but in meaning: the city's mobile sense of place."[45]

The Skirball museum took fifteen years to build from the birth of the idea to the opening of its doors on April 21, 1996. Its full name is the Hebrew Union College–Skirball Cultural Center. Like its cousin down the road in West Los Angeles that has a hyphenated name, the Skirball's full name reveals much about the conception and orientation of the museum. First, the decision to call it a "cultural center" rather than a "museum" demonstrates how much the center's board and directors want this institution to be more than simply a showcase of artifacts for edification and how the concept of museum space is changing. The Skirball is not an American Jewish history museum in the traditional sense. There is, for example, no mention of the German Jewish migration to the United States in the nineteenth century. Perhaps a more embarrassing example of how the Skirball is not a history museum was the charming and affable docent who took us through the permanent exhibit, who made several glaring factual historical errors on his tour. In place of the history of Jews in America, the museum's permanent exhibit, its temporary exhibits, lectures, concerts, and other programs, in the words of its founding director, "tell the story of how Jewish tradition, Jewish values, and Jewish vision intersect with the fabric of American life."[46] In line with this mission, while he may not have known his history, our docent was a wonderful elderly man who has worked with the Skirball for many years and evoked nostalgia for Jewishness, which may have been his real role. In contrast to the function of the Museum of Tolerance, with its outreach to diverse audiences, the Skirball is meant to be a place where Jews come to hear lectures, to have lunch, even perhaps to hold a wedding ceremony in its beautiful inner courtyard. Several supporters have described it as an oasis, "a place where weary commuters can revive their spirits with art, music, family get-togethers and lively discussions."[47] In this way, its overarching mission is the polar opposite of that of the Museum of Tolerance, which is largely concerned with moral education and vigilance and has no intention of being a "home" for Los Angeles's Jews.

Like the Museum of Tolerance, the Skirball Museum uses technology, but not in the same way, and certainly not for the same educational or ideological goal. The Skirball relies on hands-on computer displays and even a simulated archaeological dig in its children's exhibits. But the Skirball also uses technology through its powerful Web site to extend the reach of its museum to those not even present. Its Web site incorporates the museum's permanent exhibit, "Visions and Values: Jewish Life from Antiquity to America," in ways that no other Jewish museum's Web site does. It presents a Web viewer with a virtual museum experience by putting the artifacts and, more important, the narrative of the permanent exhibit online. The Skirball not only presents its artifacts in the way many high-powered art museums now do to entice visitors but also gives away its "shtick" by telling the viewer the narrative linking various artifacts.

On our live visits to the Skirball Museum, everyone from the curators to the ticket takers tried to make visitors feel relaxed and comfortable.[48] If the visit to the Museum of Tolerance leaves visitors with a sense of acute emotional exhaustion, anxiety, and moral discomfort, the Skirball, by contrast, seems to exude a certain level of upper-middle-class comfort and spaciousness, an invitation to explore and relax. The café, for example, is located right next to a space for temporary exhibits, suggesting that one can come in for a cup of coffee, see some art, hear a lecture, and shmooze with the mostly retired docent staff. The architect explicitly envisioned a place in which a visitor would feel comfortable, one might say "at home." The main auditorium has only 350 seats so that people will "feel safe and important," rather than overwhelmed, according to Uri Herscher, the museum's executive director. The café's kitchen is open and in the center of the restaurant so that people dining are not separated, physically or ideologically, from the people who cook their meals.[49]

The ideal of dismantling class and racial barriers implicit in the previous statement is clearly another, perhaps unintended, part of a visitor's experience at the museum. In our several visits, we conversed as freely with African American security staff as with our docent; our waiters in the café were, at different times, Asian, Latino, and people of European descent. This apparent effort to create a staff that reflects Los Angeles fits into the museum's overarching goal of ethnic pluralism, even if it elides the reality of class inequality in salaries and the racially stratified division of labor. The Museum of Tolerance has just the opposite feeling—spaces are tightly regulated, the staff's job is to enforce rules, not to talk with visitors, and the main exhibit is distinctly segregated from the temporary exhibits, café, and other sections of the museum.

This emphasis on pluralism at the Skirball is also a reflection of its sponsoring institution—the Hebrew Union College (HUC), which is American Reform Judaism's rabbinic seminary. The museum had been an integral part of the seminary. The original HUC seminary in Cincinnati housed the museum from 1912, when the museum was founded, until 1972, when it was relocated to HUC's burgeoning new West Coast seminary building, located on the campus of the University of Southern California. It remained at HUC until 1996, when it was relocated once again, this time to its current perch in the Santa Monica Mountains.

Many Los Angeles Jews remember the "one visit" they made to the old Skirball Museum at the University of Southern California. It was a small Judaica museum, integrally and physically attached to the rabbinic institution. Its Los Angeles sponsor, Jack Skirball, was himself ordained at the Hebrew Union College in Cincinnati in 1921. In 1932, he took a leave of absence from his congregation in Evansville, Indiana, to develop educational motion pictures in Hollywood. He subsequently went on to become a prominent independent film producer and entrepreneur. With his fortune made in the entertainment industry, he underwrote many of HUC's programs, funded the establishment of the Los Angeles museum in 1972, and gave $30 million to the building of the Cultural Center before he died in 1985. Thus, like the Museum of Tolerance, which relies on Hollywood moguls for its funding, the Skirball Museum was also founded with film dollars, situating it firmly within the distinct cultural and economic landscape that is Los Angeles.

In its new expanded space separate from the rabbinic seminary, the director, Uri Herscher, envisions the Skirball as a place where divergent ethnic groups can convene. For him, "The Skirball Cultural Center is dedicated to exploring the connections between the age-old Jewish heritage and American democracy. We offer hospitality to every ethnic and cultural identity in American life. Guided by our respective memories, we seek together to continue building a society in which all of us can feel at home. The Skirball takes particular pride in its educational and cultural programs for thousands of schoolchildren and their teachers—people of every background who are finding common ground in our pluralistic America."[50] Herscher and Jack Skirball's widow, Audrey Skirball-Kenis, say that despite the "Hebrew Union College" label, the center is not just for the Jewish community but for everybody. Herscher also hopes that the center will interest nonpracticing Jews in their own history.[51] From its original founder to the current executive management, the discourse that guides the Skirball Cultural Center focuses on the celebration of pluralism and universal "American" values of democracy, upward mobility, and entrepreneurial spirit. The Skirball strenuously avoids emphasizing Jewish difference from others, unlike the Museum of Tolerance, which places Jews in a special category of historic victimization and oppression. In that sense, for new Jews, the Skirball is the quintessential liberal museum, trumpeting the themes of progress, hope, and faith in American democratic principles.

Skirball's vision of a Jewish cultural museum that shows how Jews were part of the American social fabric dovetailed with the director's vision of a museum that celebrates diversity and multiculturalism. On the HUC Web site, one can read the following description of the Skirball:

> The HUC–Skirball Cultural Center, an affiliate of Hebrew Union College–Jewish Institute of Religion, located at Skirball Center Drive in the Sepulveda Pass, contains the Hebrew Union College Skirball Museum as its core component. The Center is designed to heighten consciousness of the role religious and ethnic pluralism plays in American society.

Critics have also seen the Skirball Museum as a "Jewish melting pot museum."[52] Herbert Muschamp, the architecture critic of the *New York Times,* in responding to the question "Why should the Skirball exist?" (a question that Herscher has been asked dozens of times during fundraising junkets), answers that the museum exists

> because the experience of Jews in America has much in common with the experience of most Americans. The particular is the universal; or rather, American cultural vitality stems from the impulse to negotiate between individual and collective experience.[53]

And Michael Schuman of the *Boston Globe* says that the permanent exhibit "could easily represent the story of any other group of people whose first stop in America was Ellis Island." (It is important that Ellis Island was the first stop only for East European Jews, the largest ethnic Jewish group in the United States; thus, again, the story of Sephardic or German Jews is ignored.)[54] The museum's namesake had a more straightforward goal in founding a Jewish museum at the Hebrew Union College: "to enable Christians and Jews to understand their common heritage, shared roots, and in that way to 'dissipate' anti-Semitism."[55]

The Skirball's appeal and commitment to American pluralism can be seen in several of the programs it has sponsored: a conference on gay rights, one on American values, a book reading by the African American writer John Edgar Wideman (who has been criticized by some African American intellectuals as a neoconservative), a *klezmer* music festival and a "Reggae Passover" musical tribute to the Jewish and African diasporas.[56] Finally, to reach families, the Skirball, like the Museum of Tolerance, is currently constructing a children's museum.

The site in the Sepulveda Pass of the Santa Monica Mountains is ideal for a Jewish culture center in Los Angeles for several reasons. First, it lies halfway between the two Los Angeles Jewish nerves centers—the Westside and the San Fernando Valley. If the Museum of Tolerance is located in the older, more observant, and more immigrant Jewish part of town, the Skirball is closer to the centers of upper-middle-class and wealthy Reform and Conservative Los Angeles Jewry—Encino, Sherman Oaks, Brentwood, and Beverly Hills. The other reason the location is ideal is that it is easily accessed by car, which in Los Angeles is the only way to get around, and is "next door" (a few miles by car) to the monumental Getty Center. In other words, the pass in the Santa Monica Mountains is quickly becoming L.A.'s answer to Museum Mile in New York, except that in L.A. they carve up mountains and drive on freeways. Last, and perhaps more important, the Skirball Museum is across the street, actually across the San Diego Freeway, from both the University of Judaism, a rabbinic institution for the Conservative movement, and Stephen S. Wise Temple and the Leo Baeck Temple, two of the largest Reform synagogues in Los Angeles.[57]

The Skirball Museum's Message

The Skirball Museum explicitly roots itself in the (post)modern American landscape and rejects the idea of diaspora, or the sense that Jews in America are not living at home. Herscher, the center's founder and chief executive officer, explicitly rejects the term "diaspora" to categorize the status of American Jewry. "There are different centers of Jewish life. One is in Israel, one is in North America, and there may be one in the former Soviet Union."[58] The permanent exhibit celebrates the idea that Jews have always had, and continue to have, multiple homes throughout the world. This runs counter to other museums that document Jewish history, especially the Diaspora Museum in Tel Aviv, which frame Jewish history in a Zionist narrative. Given the Skirball's explicit goal of rooting Jews in the American landscape, it is no wonder that the idea of diaspora, of not being at home, is not a compelling narrative, nor is Israel a central theme in the museum's iconography or textual display aside from the archaeological resources from Israel in the Discovery Center. The section on Jews' living around the world, which most museums would label "diasporas" or "exile," words that most Jews themselves use, is called "Journeys," imbuing Jews' settlement worldwide with a sense of movement and adventure without the value-laden judgment that the word "diaspora" implies. "Journeys" allows Jews to be home wherever they are in ways that "diaspora" and "exile" do not.

Herscher's own biography embodies the destabilizing of the idea of diaspora that the Skirball is actively engaged in. He was born in Tel Aviv, Israel, of German Jewish immigrants but left shortly before his Bar Mitzvah when his parents decided to move to California. They ended up settling in San Jose. Rather than seeing himself in a state of lesser existence by not being in the homeland, Herscher, through his lifetime work at the Hebrew Union College and the Skirball, personifies the rootedness of American Jews, even those who were not born here.[59] Herscher went to the University of California at Berkeley and was ordained at Hebrew Union College, a pursuit that he has described as "not theologically driven. . . . Though I have never held a congregation, I still feel that being a rabbi allowed me to deepen my knowledge of my own story, and to become a storyteller." He was on faculty as professor of American Jewish history and has served as dean of faculty at the Los Angeles campus of Hebrew Union College.[60]

The Skirball is indeed a celebration of American Jewish life, deemphasizing differences between Jews and other groups and sidestepping entirely the notion of tolerance as a necessary requirement for collective well-being and survival in the diaspora. Muschamp felt the optimism imbued by the museum on his visit: "If you do pull in [to visit], prepare to toss negativity by the roadside. Under the direction of Uri D. Herscher, the Skirball's spirit of optimism is opulent to the point of contagion. Without diminishing the meaning or magnitude of the Holocaust, the place gathers rays of light that have penetrated through a dark century."[61] In describing the exhibit itself, he suggests that the message of the Skirball contrasts with that of the Museum of Tolerance: "Building on the idea that the power to create is stronger than the will to destroy, the display adds up to the stunning proposition that the twentieth century has been nothing less than a golden age of Jewish achievement."[62] Muschamp makes this reflection upon viewing the closing movie of the permanent exhibit—a 360-degree panorama of Jewish American achievements. The film, *Visions and Values*, combines "famous Jews in history in all professions" and broader themes of diversity and inclusion. Images of Aaron Copland and Leonard Bernstein conducting, covers of books by Philip Roth, Arthur Miller, Adrienne Rich, and Leon Uris, and photos of famous

Jewish doctors and medical professionals (who are mostly women) cross the screens, accompanied by music alternately rousing or sentimental. Viewers see paintings by Mark Rothko, Marc Chagall, and Roy Lichtenstein, and musical clips of Benny Goodman, Simon and Garfunkel, Bob Dylan, and Isaac Stern, a triumphant and inspirational celebration of the cultural contributions of Jewish Americans and American Jews in the twentieth century. Quite the contrast to the *This Is Called Genocide* video that serves as the conclusion to the Tolerancenter.

Leading up to this heroic finale, the second half of the permanent exhibit is the story of Eastern European Jews in America, beginning with an American eagle menorah crafted by a German Jewish immigrant, a twelve-foot replica of the Statue of Liberty's torch, and benches at Ellis Island. The majestic power of the statue's replica, a symbolic talisman and the Reform movement's equivalent of the stone slab of Jesus in the Church of the Holy Sepulcher, is not lost on museum visitors, as it clearly signals the triumphant arrival into the heart of the exhibit, the most carefully curated section, and the cornerstone of the Skirball's museum ideology.

According to Herscher, "Early Jewish life in America mirrors the experience of most immigrant groups."[63] Or, in the words of former museum director Nancy Berman, "The basis for the museum and the center is to strengthen understanding and also to be a place of interaction for the people of Los Angeles, from, quite frankly, an intercultural point of view."[64] Echoing Herscher's comment about the universality of the immigrant experience, Robert Kirschner, the core exhibit director, says, "We set out to create something that would be an attraction for a larger public. It's one in which every population can see themselves [*sic*]."[65] The exhibit strives mightily to embrace the goal of public civic engagement through its displays of video segments, artifacts (steam ship trunks, texts and historical documents, canned goods, kitchen tchotkes, and business signs), and posters in English and Yiddish, urging frugality and thrift during wartime. Textual narration explaining the artifacts lauds notions of upward mobility, assimilation, education, and the embrace of capitalism through entrepreneurialism, captioning various displays with titles such as "Struggle and Opportunity." Herscher even added the almost utopian vision that the tracking of the Jewish American story will engender more empathy for the current waves of immigration to Los Angeles from all over the world.[66]

In this museum, Jews' sameness as Americans is emphasized as a strength and measure of ethnic success. In the Museum of Tolerance,

Jews' difference from everyone else is emphasized, as is the historical legacy of vulnerability, suffering, and loss. The Skirball is the American Dream and immigrant story; the Museum of Tolerance is ethnic conflict. In the words of one critic, "In the twentieth century, Jewish culture has become one of the most vivid ingredients in the national melting pot and one of the most deeply integrated."[67] The Skirball works within the tension of assimilation and separateness, sameness and difference. If it is a celebration of the melting pot or cultural quilt, it is also an assertion that Jews can maintain and have maintained a distinct Jewish identity in America even while being an integral group in American culture. It is the mythic narrative of acculturation without assimilation, something, the museum thinks, American Jews should be proud of. This is also one of the things that makes this museum a reflection of American Reform Jews, who strive toward modernity and integration, as opposed to the Museum of Tolerance, which has the imprint of American Orthodoxy, with its emphasis on separateness and difference, on it.

How Jewish Is the Skirball?

Although the professional staff sees the museum as a universal immigrant success story open to all American ethnic groups, this multicultural ethos is not necessarily reflected in visitor audiences. Whereas on our visits to the Museum of Tolerance we saw African American, Asian American, Latino, and white kids on school field trips, we never saw any people of color visiting the Skirball, although school groups do make up an important segment of the museum's audience. In anecdotal evidence from the curators, they suggest that most of the visitors to the museum are Jews.

Given the Skirball's affiliation with a rabbinic institution, the museum is obviously Jewish, despite its marketing efforts to position itself as a place for everyone. The primary target audience, in fact, is the "nonpracticing Jew" referred to earlier. It seems to be less geared toward the school children who come to visit the museum, but perhaps this will change with the construction of a space aimed specifically at kids. And its temporary exhibits are always geared toward a middle-class, well-educated, museumgoing audience, rather than children. Some recent exhibits have included a special exhibit on September 11 and one on Jewish wedding dresses, neither of which was particularly aimed at or would have captured the attention of teenagers or young children.

As much as the focus of the museum is on Jews and the celebration of Jewish life in America, the entire first half of the museum is an "Introduction to Judaism" course, using the Judaica collection of the original Skirball Museum. In many ways, it makes the perfect introduction to the assimilation story told in the second half of the museum. American Jewish visitors, who are the success story of Part II, need the educational material presented in Part I. This structure deftly sews up a tension that runs throughout the museum. Although the museum celebrates the American dream that so many modern Jews have embraced, the curators recognize the emerging function of Jewish museums and exhibits as teaching tools. Part I of Skirball's permanent exhibit effectively functions as a primer to the rituals, folkways, and cultural myths of twentieth-century Reform Jewish religious, popular, and civic culture. This narrative structure serves four distinct audiences: adults who often experience nostalgia for their childhoods, adults who know very little and/or are interested in "recovering their roots," to whom the exhibit demonstrates the richness of Jewish culture, non-Jews interested in learning about Judaism, and children.

The museum opens with large stone walls and replicas of ancient clay pots to suggest how ancient and permanent Jewish life has been. After a very brief history of Jewish life in biblical times, the exhibit moves to the "Journeys" of Jews throughout the world, with a special emphasis on "exotic" Jews—Sephardic Jews, Chinese Jews, and others. There is very little on the history of Ashkenazic Jewry here, although the assumption of Ashkenazi culture predominates through most of the exhibit. There is even a portable Sephardic Jewish learning center floating around the "Journeys" exhibit. Like that of the Museum of Tolerance, the Skirball's permanent exhibit is divided between the historical narrative of Part II —Ashkenazic Jews making it in America—and Part I, which is nearly silent on the thousand-year history of Ashkenazic Jewry. Part I emphasizes the dialectic of Jewish diversity and Jewish unity. It shows that Jews live everywhere and that in every place they become like the place they live. It shows what binds Jews together. Even the museum's architect, Moshe Safdie, expresses this sentiment about Jewish architecture: "Jews built in the architecture of the place [they lived in]." But they always built synagogues, schools, cemeteries, and bathhouses known as *mikvehs*.[68]

The next sections of Part I on the unity of Judaism use artifacts to discuss Jewish life cycles, holidays, and Jewish sacred space—all of the things that have traditionally made Jews Jewish—as opposed to Part II, which shows what makes Jews American. The irony is that in the twenty-first century, many Jews go to museums rather than synagogues, schools, or *mikvehs* to be Jewish, to learn about the places that their parents and grandparents actually went to.

The museum attempts to tie Parts I and II together by having the theme of Americanness run through Part I. In each of the glass cases that display artifacts and ritual objects, an institutional narrator returns, signaling important fusions of American civic and Jewish values through the symbol of an American flag wrapped around the torch of the Statue of Liberty and a description of how and why American Jews have embraced certain values such as democracy and gender equality. The symbolic melding of two specifically American symbols, rather than a Star of David with an American flag, or some other merger of Jewish and American symbol, mirrors the ideological underpinnings of the entire exhibit, indeed, the larger institution as well. The themes in Part I that were marked by the American flag/Statue of Liberty symbol included religious liberty, shelter and community, minority rights, ethical standards, "an ancient hope," the dignity of freedom, the rule of law, equality of women and men, and new directions in art.

These categories seemed to be based on ideal aspirations of the Jewish community, a popular rendition of what Jews might *hope* to be in a liberal democracy. But reality is far more complicated, and there is a lack of consensus *within and among Jews* about whether these aspirations are indeed shared values and actual practices in diverse Jewish communities. What are these (literal) flag markers intended to produce in audience members? A sense of pride and self-congratulation? A smug complacency that "we already support those issues, so I don't need to do anything about them as an individual"? A sense of belonging to the wider American culture that ostensibly values abstract notions such as democracy and freedom but falls short in practice?

In many of the displays in Part I, the curator has made explicit the connections between Jewish and American values. Each exhibit has notes that ask the viewer to reflect on the object in the case, the aspect of Judaism that it represents, and how that aspect of Judaism reflects "American values and ideals" as the core exhibit calls them.

1. *Observance of Shabbat, the Fourth Commandment*: "The Israelites believed that human beings, along with their livestock, were enti-

tled to one day a week free of labor. This ethical standard, long since adopted in Christian and Islamic practice, has become in America both a spiritual and a secular ideal."

2. *The story of Hanukkah and the Jewish zealots known as Maccabees*: "The spirit of the Maccabees lives on in the State of Virginia's declaration of 1785: "Our civil rights have no dependence on our religious opinions." Religious liberty is affirmed in America's Bill of Rights and in the Supreme Court's endorsement of separation between religion and state."

3. *On the liberation story in Passover*: "Passover, recalling ancient Israel's exodus from slavery, celebrates the dignity of freedom. Throughout American history, from the struggle for independence to the struggle for civil rights, those seeking to escape oppression have looked to the example of the biblical Israelites. New versions of the Haggadah (Passover narrative), exploring a range of modern understandings, have flourished in the United States. American Jews continue to embrace Passover's message of freedom by taking active roles in civic life and supporting the global struggle for human rights."

4. *The Jewish wedding*: "American Jews combine ancient and modern elements when celebrating the cycle of life. In many synagogues, rituals have been expanded to stress the equality of men and women. Modern *brit* (covenant) ceremonies for baby girls combine new prayers with older customs. Boys and girls alike celebrate their coming of age in Bar Mitzvah and Bat Mitzvah ceremonies. Jewish weddings, too, reflect changing gender roles in America. Many *ketubbot* (Jewish marriage contracts) are now personalized to reflect the equal standing of husband and wife."

5. *The role of synagogues in American Jewish life*: "American Jews continue to view the synagogue as a house of study, especially for children. Supplementary Hebrew and religious education is common in the American Jewish community. Synagogue-sponsored and community day schools are a more recent trend. For adults and children alike, the synagogue encourages a deeper understanding of Jewish ideals and historical experience. Learning is a priority in every form of American Judaism."

6. *On art and religion*: "Reflecting the contemporary trend toward affirming one's ethnic identity, American Jewish artisans have cre-

ated new art for the synagogue. While rooted in traditional idioms, their work is an exuberant expression of Jewish life in America."

The narrative created by the Skirball curators is one of symbiosis between American and Jewish values. There is little emphasis on keeping kosher, gender separation in Judaism, or other aspects that mark Jews as different from others. Even the Holocaust, the twentieth-century event that marked and separated Jews, is marginal to the museum's primary narrative. The museum also clearly expresses its Reform Jewish values by showing that these "permanent" markers of Judaism are in fact determined by time and place. So, for example, in the displays and photographs of synagogues, the curators have included replicas of the great classical Reform synagogue of Berlin (the iconic image of Reform Judaism's presence on a given landscape) and a contemporary synagogue in Mississippi that looks like a cross between a pentecostal revival hall and a Las Vegas show place.

In the Bar/Bat Mitzvah section (always both boys and girls, since this is a liberal American Reform institution), there is a videoloop of contemporary Bar and Bat Mitzvah ceremonies. The fact that there are boys and girls is a clear mark that the museum is presenting Jewish rituals as reflected through an American lens, but the very fact that the museum is showing video footage of Bar Mitzvahs, which take place on the Jewish Sabbath, a day of rest when no electric devices are supposed to be used, shows a Reform bent. Orthodox and Conservative synagogues do not permit videotaping on the Sabbath, and therefore, none of the Bar and Bat Mitzvahs used in the exhibit would have taken place in their synagogues. In this presentation, and in the Skirball as a whole, we see the intersection and the celebration of the Americanness, the Jewishness, and the Reformness of the Skirball.

Los Angeles Jewish Museums as Temples of American Jewish Rootedness

Until the 1970s, Israel's Holocaust museum, *Yad va-Shem*, had a virtual monopoly on the Holocaust museum business, except for several concentration camp sites in Europe that became memorials. The opening of Los Angeles's Museum of Tolerance broke the Israeli monopoly on presenting the Holocaust and did so in a most American way—by introducing the idea of Jewish particularity and Jewish victimhood through the lens of tolerance and ethnic violence. In Israel, the Holocaust is used as a catalyst for positive Israeli identity, showing how life in "diaspora" led to genocide and how, in the face of genocide, some Jews fought back heroically. Hence, the name of Holocaust Remembrance Day in Israel is "Day of the Holocaust and of Heroism [*Yom ha-shoah veha-gevurah*]. In place of bravery, the first part of Bet Ha-Shoah's name has the word "tolerance" in it. And, now, Los Angeles is exporting its museum culture back to Israel with the groundbreaking of Museum of Tolerance in Jerusalem, funded primarily by wealthy Jewish Angelenos. Where is the center of the Jewish world if Jewish museums are being exported from America to Israel? Michael Berenbaum, the former U.S. Holocaust Memorial Museum's director, calls this the "nativization of the Holocaust," arguing that American Jews today are "proud and self-affirming." He believes that the interest in American Jewish museums will "slowly bring an end to the Israeli-centered period for American Jews."[69]

If the Skirball is an example, he is absolutely right. The Skirball Museum turns the Israel-centered narrative on its head by placing America at the center and by presenting the past two thousand years of Jewish history not as a series of anti-Semitic events resulting from "exile" but as a series of celebratory journeys through time and place. And the twentieth century, which the Museum of Tolerance portrays as the most violent century in history, is seen as a celebration of Jewish achievement, acculturation, and acceptance.

America is the land of identity questions, hence the obsession with identity and ethnic sameness and difference in both of these museums. Unlike Russian Jews, for whom identity is something too often determined by others and who would rather avoid such questions, American Jews play with, display, and celebrate identity. (It is also no accident that it is American Jewish scholars, like us, who are most interested in the question of a post-Soviet Russian Jewish identity.) Since the turn of the century, when British Jews attempted to simultaneously make themselves British and remind themselves of their Jewishness through a museum exhibit, Jews living in liberal, pluralistic societies have used public displays as opportunities of figuring out who they are and how they are rooted in the places they live. At the Skirball Museum, American Jews show off the fact that they have made it. It is triumphalist and does not tolerate difference. There are very few representations of contemporary Orthodox or Hasidic Jewry, and even less mention of Jewish rituals that make Jews different from other Americans. The Museum of Tolerance–Bet Ha-Shoah is obsessed with the question of difference, of the violence that difference spawns, and tells its viewers to be suspicious of the comforts of America. If the Skirball's Jews foster pride in American Jews' rootedness, the Museum of Tolerance wants to shake that sense of rootedness and remind Jews of the intolerant past, present, and, perhaps, future.

4

Castro, Chelsea, and Tel Aviv
Queer Jews at Home

Home is the place you get to, not the place you came from.
　　　　　　　　　　　　　　　　　　　　　　—Paul Monette

[Gay men] have created gay communities, our semi-mythical mini-
Zions: San Francisco's Castro, New York City's Greenwich Village
and Chelsea, Provincetown, Fire Island's Pines and Cherry Grove,
West Hollywood, Key West, Amsterdam, sectors of Berlin and London. (There are also lesbian Zions as well: Northampton, Park
Slope, Palm Springs, etc.) These are our cultural homelands, and
our visits feel like a return home, even if we've never set foot there
before.　　　　　　　　　　　　　　　　　　—Lawrence Schimel

I belong to the groups that I choose for myself, and not to any
homeland.　　　　　　　　　　　　　　—Walid, a queer Israeli Arab

We have spent many years living at and studying the intersec-
tions of sexuality and Jewish community. In our book *Queer Jews,* we
showed how lesbian, gay, bisexual, and transgender Jews are expanding
Jewish communities and changing how *all* Jews understand such foundational relationships as family, community, and nation. It was not an accident that, although we did a worldwide search for contributions to the
anthology, nearly all of our submissions came from the United States,
where queers are claiming space for themselves in Jewish communities.
The few submissions we received from Israel focused less on Jewish community and identity than on basic civil rights and on how sexuality complicates one's ability to belong to the Israeli nation.

The measure of Israeli queers'[1] rootedness in Israeli society depends on
how ambivalently or deeply they embrace or reject Israeli ideologies of

national belonging. Like all Israelis, Israeli queers must engage with Zionism, the political conflict with the Palestinians, and the religious/secular divide that informs so much of the nation's cultural and political discourse. But they also simultaneously negotiate such ideologically fraught issues as how much or how little they identify with Palestinian queers or the ways in which Israeli notions of masculinity and femininity enable or constrain their sense of self. In coming out, building communities, finding partners, and forming families, Israeli queers encounter contested ideas about religion, "race," ethnicity, and gender—all of which are folded into larger questions about what it means to be an Israeli.[2] Today, that answer is by no means clear, as some Israelis increasingly bemoan the demise of Zionism and collective identity,[3] while others embrace individualism, materialism, and American popular culture as a welcome relief and salvation from the oppressiveness of enforced sameness.[4]

Meanwhile, American queer Jews have tended to form communities and identities around the ideological axis of pluralism, individualism, diversity, and the celebration (rather than suppression) of difference. The ways American Jewish queers express their rootedness and their cosmopolitanism has been informed not by the legacies of Zionist nationbuilding rhetoric but rather by American mythic ideals of assimilation, diversity, tolerance, and pluralism—whether looking at Jewish identity within discourses on race, American interests in Middle East foreign policy, or gender and feminist social change. The assumption of multiple allegiances and belonging to several communities simultaneously is almost taken for granted and celebrated as one of the strengths of living in North America.

Queer Jews in Israel use the language of tolerance and diversity, too, although in a different voice. Whereas American queer Jews embrace the language of multiculturalism to address diversity within *Jewish* communities, Israeli queers usually talk about diversity in much broader terms regarding the character and openness of Israeli society generally. Because most Israeli queers who are out of the closet identify as secular, the discourse around tolerance and diversity engages less with religion or Jewish communal practices than is the case for many American Jews. Queer rights and issues in Israel focus on creating change at the broad level of national society and culture. This chapter looks specifically at the experiences, allegiances, and relationships between global, rooted, and cosmopolitan Jews in different places who identify as queer—lesbian, gay, bisexual, and transgender. Queer Jews create identities and build a sense of community in American and Israeli national and cultural contexts and at the same time form global communities that transcend geography and nationality, as Jews and as queers.

The Promised Land: Is Israel a Haven for Queer Jews?

From the beginning of the Jewish nationalist movement known as Zionism in the late nineteenth century, Zionists have argued that Jews were not welcome in "other people's countries" and needed a refuge, a place where Jews could run their own affairs and a country that would take in Jews who were persecuted around the world. The idea of a refuge or haven implies safety, stability, and support, a place to which a person who feels threatened can come for peace. Jews around the world have looked to Israel as the physical embodiment and realization of safe space, despite its origins in British colonialism, its seemingly endless struggle and conflict with surrounding Arab states and Palestinians, and the use of military force and concrete fences to sustain the illusion of safety. This yearning for safety and desire for power helped Israel emerge as a modern nation-state after the Holocaust. It was one of the central motivations behind the government-sponsored mass migrations shortly after the founding of Israel as Jews throughout the Middle East moved to Israel. American Jews flocked to Israel shortly after the 1967 Six Day War out of Zionist pride and a desire to fully express Jewishness as a national ethnicity. More recently, Israel has prided itself on being a place of refuge for Ethiopian and Russian Jews, even if its treatment of these recent immigrants has been more than ambivalent. Indeed, there are many examples of Israel's functioning as a haven for Jews, even if more Russian Jews die for their Jewishness in Israel today (in suicide bombings and army service) than they do because of anti-Semitism in contemporary Russia.

Emerging from the closet and from centuries of persecution, gay liberationists in the 1960s sought to create their own "promised lands" of safety, refuge, and support in the gay ghettos of the Castro, Greenwich Village, and West Hollywood. The notion of "going west," popularized by the 1979 Village People song with that name, suggested that gays and lesbians in the United States were "in diaspora" from their true homes. They were already dispersed and needed to come together, but where? As the narrator in Andrew Holleran's *Nights in Aruba* says, "The West in the end meant only one thing: San Francisco."[5] But what does "going west" and being "at home" mean in this context? Is the notion of safety and liberation an illusion, as well? Wayne Myslik, a geographer who studies queer "promised lands" and queer safe space and havens, asks the question "What makes a place feel safe?" He shows that antigay violence occurs in *higher* rates in gay neighborhoods, in those places that queers call havens. Moreover, he shows that most queers don't even live in gay neighborhoods.[6] For lesbians and transgender people, who face economic discrimination, invisibility as queers, and potential sexual/gender violence, the idea of safe space can seem even more tenuous, regardless of where one happens to live. For queer people of color who face housing discrimination, and queer working-class and poor people who cannot afford expensive rents due to "guppification," gay ghettos and promised lands often are the provinces of wealthy gay white men.[7] A sense of liberation, safety, and refuge depends on who is being liberated and who is fleeing and arriving.

The same might be said for the idea of safe space for Jews and the physical state of Israel. As a direct result of entrenched political conflict between Israeli governments and Palestinians, more Jews die or experience violence as Jews in Israel than anywhere else in the world. Many Israeli Jews do not feel safe in their own country. The notion of security occupies center stage in Israeli political debate and government budgets. In fact, most Israeli Jews feel exhausted by the political conflict with Palestinians, voice despair about ever seeing safety come to realistic fruition, and yet continue to elect leaders who employ policies in the name of safety that result in just the opposite. Greater numbers of Russian Israeli Jews now are leaving Israel to return to Russia than are immigrating to Israel.[8] It is precisely the combination of nationalist ideologies and claims of homeland and the exercise of political power that contributes to so much instability and violence.

The statistics offered by Myslik seem to debunk the idea that a gay neighborhood is a refuge. But, in fact, his argument points to an unwitting and ironic parallel: "Queer spaces such as San Francisco are for gay men (and lesbians) [*sic*] more akin to what Jerusalem is for Jews: most of us live somewhere else, fewer of us make the pilgrimage than in the past, our political power has moved elsewhere, but the cultural and emotional significance of the place cannot be overestimated." It is emotion, culture, and, most important, symbolic and political power over a place that makes one feel safe in that place. This link—between Jerusalem for Jews and gay ghettos as the metaphorical Zion for queers—highlights how space and place are compelling ideas around which to develop the political notion of citizenship, peoplehood, and belonging. To take Myslik's argument a step further, it is this very symbolic and political power over place (and how that power is used and abused) that makes it a target for violence.

The 2002 LGBT Pride Parade in downtown Jerusalem is a case in point about the struggle to define and claim safe space. Flamboyant and joyous Pride Parades and rallies have taken place in Tel Aviv since 1998, with increasing numbers of attendees and international media coverage of the event. Jerusalem, however, remained off-limits in claiming queer public space because of security concerns, fears about potentially violent backlash by religious homophobes, and lack of support from the city administration.[9] The city first promised to provide partial funding for the parade, which prompted a petition of protest to the Israeli Supreme Court —and the city reneged on its promise. Just prior to the scheduled parade, the Jerusalem Open House, Jerusalem's gay community center, established in 1997, flew the ubiquitous symbol of gay pride, the rainbow flag, in front of its building. The flag was viciously torched and burned in an attempt to intimidate organizers and to prevent the march from happening. Despite these institutional hurdles,[10] roughly five thousand people marched under heavy police protection, waving flags and banners such as one that said *"Ahavah lei'lo gvulo* [Love without borders]." And more recently, religious clerics from three faith traditions met in Jerusalem to protest the 2005 WorldPride Festival.

But is Israel a haven for a queer Jew? Does that idea of safety and refuge depend on where "home" is located—either in Tel Aviv or Jerusalem? And does it depend on who does the defining? Does the fact that someone identifies as gay, lesbian, bisexual, or transgender affect how she or he views Israel, especially when it comes to questions of sex, sexuality, and gender? How is it possible that in some quarters of Israeli society and culture, conservative ideologies view homosexuality as a grave offense against the Jewish nation, even though Israel offers more legal protections for gays and lesbians than the United States? Queer Jews' queerness can make any place feel less safe, precisely because of a lack of power in that place, but we argue that it is precisely the diversity and pluralism of American Jewish life, and not the legal protections of Israel, that makes the United States feel safer than Israel to many queer Jews.

Our first case study, Steven, in his early thirties, was born and raised in California and used to live in Berkeley, California. In 1996, he graduated from the University of California, packed up, and moved to New York City. Steven identifies as gay, but has struggled to reconcile being Jewish and being gay, because he sees Jewishness as foundational, the sense of self that connects him to the past, present, and future. His gay identity is an added and relatively recent layer to that foundation. Steven was raised as a Conservative-Orthodox Jew and desires to continue this level of Jewish practice and affiliation. He is a Zionist, holds right-wing Israeli (and moderate conservative American) political beliefs, and spent a year during high school in Israel. But, for him, there was only one place on earth where his two identities—Jewish and gay—could meet in the way he wanted, and it was not Israel, nor was it San Francisco. For Steven, New York was the only place on earth that was both a gay and a Jewish Zion. Steven cannot imagine living anywhere else in the world. "Where else," he comments, "could I organize a monthly *Shabbat* dinner for gay Orthodox men on the Upper West Side of Manhattan and have to turn away people for lack of seating?" Steven has no desire to move to Israel, even as he supports the right-wing government of Ariel Sharon.

Less Orthodox queer Jews often struggle less with their connection to Israel and feel more comfortable in their status as new Jews. The New York–born writer Lawrence Schimel identifies himself as a "post-Zionist," by which he says he is "primarily talking about a change in Israel-diaspora relationships . . . I am a diaspora Jew, meaning I am descended from the tribes that have scattered across the globe and have not made *aliyah,* have not returned to the homeland of Israel. I have no desire to make *aliyah*; I plan to stay right where I am." Ironically, this New York Jew left the queer Jewish Zion for Spain, where he finds himself the only Jew around, although he desperately hangs on to his rent-controlled apartment in Manhattan. Schimel sees himself as part of the generation of Jews who "construct our Jewish identities closer to home and embrace our diaspora identity." We wonder whether the fact that he and Steven identify as gay also helps them challenge the idea that Israel is their haven.

Queer and Jewish Politics in the United States

Compared to other secular democracies, the United States does not grant many legal protections for queer Americans. Currently, people who identify as gay and lesbian, let alone transgendered, cannot serve openly in the military, cannot get married (except in Massachusetts), cannot file taxes jointly if they are partnered, cannot adopt children in certain parts of the country, cannot bring a noncitizen partner to the United States, do not automatically inherit property, and do not have access to a whole list of rights and responsibilities that are automatically and effortlessly granted to people who identify as straight. Unlike the Israeli government and legal system, the U.S. government and courts are generally not activist in the liberal sense.[11] With occasional exceptions, they cautiously follow social trends, rather than lead American culture toward large-scale social change through legislation and court rulings. Social change in the United States tends to start not in legislatures but in nonprofit organizations, street protests, legal challenges, or other forms of social activism. Queer Jews in the United States are active in these broad-based political and legal movements for social change. They are prominent participants in general queer activism and work for social and cultural change through arts, letters, and scholarship.[12] In these forms of activism, queer American Jews resemble their Israeli counterparts, who work toward increased civil protections and rights under Israeli law.

But queer Jews in America diverge from their counterparts in Israel in the degree to which they claim power over their Jewishness, something that many Israeli organizers are simply not that interested in. American queer Jews organize primarily around synagogues and Jewish cultural and social organizations. In the United States, many queer Jews struggle with the desire either to integrate into established Jewish communities, changing them from within, or to preserve the comforts of creating and maintaining separate spaces for themselves. The question of whether to integrate or separate depends largely on how rooted or displaced one feels, and increasingly, queer Jews in North America are using the language of pluralism to claim their roots (and rootedness) *within* their communities of origin. Queer Jews are beginning to openly serve as rabbis, school directors, camp counselors, and Hebrew school teachers and in other positions of authority and power in the American Jewish world.[13]

The examples of this queer Jewish move toward transforming and integrating into American Jewish communities have multiplied exponentially over the past five years. The largest rabbinic organization in the United States, the Reform movement's Central Council of American Rabbis, permitted its clergy to conduct same-sex wedding ceremonies in 2000. (This move also put Jewish communal power in the center of broader legal issues around marriage and family in American society.)

The Hebrew Union College–Jewish Institute of Religion, the Reform movement's professional and rabbinical seminary, recently admitted Reuben Zellman, the first openly transgender rabbinical student, a decision that received unprecedented international media coverage.[14]

Similarly, the Conservative movement is wrestling with issues of sexuality and diversity by reopening the question of ordaining openly queer people as rabbis and cantors. In March 2003, the student-led *Keshet* (rainbow) group at the Jewish Theological Seminary, in New York, organized a daylong seminar about queer issues in the Conservative movement, entitled *Tse U'lemad* (Go and Learn).[15] More than 350 people attended the seminar, which prompted a wave of petition-signing to repeal the movement's ban on openly queer rabbis.

However, this public claiming of space and entitlement within Jewish communities has not occurred without tremendous personal costs and encounters with overt, wounding homophobia that forces American queer Jews to question their rootedness in the American Jewish cultural and political landscape. In a recent skirmish, a day school in the Midwest offered a position to Benay Lappe, a Conservative rabbi, only to rescind the offer when she divulged that she was a lesbian. The experience was a near-repeat performance of Rabbi Lappe's previous experience with institutional homophobia at the end of her rabbinical school training, when the Jewish Theological Seminary threatened not to ordain her. In reaction to the day school administration's homophobia, a grass-roots group of parents, the majority of whom were straight, lobbied the school's board of directors, and Rabbi Lappe wrote an impassioned letter to the principal, arguing in favor of changing the school's hiring policy. She wrote:

> The hiring of a gay or lesbian teacher is not a *halachic* [Jewish legal] issue. As you well know, the Law Committee of the Conservative movement has expressed a range of opinion on the issue of homosexuality, and has expressly given the individual institutions affiliated with the movement—schools, camps, synagogues, etc.—the autonomy to decide their own policy on the issue of the hiring of openly gay or lesbian faculty, clergy, and staff. We are a movement which allows for a range of opinion on many issues, including *halachic* issues. I do not ask you to agree with my understanding of Leviticus, or of human nature. But I ask you to give your students the opportunity to learn another Conservative opinion on the matter. In our professional careers, we are given few chances to do something truly momentous. We are given few chances to

make a historic difference. We are given few chances to literally change the world. We are given few chances to literally save the lives of our students. You will not be universally popular if you decide to retract your objection to the hiring of a gay or lesbian teacher. It will not be easy for you to withstand the criticism of some of your *ba'alei batim* [financial supporters]. But you will have few opportunities to ever do something this important again.

After a public forum at which several rabbis presented divergent arguments about "Judaism and homosexuality" and an open board meeting, the parents' group successfully lobbied the board of directors to change the school's hiring policy. However, their victory was bittersweet and somewhat hollow, as the board instituted a policy that applied the sexual orientation nondiscrimination clause to teachers only and did not include rabbis or cantors, thus excluding the possibility of rehiring this particular lesbian rabbi. The move toward inclusion of queer Jews in all movements and at all levels of community organizations is uneven at best but is advancing rapidly, when one considers the extent of social change in historical perspective.

The claims and gains by queer North American Jews over power, space, and visibility is relatively recent. The movement to establish American gay and lesbian synagogues began in the early 1970s in New York and Los Angeles, and by the turn of the new century, there were more than twenty-five queer synagogues throughout the United States and several in Canada.[16] Most LGBT synagogues are affiliated with broader Jewish movements (primarily the Reform movement), receive money from general sources of Jewish funding, and are engaged in outreach to diverse populations that include heterosexuals.

Established Jewish institutions, rather than queer Jews, are now the ones having to react. Some (but not nearly enough) are taking steps toward actively expanding their scope and programming to include this new constituency. (Of course, LGBT Jews have always existed, but only recently have issues specific to queer Jews become part of the agenda for many progressive mainstream Jewish institutions.) In 1999, the Shefa Fund, a progressive Jewish foundation, established a fund for LGBT issues to provide seed money to fledgling projects around the country. Boston is the home of *Keshet*, an LGBT Jewish organization that receives significant funding from Boston's Combined Jewish Philanthropies. In Atlanta, Joshua Lesser, the rabbi of Congregation Bet Chaverim, founded in 1985 as a gay and lesbian synagogue, has established The Rainbow Center (*Mircaz Keshet*), in partnership with Atlanta's Jewish Family and Career Services agency, as a resource center for LGBT Jewish adults, families, and youth and for the broader Jewish community. A similar model is emerging at Jewish Family and Children's Services of San Francisco, which maintains programs focused on providing social and psychological services and relevant programming for queers and their families. And in 2003, we founded Mosaic: The National Jewish Center for Sexual and Gender Diversity, the first national organization to work for LGBT inclusion in the Jewish world. Mosaic's staff went from zero to five in just two years, and it receives funding from mainstream foundations across the country.

In the San Francisco Bay Area especially, queer Jewish issues are "hot" among mainstream Jewish organizations, and the region offers one model for integration that other cities may learn from and follow. San Francisco's Israel Center conducts LGBT outreach efforts that include a "Journey of Pride" Israel–San Francisco travel exchange program. The largest conservative synagogue in San Francisco has a gay and lesbian committee, and a gay man served as president of the congregation. Even the Koret Foundation, a well-known philanthropic foundation, is in on the action, having supported the gay and lesbian synagogue of San Francisco with a three-year grant to "improve its member services."

Recognizing the need to fund all these initiatives and to develop leadership at the larger institutional level, the Jewish Community Federation of San Francisco established an "LGBT Alliance" that conducts programming and fundraising for Bay Area queer Jews—an important measure of change and recognition by the established (and what critics would decry as corporate) Jewish community. Indeed, the mission statement of the Alliance trumpets the language of individualism, diversity, and inclusion that marks so much of American Jewish discourse about identity, while hinting at institutional relationships with Jews elsewhere in the world:

- To reach LGBT Jews in the Bay Area to strengthen their Jewish identity through community building and fundraising in support of the Jewish community, locally and abroad. Special attention is given to reach unaffiliated Bay Area LGBT Jews.
- Provide a secular space for queer Jewish community building that is culturally—not religiously—affiliated.

- To promote a sense of pride in being twice blessed (both Jewish and queer).
- To provide opportunities for meaningful and joyful involvement by LGBT individuals in the Jewish community.

> The Alliance fosters ties between the Bay Area LGBT Jewish community and the LGBT community in Israel. The relationship between these two communities was established during the "Journey of Pride" mission to Israel in 2001, and continues to grow and thrive today. The Alliance directly supports programs in Israel that have made a significant impact on the lives of LGBT Jews there through the fundraising efforts of the JCF annual campaign.

The statement recognizes that Judaism's relationship to homophobia and American Jews' sense of rootedness may be the reasons that so many LGBT Jews are unaffiliated. The mission statement addresses this issue explicitly and suggests that through institutional change, American LGBT Jews will begin to feel more rooted in American Jewish communities.

In the center of American progressivism, queer Jews are effecting change in mainstream organizations. They are the force behind changes that tend to be more proactive than reactive, and they seek to transform institutions, rather than leave them. These signs of queer Jews' increasing symbolic and tangible political power demonstrate the shifting meanings of home and belonging. By embracing the distinctly American discourse of diversity and pluralism, they are asserting the emotional and cultural importance of rooting within their own Jewish communities, rather than leaving them altogether, and enriching those communities from within.

Queer Politics in Israel

Israeli queers have organized their political model differently from American (Jewish) queers. The American model of LGBT activism, as outlined by historians such as John D'Emilio, suggests that LGBT social and cultural integration and migration to urban areas happened before social and political progress could begin in earnest. In other words, the achievement of a critical mass and people's consciousness of themselves *as a community* coalesced as the recognition of the need for change slowly emerged.[17] Such has been the case for queer American Jews, who needed to find one another and to form their small communities, usually in the form of synagogues, before they could advocate for social, legal, and political change in the wider community. In contrast, much legal and political change in Israel happened through the legislature and courts on a case-by-case basis, at the same time that, if not before, a significant social and cultural queer movement developed in the city centers. According to Lee Walzer, what makes the situation in Israel so interesting is that the legal and political victories of the 1990s, which have made Israel one of the most progressive countries on gay rights issues, "happened without a visible lesbian and gay community publicly mobilized to demand its rights."[18] The Israeli government, an activist government that pushes Israeli society to change its social and cultural beliefs, has allowed gays in the military since 1993, same-sex partner benefits since 1994, and full rights for second-parent adoption, which allows two people of the same sex to be legal parents, since early 2005.[19]

The story of the opening of the Piccolo bar in Tel Aviv, in 1991, is reflective of the disjuncture between Israeli law and society. The bar, opened shortly before the Persian Gulf War in 1991 (and closed down shortly after), was located on top of the popular City Garden (Gan ha-Ir) Shopping Mall in Tel Aviv. When the owners of the mall found out that Piccolo was going to be a primarily gay establishment, they tried to rescind the lease, and Piccolo sued. A Tel Aviv district court held that City Garden could not rescind the lease because of the sexual orientation of the bar's patrons and owners. Using tropes of identity and persecution, the judge compared the general intolerance toward gays and lesbians with the trials of the Jewish people in exile from their homeland.[20] He suggested that homophobia and anti-Semitism prevented queers and Jews from feeling rooted.

But while the government may be activist in its embrace of queer civil and political rights, Israeli society is still much more overtly intolerant of queer sexualities than American society. Raz Yosef, an Israeli professor of film and television at Tel Aviv University, writes, "Israeli . . . masculinity is constituted through the force of exclusion of the queer, the (homo)eroticized Mizrachi, and the Palestinian male 'others,' a repudiation without which the national subject cannot emerge."[21] Despite increasing visibility in Israeli popular culture, many queer Israelis remain "in the closet," maintaining heterosexual marriages, using aliases in queer contexts, and leading double lives, at the same time that more

Americans are coming out at earlier ages and living openly as queers.[22] Ruti Kadish points out that even though laws protecting the rights of gays and lesbians exist in Israel, few queer Israelis take advantage of the new political and legal space. "This phenomenon illuminates the great discrepancy between legislative and political gains achieved by a few 'out' activists and the closetedness of the vast majority of the community. At numerous events, whether widely publicized or small gatherings in private homes, it is common to see participants duck at the sight of a video camera and request not to be included in pictures. Use of only first names and/or initials is common practice in gay and lesbian publications."[23] Israeli queers have legal rights, but their visibility as a community is still somewhat tenuous.

The tension in Israel is between extensive legal rights and lack of visibility (unlike the United States, which has the opposite tension—high visibility and few legal rights). Therefore, the primary way gay and lesbian Israelis have historically organized themselves into a community has been through informal social gatherings that have eventually morphed into political activism, even if the numbers of people involved in activism constitute a small minority. Lesbians and gay men in Israel began organizing in living rooms (not bars, as in the United States) in the mid-1970s (at the same time, American and British Jews began organizing themselves in gay synagogues), when eleven men and one woman founded *Ha'agudah le'zchuyot ha'prat* (The Society for the Protection of Personal Rights), known as the *Agudah*. Lesbians also founded a feminist organization, known as ClaF, an acronym for *Kehilah lesbit feministit* (Lesbian Feminist Community). The *Agudah*'s full name demonstrates its broad-based mission for individual rights, as distinct from gay or Jewish rights—a marked departure from the collectivist orientation of Israeli society in general. ClaF's overtly feminist politics delineates its allegiances beyond the narrow sphere of gay issues. For example, Chaya Shalom and Gila Svirsky, two veteran activists in ClaF, have also been key players in the success of the peace activist groups Women in Black and Bat Shalom/The Jerusalem Link, both of which have worked with Palestinian feminist peace activists to advocate for a two-state solution to the Israeli-Palestinian conflict.

The desire to have separate lesbian and gay movements in Israel is not accidental. Reflecting the wider patriarchal culture in Israel more generally, queer advocacy and organizing in Israel, as in many other countries around the world, has historically been dominated by gay men and is by no means deeply influenced by feminist theories of gender equality. In the

Israeli case, secular gay men have tended to define the agenda and the unspoken boundaries of inclusion, despite the personal and political links between activists in queer rights, feminist, peace, and human rights groups.

In contrast to the dominant queer men's party scene in Tel Aviv, which could easily resemble a Saturday night in West Hollywood or Chelsea, many lesbian women seek out community in informal social networks. Unlike the visible sexuality and questioning of monogamy among many Israeli gay men, many Israeli lesbians eschew nonmonogamy and the traditional discourse of sexual liberation and profess relatively conservative ideas about family and the desire for children, even as they increasingly and creatively use the State's resources to pay to have those children through alternative reproductive strategies.[24] This is not to reify gender differences among lesbians and gay men along biological lines but rather to point out how gender ideologies shape socialization processes *in general* as well as specifically vis-à-vis queer politics and subcultures.

Perhaps this lack of common political agenda slowed down the process of forming a public LGBT political culture in Israel. Gay Pride festivals, the most obvious symbol of queer visibility, came to Israel only in the mid-1990s but, not surprisingly, were initiated by a member of the Israeli parliament, Yael Dayan, who started "Pride Day at the Knesset" in 1993. One of the first big demonstrations for gay and lesbian rights took place in 1996 in front of the home of the late Ezer Weizman, Israel's then-president, after several of the biggest legal and political battles had already been won. Weizman had, earlier in the week, said that he was not in favor of gays and lesbians coming out of the closet, and this prompted several LGBT groups to mobilize, organizing three hundred people for Israel's first big public queer protest. Visible Israeli queer activism was born, then, about twenty-five years after American queer activism. Interestingly, Weizman's complaint was not about gay and lesbian rights, which had already been won, but about gay and lesbian visibility, again showing how law and society in Israel often move in opposite directions.

The first full-fledged parade that shut down Tel Aviv's north-south axis, Ibn Gvirol Street, took place in 1998. Organizers planned the parade for the end of June to commemorate the Stonewall Riots of June 1969, when American queers revolted against a police raid at a Greenwich Village bar. Israel had its own "Stonewall," its own public display of queer street radicalism, later in 1998 during the "Wigstock Riots," after a popular drag show benefit was abruptly canceled by the police because the show had not ended after sundown on *Shabbat*. Many present took to the streets, marking the birth of an aggressive, Israeli queer activism. It also ironically reflected the seeming gap between Israeli queerness and Israeli Jewishness, since the tension was between the enforcement of traditional Jewish law and the desire of (secular) queer Israelis to continue celebrating after sundown. In terms of political visibility, in 1999, voters elected Michal Eden the first openly gay member of Tel Aviv's city council, and, in November 2002, Uzi Even became the first openly gay member of the *Knesset,* the Israeli parliament; his election made international news. In 2003, two gay men were elected to city councils. This increasing political visibility of the LGBT vote has led gay political activists to refer to "the pink vote," which some activists estimate to be as much as 20 percent of likely voters in any given election in the gayest city in Israel, Tel Aviv.[25]

The Jerusalem Open House (JOH) makes for an interesting case study in how discourses of multiculturalism and relationships between new Jews around the world contribute to the creation of institutions and social change.[26] Founded in 1997, JOH was led by veteran *olim* (immigrants) from the United States and Canada, who had seen the birth of successful LGBT community centers in North America and who felt that the time had come to organize a center of their own as a counterforce against the conservative political culture of Jerusalem. Given the polarized context of Jerusalem, does the JOH manage to unite queers in the city under the banner of multiculturalism and diversity as promised? With the severe segregation between Israeli Palestinians and Jews, and the hegemony of Orthodox Jews in key municipal posts, the answer is unclear. Despite these severe obstacles, the JOH enlists the metaphor of rootedness in staking a claim for legitimacy within Israeli culture. Hagai El-Ad, the JOH's first executive director, has said repeatedly, "There's only one place in Jerusalem where you feel at home."[27]

Indeed, the striking difference in the visibility of Jerusalem's and Tel Aviv's queer subcultures is a symbolic lesson in thinking about claiming space and power. Whereas it is easy to spot queer Israelis on Tel Aviv's Sheinkin Street and in bars and cafés throughout the city, Jerusalem's queer culture feels much more underground and discreet and is more likely to be conducted within the space of private homes. The rainbow flag of Jerusalem Open House, hanging from the fourth floor of a downtown building, stands as a glaring exception. Nonetheless, El-Ad's optimism echoes Wayne Myslik's argument about space and the conditions necessary to create a sense of safety and home, even in one of the most repressive and intolerant cities—for both Jews (of unorthodox persuasion) and queers. The JOH has been so successful in its attempts to make Jerusalem a safe place for queers that it won the right to host WorldPride 2005, an international gay pride celebration, on its home turf in Jerusalem. Undoubtedly, WorldPride would have marked the largest LGBT gathering in Israeli history, had it not been cancelled by organizers because of the planned Isreali pullout from the Gaza Strip that same month.

Queer Organizing across National Boundaries

Queer Israeli activists often come to the United States on fund-raising missions or to look for new ways of political organizing. In the past few years, Israeli queer organizing has begun to look much more like gay and lesbian lobbying and activism in the United States. Indeed, Israeli queers are increasingly coming to the United States to learn from well-established political groups, borrow strategies, solidify their contacts, cultivate donors, and incorporate American queer activist lessons into the Israeli national context. This trend toward putting American queer Jews at the center of global LGBT Jewish activism has expanded to the former Soviet Union and Argentina. In fall 2004, two lesbian Jewish activists from St. Petersburg, Russia, traveled to San Francisco to learn how to organize queer Jewish communities. These Russian queer Jews saw the United States in general, and San Francisco specifically, as the center of the queer Jewish universe. In 2004, German Vaisman founded Keshet Argentina, whose mission is to create a fully inclusive Jewish community. Vaisman learned his organizing in Boston.[28]

In 1991, the *Agudah* sent two activists across the United States to raise money for a gay and lesbian community center. Their appeals were so successful that the Center opened in Tel Aviv in 1994.[29] Leaders of the *Agudah* have made periodic visits to the United States to increase visibility for LGBT issues in Israel but also to raise money among wealthy queer American Jews. On a 2000 trip to San Francisco, *Agudah* leaders met with individual donors, spent time at the LGBT synagogue, and even met with members of the San Francisco's Board of Supervisors to talk about LGBT issues in Israel.

The *Agudah* has become even more sophisticated in developing its relationship with American queer Jewry. After the successful fundraising trip in 2000, the leadership of the *Agudah* formed the American Friends of the *Agudah* (AFA), whose goal is to make the *Agudah* and Israeli LGBT issues more visible to American Jewry.[30] The AFA was incorporated in 2001 and has obtained IRS 501(c)(3) tax-exempt status, which allows for tax-deductible contributions from Americans to the AFA. The *Agudah* is also making its magazine, *Zman Varod* (Pink Times), available for purchase in the United States. If Israel is supposed to provide American queer Jews with spiritual sustenance, America, with its vast wealth and culture of philanthropy, is supposed to provide Israeli queers with financial support. Both sides need each other to maintain a transnational relationship, but each side comes to the table rooted in its particular national, cultural, and political context.

Like the *Agudah*, the Jerusalem Open House looked to Jewish queers around the world and to American queer Jews in the United States and in Jerusalem to fund its endeavors. Like the *Agudah*, it set up an American Friends of the Jerusalem Open House nonprofit organization in order to solicit tax-deductible donations from wealthy American donors. This philanthropic donor-recipient process replicates an entrenched custom that developed long before the establishment of the state of Israel, in which global Jewry funded the organizing and activism of Jews in Israel. Given the relative lack of philanthropic giving to the nonprofit sector within Israel, the JOH has managed to secure 90 percent of its funding from foundations, Jewish federations, and individual queer Jews in the United States, and only 10 percent through local giving and membership dues, much of which comes from American and European immigrants to Israel. In crass terms, American Jewish queer organizing made the Jerusalem Open House a reality, for its founders could not have institutionalized to the fullest extent possible without significant financial capital from their rooted cosmopolitan peers. But the Open House's and the *Agudah*'s dependence on American (queer) Jewish dollars means that the two organizations compete for those dollars and are often at odds when American queer activists and donors visit Israel.[31]

Whereas critics might decry the power of the American dollar as yet another example of American Jewish philanthropic paternalism, in fact, this shows the mutual dependence of queer Israelis and American queer Jews. Both the San Francisco Federation's LGBT Alliance and the Jerusalem Open House felt the need to connect with communities "locally and abroad." These relationships and ideas circulate transnationally, rather than one way.

Queer Jews Traveling: Here to There, and Back Again?

Like all American Jews, those who are queer are raised with the belief that Israel is the Jews' homeland, suggesting connection and entitlement. American Jews give money to Israel, make pilgrimage-like trips to Israel, and study Israel in Hebrew school, and some, although not many, choose to move to Israel.[32] Queer American Jews travel to Israel for a variety of reasons, but in so doing they often learn more about what it means to be a rooted American Jew than about what it means to be an Israeli or about the complicated meaning of Jewish identity in Israel.

Some communal organizations in the United States have organized travel to Israel especially for queer Jewish Americans, operating under the assumption that this niche group has special interests and special needs. San Francisco's Israel Center, a program of the Jewish Community Federation of San Francisco, organized a Journey of Pride, a trip for LGBT American Jews to Israel. And, to create a "bridge," the program also sponsored the *Agudah*'s visit to San Francisco in fall 2000, building the bridges in both directions. The goal, then, was not simply to take a group of queer American Jews to the Holy Land but also to develop a specific diaspora business for queer Jews—to network queer Israelis and queer American Jews for mutual community and identity building.

The Israel Center organized two trips, one in 1999 and a second in 2001, as part of the Federation's "Living Bridges Program," which aimed to create lasting personal and professional relationships between queers in the Bay Area and in Israel. According to Meirav Yaron, then director of Living Bridges, these personal connections were supposed to effect institutional and organizational change. In our interview about the Journey of Pride, Yaron discussed what each side gains from its participation in the trip: "the Israeli LGBT activists get financial support for their programs and also learn about LGBT organizing more generally. Israeli activists visited Lyric [a gay teen organization], AIDS organizations, and other LGBT community groups." Yaron suggested that these activists gain serious nonprofit management skills in financial management, fundraising, and capacity building, while also seeing what models of LGBT organizing work in, as she called it, "the capital of gay life," San Francisco. "Israeli LGBT activists have so much to learn from San Francisco."[33] Yaron had a harder time articulating concretely what the American queer Jews gained from their trip to Israel. "They wanted to go to Israel, to experience gay life in Israel." Some of the Living Bridges trips, like its trip for early childhood educators, had a more reciprocal relationship. In this case, Yaron said, the Americans learn a great deal from the Israelis, who have a more developed early childhood education program and better curricula. But, for LGBT Jews, the connections seemed to benefit the Israeli organizers more than the American ones.

The Journey of Pride itinerary included traditional Holy Land tourist sites and activities that any American would visit, such as a Dead Sea dip, with added queer events such as a dinner held by the JOH and an Israel Independence Day (*Yom Ha'Atzmaut*) barbecue with the *Agudah*.[34] The itinerary showed off as much of Israel as possible, while also offering the particular transnational queer Jewish identity experience the Journey of Pride aimed to create. The *Agudah*'s trip to the United States, on the other hand, had much less to do with identity building than with the development of nonprofit management skills and relationship building with current and potential donors.

In 2001, because of rising tensions in Israel, the Israel Center had difficulties recruiting people for the trip. Only twelve people went on the 2001 Journey of Pride, although one journalist and a San Francisco city council member attended, as well. The most notable outcome of the Journey of Pride trips was the development of the LGBT Alliance at the Jewish Community Federation of San Francisco. In other words, shuttling queer Jews to Israel encouraged them to envision their own communal development at home. Other American Jewish organizations jumped on the queer bandwagon, most notably when, in 2003 and 2004, taglit-birthright israel sponsored all-expense paid tours of Israel for queer Jewish youth. Twenty-five North American Jewish youth participated in the 2004 trip, including Jonathan Goler, who said that meeting gay Israeli soldiers was the highlight of his trip. "They symbolize the way we should all be—free and unafraid."[35] Similarly, the 2005 WorldPride conference in Jerusalem prompted Jewish organizers from several LGBT synagogues, Boston's *Keshet,* and even the United Jewish Communities (one of the largest communal organizations in North America) to sponsor trips to Israel, although these trips were subsequently cancelled, along with World Pride Itself.

We have each traveled to Israel as queer Jews, although never on an organized tourist trip like the Journey of Pride. Caryn lived in Jerusalem for two years just as the JOH moved into its space in downtown Jerusalem; David visited for three weeks in June 1999, taking part in Tel Aviv's annual Gay Pride parade and meeting with Israeli queer activists.

From Caryn's field notes at the Jerusalem Open House, December 1998:

Last night was the Open House's inauguration party for the new space downtown. It's right on the main pedestrian thoroughfare, with a gigantic rainbow flag hanging from the balcony. Just by claiming visible space on the most well-traveled street in the city feels like an enormous symbolic statement, and a welcome respite from the pervasive feeling of religious intolerance and homophobia here. The space is generous but spartan, with a reception area, a small kitchen, a library, and a few meetings rooms. The central room was set up with a small stage and folding chairs, where the founders and a few political allies made happy speeches amidst much applause. Everyone in the room seems to agree that moving from idea to reality to create a queer space in the city of Jerusalem is quite an accomplishment, and I felt as if I were witnessing queer history in the making. After the speeches, the crowd mingled and flirted in small groups, around seventy-five people mostly over thirty, more men than women. Although the center claims to be multicultural and open to everyone, the JOH has some work to do. Almost everyone was secular, or at least not identifiably religious (through clothing or wearing a *kippah* [skullcap]), and I couldn't tell if any Palestinian queers showed up, because no one was speaking in Arabic. Almost everyone spoke Hebrew: I heard no Russian, but I knew a few English speakers, mostly some of the original founders, who are immigrants that have been here for years. Although it was moving to observe the tangible development of queer community in Israel, I still felt oppressed by the conservative politics and outlook of the city, and knew that the JOH had its work cut out for it.

Many of the organizers of queer Jewish trips to Israel presume that, like all diaspora business identity tourists, queer American Jews are looking for transformative Jewish and gender experiences in Israel, experiences that they could have only in Israel. Although for some, like Caryn, Israel's strict gender divisions and entrenched Orthodoxy make Israel a less spiritual place, others do have such transformative experiences. Ali Cannon and TJ Michels, two transgender writers and activists, have written about their experiences as transgendered people at the Western Wall in the Old City of Jerusalem, the holiest site in Judaism. Cannon, who was born and raised as a woman but who now identifies as a transgender Jewish man, legally came to Israel as a man; at least that is what was written on his passport. One of the most powerful experiences he had in the crystallization of his male Jewish identity was his visit to the Western Wall. The Wall is divided into a male and a female side, and Israel places "gender police" at all the entrances to Judaism's holy sites. Their job is to make sure men and women stay separated. All Bar Mitzvahs take place on the male side, while the women peer through the gate between the two sections. Cannon had become a transgender man and was therefore able to walk into the men's section. There he prayed as a transgender man for the first time in his Jewish life. Ironically, the Wall (and Israel more generally) helped him solidify his identity as a *Jewish* man precisely because of its rigid understandings of gender.

Michels had a less liberating experience. She identifies as transgender butch but uses female pronouns, and most people see her as a "she." She dresses, however, as a "butch dyke." Her agenda for coming to the Wall was simple. In her words, it was "to pray to God." She approached the wall with her two sisters, "with [her] baggy shorts, T-shirt, and shaved head." Michels generally operated under the assumption that people read her as female, since she has breasts. But not the day she approached the Wall. The gender police stopped her from walking with her lesbian sister to the women's side and instead sent her to the men's side. The emotional experience of having her body and identity defined for her by a police officer was traumatizing. She cried and told the guard, in broken Hebrew, that she belonged on the women's side. For these two transgender American Jews, coming to Israel had an intense spiritual and emotional effect on them that changed the way they viewed the world and themselves. It functioned the way some of the original Zionists thought it should—as a place for Jews to wrestle and reconnect with Jewish identity and culture.[36]

Queer Jewish Israelis travel to the United States for many of the same reasons that other Israeli Jews travel to the United States—not so much as tourists but as global Jews. When Israelis take vacations, they roam the globe and often end up in locales like India, South America, Turkey, and, as the 2002 terrorist attack highlighted, beach resorts in Africa. They come to the United States to see family, tour New York or Los Angeles, attend graduate school, or flee the narrow confines of Israeli society. Many come to the United States for economic opportunity, as Naama Sabar found in her study of Israelis in Los Angeles, and, in times of violence like the second intifada, many choose to come to the United States as a kind of respite from the harsh realities of day-to-day life. The vast body of academic research about "Israeli émigrés" and the dearth of studies on Israeli tourists (the reverse of the abundant research on American tourists to Israel and the dearth on American immigrants) suggests that these different Jewish peoples are moving around for different reasons.

The gay Israeli poet Ilan Sheinfeld, in his poem "My Identity," adds that, at least for queer Jewish Israelis, travel is a source of identity formation:

> *My Identity*
>
> My identity is all of those things that save me from uncertainty and
>   The detachment of a cold rest in a foreign city:
> Homosexuals, Jews, writers. Three minorities whose sites I pursue in London.
> Every bar seems to me like a homeland, although I'm not a
>
> Follower of its citizens. Every hint of a man's Jewishness in the street, in the library brings me great comfort. . . .[37]

Although the poem's narrator crafts identities in England, rather than the United States, Ilan Sheinfeld's narrator sees safety and refuge in gay bars and at Jewish gatherings in London. Sheinfeld also overturns one of the key Zionist ideals—that to be truly Jewish, one has to be in Israel. The narrator, an Israeli Jew, seeks solace and refuge in "the diaspora," where he finds his "homeland." His characters think globally, rather than diasporically. Our own experiences in Israel at gay pride celebrations suggest that queer space in Israel proved to be a place of refuge from the alienation we each often felt in Israel generally.

Many gay Israelis leave the country in order to explore their sexuality and sexual interests. Several of the subjects in the book *Independence Park,* a collection of interviews with gay Israeli men, discuss the connections of sex, sexuality, freedom, and travel to the United States, the queer mecca. Rafi Niv, one of the voices in the book, for example, believes that many gay Israeli men leave Israel in order to come out. "They mostly go to New York or San Francisco. Maybe if I had money, I'd do it, too."[38] So queer Jews going in both directions are forced to confront the different sexual and gender regimes of Israel and the United States. If the strict enforcement of two genders in Israel liberated a transgendered person transitioning from female to male, Niv believes that the seemingly liberatory sexual culture of the United States would liberate him.

How do money, tourism, ideas, and people highlight the question of national, symbolic, and intimate boundaries and citizenship? How are borders constructed through law, and how are they policed? How do queer Jews around the world engage with these boundaries differently and sometimes transcend them?

Building the Nation: Queer Politics across National Borders

Israel's legal relationship to sexuality is in some ways more liberal than that of the United States, and this affects international queer Jewish relationships. Immigration to Israel is a highly contentious issue that is based on the 1950 Law of Return, which says that any Jew (the definition of a Jew is one of the contentious issues) can gain citizenship in "the Jewish state." If a couple made up of a queer Israeli and an American Jew wanted permanent residency status together, moving to Israel would be easy. The American Jew could gain Israeli citizenship instantly, and the couple could live together in Israel as citizens. Of course, if the American Jew was of age, he or she might have to serve in the army, as well, since Israel has mandatory conscription, but that's another story. If, however, the couple wanted to move to the United States, the Israeli would have a much harder time gaining citizenship. Since the United States does not offer same-sex partners residency rights, the couple could be broken up by U.S. immigration, and the Israeli would be deported to Israel. With its more liberal laws and its contentious policy of offering generous subsidies to immigrants to "in-gather the exiles," Israel is an easier immigration option than the United States for two queer Jews.

If one of the couple is an Israeli citizen and the other is an American non-Jew, the balance is still dramatically in favor of settling in Israel. The U.S. law would still hold that the Israeli has no right to settlement in the United States. In Israel, for many years, according to Aeyal Gross, professor of law at Tel Aviv University and the leading specialist on LGBT legal issues in Israel, the Ministry of Interior has had a policy that the same-sex partner of an Israeli (whether Israeli by birth or by naturalization) may be granted a tourist visa for six months with a work permit that can be renewed. After about three years of this status, the non-Jewish partner can gain temporary resident status and, eventually, permanent residency. In 2004, the law became even more generous to binational couples by recognizing same-sex couples as common-law marriages, thus allowing noncitizen same-sex partners of Israeli Jews automatic right of residency.[39] In all cases, Israel's government works to maintain its status as the Zion for all Jews, no matter their sexuality or their partner of choice, and is even willing to bring in non-Jews if it means keeping a Jewish Israeli in Israel.[40] This, of course, hinges on the nationalist idea that Jewish identity supersedes, or even erases, other identities, even those that the state, in other situations, might find objectionable. In cases where demographic anxiety drives immigration policy, as is the situation in Israel, queers are acceptable to the government as long as they're Jewish, in spite of their queer sexuality.

In other words, for the Israeli state, the drive to build and reproduce the Jewish nation and to encourage Jews to move to Israel is more important than sexual identity, in law and politics. In America, to many people, one's queerness is far more important than one's Jewishness, something that might not have been the case fifty years ago. In the United States, Jewish identity is not solely determined by or in conflict with nationalist ideology. Jewishness is also not automatically coupled with the idea of a demographic imperative to produce as many Jews as possible, although American Jews themselves wrestle with the question of Jewish continuity, often, we've observed, obsessively. Rather, in America, Jewish identity is just one of many potential identities to choose from in an array of diverse names, labels, communities, and locations that one might claim. This seemingly celebratory discourse of pluralism and difference paradoxically can erase certain important aspects of who we are. For example, Lesléa Newman, author of *Heather Has Two Mommies* and one of the foremost Jewish lesbian writers in the United States, is consistently frustrated by the labels people place on her and her work. More often than not, she is marked as a "lesbian writer" rather than a "Jewish writer," because in the United States, "lesbian trumps Jewish even if there are no lesbians in the story."[41]

In Israel, nationalism and national identity outweigh claims for recognition of diverse sexualities; in the United States, especially for middle-class white gay men, sexuality can often overshadow other forms of identities and citizenships. Some Israeli gays and lesbians cite this trumping of nationalism over sexuality as the reason why antigay violence is virtually nonexistent in Israel. According to one scholar and activist, "aggression against Arabs perhaps has something to do with the lack of gay bashing. The fact that we're [gays and lesbians] all Jews helps us be adopted into the national consensus."[42] In fact, surveys show that a majority of Israelis are willing to grant civil rights to gays and lesbian Jews, while at the same time denying them to Palestinians and Arab citizens of Israel. This may also have to do with the fact that, according to Ruti Kadish and Lee Walzer, Israeli gays and lesbians try to become part of Israeli society, rather than transform it.

Queer Orthodoxy

An additional wrinkle in the knotty nationalism/sexuality/gender question concerns religion and observance. Although Israel by definition remains a Jewish state, unlike American queer Jewish communities, the mainstream queer political movement in Israel has not centered on issues of reclaiming Jewish spiritual identity and religious practice. Most Jewish Israeli queers define themselves as secular and, in many cases, see Judaism, as represented by Orthodoxy in Israel, as a source of their oppression, rather than a potential site of change and transformation.

Those queer Israeli Jews who are religiously observant definitively do not feel Israel to be a safe haven, even if Israel represents spiritual rootedness and the site of Jews' religious homeland. In Israel and, to a lesser degree, in the United States, to be religiously observant often translates into adherence to traditional Jewish law (*halacha*). Most traditional interpretations of *halacha*, in both the Orthodox and the Conservative movements, consider homosexual sex acts sins, harbor social and legal disdain for queerness, and stigmatize those who openly identify as queer. To identify as religious and queer (in Israel, and within many religiously traditional communities in the United States) is seen as a destabilizing threat because out queers draw attention to distinctive sexual differences among Jews and call into question the norm of heterosexuality. Steven, for example, has said that if he were straight not only would he be more religious but he would be more likely to move to Israel. His queerness gets in the way of his accessing traditional Judaism and Israel to the extent that he might like. His queerness makes him feel less safe in Israel and in the world of Orthodox Judaism.

The intersection of religious observance and queer sexuality has only recently emerged as central to the debate about belonging and home in global Jewish communities, especially after the successful release of Sandi Dubowski's *Trembling before G-d*, which documents the lives of gay and lesbian Orthodox and Hasidic Jews, and the recently released *Keep Not*

Silent, a poignant documentary by Ilil Alexander about lesbians in Jerusalem. In *Trembling,* the character Deborah painfully expresses the lack of pluralism in Israel that affects queer religious Jews on multiple levels. Deborah encounters the rather monolithic radical secularism of Israeli queer communal identity and politics and the subsequent lack of space for religious queer Israelis, while struggling with the seemingly impossible idea of coming out in her religious community. Deborah's Israeli coming-out experience is not liberating, as she feels that there is no place for herself. Particularly for Orthodox women, who are pressured to get married early, have lots of children, and devote their lives to their families, being lesbian poses significant challenges that make it difficult to both remain religious and remain in Israel.

One of our informants, Chani, raised Orthodox and now a secular Jewish lesbian, explains why Israel doesn't feel safe for queer Jews. She grew up in a rigorously Orthodox home with many siblings. Chani realized she was a lesbian in her early twenties and left the religious world. She identifies politically as a leftist-feminist, worked for Palestinian and feminist rights in Israel, and currently lives in the Bay Area. She moved there because, in her own words, "I could be totally free to explore my sexuality and get away from my family. I can be out, radical, kinky, all these things here and no one cares." For Chani, the cost of living in Israel seemed too high a price to pay, given the possibility that her family might disown her if they discovered her sexuality. Being a new Jew for Chani meant fully immersing herself in the lesbian communities of San Francisco, while moving away from anything specifically associated with Jewish communal life in the United States, since Judaism, at least the Orthodox Israeli variant, represented repression to her. The irony of Chani's story is that her brother has recently come out, much to the chagrin of his family, while Chani, until this past year, had chosen to remain closeted to her family, even at such great distance. On a recent visit to San Francisco, Caryn asked Chani's brother if he would ever consider moving to the United States. He replied, "No way, are you kidding? You never hear the muezzin call or see religious people here! It's like there aren't even Jews in America!" The story of Chani and her brother mirrors the complicated relationships between American and Israeli Jewish queers. For Chani, America represents not just sexual freedom but also the freedom to choose whether or not to identify as Jewish altogether. For her brother, the allure of sexual freedom in the United States is not tempting enough for him to sacrifice important aspects of who he is as an Israeli Jew.

Queer Israelis and Queer American Jews: Different Strains of Ambivalence about Zionism

Many queer activists argue that the movement for equal rights for all people, regardless of sexual orientation, crosses all political and geographic borders. We agree. But we argue that it is no longer useful to think that Jews constitute a single people, regardless of political and geographic borders, particularly when looking through the lens of queer sexualities and experiences. Do Israeli and American queer Jews have much in common? Yes and no. Are their political struggles similar? Again, the answer is yes and no. Are the cultural and identity questions at all similar? Certainly not. Why should American queer Jews care about Israel, and why should Israeli queer Jews care about America?

In the past, Zionism and the trauma of the Holocaust provided a powerful ideological glue that bound American and Israeli Jews. With the Holocaust quickly morphing into museum memory, and Israeli society discovering its own internal differences, the twin pillars of secular Jewish religion no longer seem to serve that function. The irony of a post-Zionist Israel is that most secular queer Israelis could care less about the romantic notions of Zionism so often promulgated in Jewish communities outside Israel. The mythic "dream" of Zion does not match with the messy, everyday realities of Tel Aviv traffic congestion, slumping economies, political instability, and family obligations that make up day-to-day existence in contemporary Israel.

As one Israeli gay man said during an interview in 1999, "What does Zionism mean to me? I let Netanyahu [Israel's prime minister at the time] and people in New York think about that. Me, I don't have time to worry about Zionism this, the Jewish people that. I have to worry about finding a job so I can pay next month's rent." Rafi Niv, former editor of *Kol Haifa*, the gay newspaper in Haifa, says, "I don't know if I'm a Zionist. It isn't really clear to me why I live here. I mean, it's clear to me that this is my language, and that it would be very difficult for me to live in a different language, a different mentality. And I guess that sometimes I do feel what you call, like, the rootedness of the native Israeli. . . . There's something that's called home, and, yes, I miss home when I leave. And home means both this apartment and also something larger, someplace where I feel at home."[43] Shachar, another contributor to *Independence Park* who traveled between Israel and New York, answers the question about his identity: "I wouldn't say I'm Jewish. I'm Israeli. I never had anything to do with the gay synagogue in New York. My boyfriend would go there. He would bug me, like, all the time to go with him, but I would say to him, 'I've never been to a synagogue in my life, you want me to go to a synagogue just because it's for gays?' I don't have any religious thing." Most people go to synagogues "just because it's for Jews," but Shachar does not see himself that way, nor does Chani, who has escaped the religious oppression of her childhood to embrace sexual freedom in San Francisco.

Shachar and Chani, on one hand, and Steven, on the other, are virtual opposites in the scheme of global Jewish communities. Shachar and Chani's identities focus on nationalist assumptions; they are Israeli and craft their identity in national ways—in language, schools, army, passports, and cultural memory. Yet neither of them would claim the mantle of Zionism or religion. This points toward the larger crisis in Israeli academic and cultural circles over the meaning of collective identity in postmodern Israel. In contrast, Steven's identity is Jewish and distinctly American, and he constitutes his identity in the religious and cultural contexts of New York's Jewish communities. And yet, what binds all these queer Jews together is the very American yearning for freedom and sexual autonomy, for the right (or privilege?) to craft a sense of self (sexual, spiritual, political) from an array of multicultural possibilities, to transcend the limits and constraints of heterosexuality so relentlessly promulgated by mainstream and traditional Jewish texts, histories, and communities.

We have already shown that the ways queer Israelis and queer American Jews constitute communal identities are different from one another— through nationalism, pluralism, membership (or not) in synagogues, and the wide range of other avenues through which people create community. One other major complication is the fact that the identity "queer Israelis" includes non-Jews, namely recent Russian immigrants, many of whom are not Jewish; Israeli Arabs and Palestinian Arabs, who in some cases have become part of a queer Israeli communal identity; and even foreign queer laborers from Southeast Asia and elsewhere who have little interaction with the organized queer Israeli community.[44] Arabs and Jews can meet (but often don't) in the context of queer politics and queer community, precisely because Israeli identity is national, rather than religious and ethnic.

Because of the presence of non-Jews in an overarching queer Israeli community, queer Israelis as a communal presence are some of the biggest advocates for peace with Palestinians in Israel. Their political representation has come primarily from the Meretz political party, which sits further left than the Labor Party on the Israeli political spectrum, and queer organizations have been active opponents of the Sharon government. Queer Israelis, particularly lesbian feminist activists, often maintain strong relationships with peace organizations, such as Women in Black and Bat Shalom. In addition, because of the intense, violent homophobia of Palestinian society, countless Palestinian queers have found Israel to be a safe haven, often hiding out in the country illegally. According to *Agudah* sources, about one hundred gay Palestinians are living in Israel, twenty-five of whom have sought out Israeli LGBT organizations for legal and community support. These Palestinian queers seek the legal protections of Israeli society and social and cultural contacts within the Israeli queer community. In several recent cases, the *Agudah* has mobilized to halt the deportations of gay Palestinians who did not have Israeli residency papers back to the West Bank and Gaza.[45]

Many queer American Jews, while espousing liberalism on American political issues, maintain strongly held beliefs and values about Israel and Zionism. Indeed, in the past two years, the question about nationalism, Zionism, and American Jewish queer responses to the Palestinian-Israeli conflict have generated so much discussion and dissent that an entire weekend of programming was devoted to this issue at the LGBT synagogue of San Francisco, Congregation Sha'ar Zahav. For American queer Jews, there is little consensus about what to do with Middle Eastern politics. Some American queer Jews, like their Israeli counterparts, are on the left politically, both on U.S. politics and on Middle Eastern politics. Tony Kushner and Alisa Solomon, well-known queer Jewish cultural critics, have recently compiled an important anthology that explores historical and contemporary perspectives on the Palestinian-Israeli conflict by progressive and critical Jewish thinkers.[46] Meanwhile, in this current era of Middle Eastern uncertainty, other queer American Jews have more in common with the majority of American Jews and have become more entrenched as the "promised land" has come under fire. Most American Jews (queer and non-queer) ascribe to a diffuse notion of Zionist ideology and support for Israel, which all but erases the possibility of alliances between American Jews and Palestinians on queer issues (globally or within Palestine itself), as the connection between shared land, heritage, and/or symbolic language does not exist.

One striking exception to this tendentious relationship between national and sexual identity is *Precious Stones*, a play written and produced by Jamil Khoury and the Silk Road Theatre Project at the Chicago Cultural Center.[47] Khoury, a gay, Syrian Christian playwright, has worked with Jewish, feminist, and queer dialogue groups for the past ten years to produce a theatrical piece about a lesbian couple made up of a Palestinian-American and an American Jew whose relationship forms the foreground for a meditation on the Palestinian-Israeli conflict and the role of Americans in resolving it.

Queer American Jews want to make Israel a safe place for Jewish queers; queer Israelis want to make Israel a safe place for queers and all Israelis. If queer American Jews want to know when the first Israeli queer synagogue is going to open, many queer Israelis want to know when all Israeli citizens will have civil rights, when the intifada will end, and when Palestinians will have a home and state to call their own.

Queer Jews are new Jews, in that they connect emotionally and culturally with multiple places and traverse routes across national boundaries but are nonetheless rooted in a specific place they call home. Queer Jews participate in multiple communities on the basis of their sexuality and their ethnic and religious identity and show how multiple allegiances affect people's ability to make home in certain places. Queer American Jews' encounters with queer Israelis, and each group's encounters with America and Israel, show how American they are, and vice versa. This chapter questions even the idea of a global community of queer Jews by asking what, really, all of these people have in common.

5

Our Kind of Town

New York Is a Center
of the Jewish Universe

When you grow up in New York—all the world is Jewish. When all the world is Jewish, nobody is Jewish, really.
—Nathan Perlmutter as cited in *L.A. Jews*

In the New York area, the public schools are closed for Jewish holidays. It's one of the few places in the United States where an African American administrative assistant for an investment bank sends off employees with "Have a good *Shabbes*" on Friday afternoon and "Be sure you get home quickly. The sun is setting." Seeing people in Hasidic garb or a play in Yiddish, hearing Hebrew and Russian on the streets or the best *klezmer* music in the world, reading *The Forward* at a newsstand, eating a bagel with a schmear, training as a rabbi, participating in an Orthodox gay Jewish *minyan*—all of these things are unremarkable in New York.

New York is a new Zion of the Jewish world, with its complexity, density, and sheer cacophony of Jewish voices, institutions, and cultures. New York is so gigantic and multifaceted, the site of so many different communities, agendas, and visions, that any analysis of how and why New York has become a center of Jewish life and culture inevitably poses only more questions.

Woody Allen's comedy works only because most of it is set within a certain Upper West Side cultural milieu, the part of New York that much of America now seems to recognize as a "Jewish town." Many may remember Jesse Jackson's regrettable gaffe during the 1988 Democratic presidential campaign when he referred to New York as "Hymietown."

After the 9/11 World Trade Center attacks, rumors began circulating that the Israeli government had called all Jewish employees, telling them to stay at home. No such anti-Semitic urban myths circulated after the Oklahoma City bombing in 1995. One thing everyone can agree upon is New York's Jewishness. Why is New York the historic and contemporary referent for all things Jewish? How has New York become the fulcrum for Jewish points both east and west?

New York is Jewish not just because of its perceived cultural resonance, picked up by Jews and non-Jews alike, but also because New York has been, and continues to be, home to countless Jewish institutions, communities, and individuals, representing almost every imaginable version of what it means to be Jewish. It is ground zero of the diaspora business, of global Jewish tourism, philanthropy, research institutes, and nonprofit organizations. It is where Jewish identity and memory are manufactured, performed, reinvented, contested, and then circulated throughout the world. It is the prototypical home for today's new Jews, a place in which they first plant roots, even if they eventually leave there for other locales. Barbra Streisand might call Malibu her home, but just hearing a smidgen of her voice conjures up images of New York concrete. You can take the girl out of Brooklyn, but you can't take Brooklyn out of the girl.

Each chapter in this book has had some deep connection to New York. In the chapter on Moscow, we found that most Moscow Jews have family or friends living in Israel and in New York. The organizations funding the re-establishment of Moscow Jewish life are usually based in New York and Jerusalem. And, not surprisingly, the institutions that support the educational and cultural life of Moscow's Jews draw their roots to two places—Israel and New York.

In chapter 2, we showed that the strategic planning, financing, and human resources for the global Jewish tourism business come primarily from New York. In Caryn's research, she found that a large percentage of the American twenty-something émigrés living in Jerusalem traced their roots to New York. The *yeshivas,* schools, philanthropies, and summer programs that use Israel as a backdrop for performing identity are usually based in New York. Moreover, New York is also poised to become a key tourist *destination* for Jewish youth identity travel.

We then moved to Los Angeles, home to the third most diverse and multicultural Jewish community in the world. In Los Angeles, for both the Skirball Cultural Center and the Museum of Tolerance, New York functions as both a real and symbolic core of Jewish identity, as the source of historical, cultural, and physical migration, as a venue for contemporary social problems, and as a site of nostalgia and historical memory. The Skirball Museum, for example, has a replica of the Statue of Liberty at the entrance to the second half of its permanent exhibit, and much of the material the museum uses to describe what it means to be an American Jew comes from New York. The Museum of Tolerance uses the Crown Heights riot of 1991 as a symbol of the ethnic tension (and, in the museum's view, lingering anti-Semitism) that continues to haunt the United States. The museum has gone even further and established a New York branch. In this way, Los Angeles has become New York's West Coast counterpart as the anchor for Jewish communities and identities, but New York remains primary in the Jewish collective imagination as the historic and authentic site of Jewishness in the United States.

And we need not remind the reader that Steven, the man who helped establish a gay Orthodox *minyan* on the Upper West Side of Manhattan, saw New York as his own Zion, one of the only places in the world where queers and Jews intersect, making space for queer Jews to live full lives as queers and as Jews. In popular culture, queer and Jewish sensibilities meld in New York in television programs like *Will & Grace,* in theater productions like *Angels in America* or *The Producers,* in musical performances, by groups like the cheeky lesbian *klezmer* band the Isle of Klezbos, and in new forms of Jewish performance, like the "Storahtelling" project's "Shabbes Queen."[1]

In this chapter, we explore how the Center for Jewish History, the Museum of Jewish Heritage, and the Jewish Community Center of Manhattan use many of the same themes of pluralism, tolerance, multiculturalism, and universality found in L.A.'s Skirball exhibits, but with a particular New York twist. We focus on these Jewish institutions because they project a peculiarly American vision of Jewish life and show how these institutions set up New York as a crossroads of Jewish life—past, present, and future.

If You Can Make It Here . . .

We see New York as a rich site to describe the dynamic tensions that define the Jewish map and that characterize the roots Jews have to the places they call home—the tensions between unity and diversity; between tradition and (post)modernity; between past, present, and future; between here and there, nowhere and everywhere, all seemingly at the same time. New York has been home to one of the world's largest and most diverse Jewish populations for more than a century and continues to act as a magnet for migration from around the world and across the United States. If Ukrainian and Polish Jews made the nineteenth-century New York German Jewish community more diverse at the turn of the twentieth century, at the turn of the twenty-first century it is Bukharan, Iraqi, Ethiopian, Israeli, and post-Soviet Jews who force New Yorkers to talk about diverse Jewish communities and cultures. In this concluding chapter, we show how this tension is negotiated on the streets of New York, in neighborhoods, and in its educational and cultural institutions.[2]

Although Jews first settled in New York in the seventeenth century, New York was not considered a Jewish city until the late nineteenth century, when millions of immigrants began to flee from the poverty and repression of Eastern Europe to work in the factories and slums of the Lower East Side.[3] For nearly the entire twentieth century, New York City was home to more than a million Jews, making it by far the largest municipal Jewish population in the world. The United Jewish Appeal–New York's 2002 Jewish Population Study of New York, however, suggests that New York City may be losing its power; the Jewish population of the city fell below one million for the first time since the nineteenth century.[4]

Just as the historical and contemporary place of New York has been present throughout the book, so too has the tension between the past, present, and future. In New York, past and present coexist, each taking part in shaping the varieties of Jewish futures. Jewish tourists coming to New York explore the past by visiting Jewish museums or the Lower East Side, sometimes more frequently than they engage with the vibrant, multicultural Jewish world on the Upper West Side and in Brooklyn and Queens. Many Jews who live on the Upper West Side rarely venture to the more "remote" or "exotic" neighborhoods of Brighton Beach or to Hasidic Crown Heights, unless taking supervised tours. And, since the mid-1990s, the Lower East Side once again is becoming home to young Jews, after the exodus from the neighborhood in the 1920s and 1930s. Today, young hipster Jews and lower-middle-class Orthodox Jewish families are moving to the Lower East Side for its relatively affordable, but rapidly gentrifying, housing. But most tourists still come looking for the ghostly echoes and nostalgic remnants of their ancestors who lived in tenements and worked in the garment industry and can do so by taking a cell-phone-guided walking tour of the Lower East Side by dialing a tollfree number and downloading maps off the Web.[5]

We want to end this book by talking about how past, present, and future each have an active role in defining home, place, roots, and communities for Jews. This sometimes uneasy coexistence is what binds people to these places. New York is Jewish, not just because it has the largest urban Jewish population in the world, not just because it is the financial and cultural hub of the Jewish world, not just because nearly every rabbi trained in the world will spend some time there, not just because it has the best Yiddish-language study program in the world, but also because it is the place to which so many global Jews trace their histories and through which they envision their futures. For Jews, since the turn of the twentieth century, New York has been overpopulated with people, ghosts, ambitions, and dreams.

The Jewish Ghosts of New York

In New York, past and present compete for power over place. New York is home to the greatest number of living Jews in the world and is also the former home of many American Jews, who envision New York, especially the Lower East Side and Brooklyn, as a place of memory. Many sites in New York most visited by Jews are places of memory making, not places of contemporary activity.

Like all other examples of travel and shuttling in this book, Jews living in and headed to New York want to see both past and present. They want to inhabit an authentic contemporary Jewish experience while they also remember their past. Like Jews traveling to Eastern Europe who want to see concentration camps and then meet the "one surviving Jew" of a *shtetl,* like the queer American Jews who go to Israel to do history and memory work at the Western Wall while also wanting to meet living, breathing Israeli queers, New York's Jewish landscape is similarly shaped by past and present.

As Jeffrey Shandler has noted, "the Lower East Side of today resembles other iconic sites that Jews have called 'home': the Land of Israel during the period before the modern State of Israel was established, and Eastern Europe after World War II. In all three of these places there is a 'Jewish absence' of some kind, and it is this, I think—rather than simply a Jewish *presence* . . . that inspires visitors . . . to re-animate the environment with their visions of a vibrant past."[6] These absences or ghosts are what allow today's new Jews to feel at home in places where they may not live, and to make home in places we might not expect.

In the next breath, Shandler goes on to describe young Orthodox Jews, gen-X and gen-Y Jews, and others who actually live, pray, and sometimes work in the present-day Lower East Side, Jews whose presence poses challenges to those who can see the Lower East Side only as a mythic home of the past. Beth Wenger, the historian of American Jewry, reveals the competing claims over Jewish space when she says, "While some New Yorkers have created a new, cutting-edge culture on the Lower East Side, most American Jews still come to the neighborhood to imagine the old, immigrant world."[7] What kinds of conflicts occur when New York, and in this case the Lower East side specifically, comes to serve as both a mythic and a real home?

Field notes from the Lower East Side:

Walking the streets of the Lower East Side, one can't help but notice the competing claims over place, from historical landmark signs to trendy, self-assured coffeehouses that scream gentrification. The knish salesman still has his cramped shop on Houston St., but rather than speaking Yiddish, as many Jewish tourists hope to find, one hears Russian news blaring on the radio, and a bilingual menu in Russian and English. In the search for nostalgia, one finds poor Russian Jewish immigrants. After purchasing a knish and saying "*do svidaniia* [goodbye]," we turned the corner down Rivington Street to find several boutique shops competing for public recognition with the new "shmatta" dealers—the dozens of Asian-American merchants selling cheap clothing, knock-off luggage, and other wares. A trendy French bistro sat next door to what seemed like a modern-day tenement. Our ultimate destination was the Lower East Side Tenement Museum, just a few doors down the block. But on the way, we looked for ghosts and found real people, who—rather than claiming a past in Eastern Europe—spoke Spanish, Cantonese, Vietnamese, and Korean.

Upon arriving at the Museum gift shop filled with books, *tchotkes,* posters, and calendars celebrating the multicultural history of New York (and, by extension, the United States), we found tourists and students milling about—some clearly Jewish, but most were, at least by appearance, white, middle-American visitors touring New York. A group of kids on a school fieldtrip were there to learn about American immigration, and there we were, two academics wanting to find out why people come to the Tenement Museum.

Why preserve a dilapidated site of impoverished immigrants whose descendants have long left the neighborhood behind for the Upper West Side and the suburbs of New Jersey? It's an odd landmark as landmarks go. According to Ruth Abram, the executive director of the Tenement Museum, a U.S. National Historic Site, the mission is "to promote tolerance and historical perspective through the presentation and interpretation of the variety of urban immigrant and migrant experiences on Manhattan's Lower East Side, a gateway to America."[8] Even though the founders of the Tenement Museum, the tourist hub of the Lower East Side, see it as a universal and culturally diverse site of memory, Jewish visitors see Jewish ghosts there. Many visitors are shocked to see well-established, thriving Latino and Asian-American immigrant shops and communities competing for space with the newly gentrifying apartment buildings on the same block as the "Jewish" Tenement Museum. In the words of the anthropologist Jack Kugelmass, "Family and ethnic genealogy give most American Jews a legitimate and continuing connection to the Lower East Side and the past that its remaining landmarks connote. But it is the idea of uniqueness, of singularity, that has fixed the Lower East Side in Jewish memory and has given it a continuing connection to American Jewish life long after its most noted Jewish institutions have become nothing more than restaurants and discount stores."[9] American Jews in New York often come to bear witness to their lost homeland of New York only to find that the famous Ratner's deli has closed and a hip new music lounge has opened in its absence.

The Center for Jewish History

Just as New York is becoming an institutional home of the American Jewish past, it also remains the institutional center of the Jewish present. New York is home to scores, if not hundreds, of Jewish organizations, many of which are dedicated to Jewish learning and scholarship. The city is the home of rabbinic institutions, some of the oldest Jewish Studies university programs, day schools, synagogue schools, research centers, Jewish think tanks, and other institutions that create the foundation for modern Jewish learning. One of the newest institutions is the Center for Jewish

History, located not far from Union Square. It is the largest repository of Jewish knowledge in the world outside Israel. The choice of the name "Center for Jewish History" without any modifiers like "in the diaspora" or "in New York" was no accident.[10] The Center for Jewish History symbolizes several trends—the move to consolidate and centralize Jewish institutional life, the need to project diversity and multiculturalism in the Jewish world to the wider world, and the desire to be located at a physical and historic center of Jewish life.

In the mid-1990s, several scholarly organizations came together to form the Center for Jewish History, an institution that has been called the "Library of Congress of the Jewish people."[11] Since its founding, other Jewish scholarly institutions have joined the Center, including the Association for Jewish Studies, which moved in 2003 from Brandeis University.[12] In its initial constitution in the early 1990s, the Center had four founding groups: the Institute for Jewish Research (YIVO), the Leo Baeck Archives, the American Jewish Historical Society, and the Yeshiva University Museum. In 1998, it added its fifth institution, the American Sephardi Federation, and the Center continues to find ways to build bridges and incorporate other scholarly Jewish institutions under its big-tent approach to preserving Jewish cultural and historical diversity.

The oldest of the constituent institutions is the American Jewish Historical Society, founded, in 1893, to serve as a repository for documents related to the fast-changing and fast-growing experiences of Jews in America. It is the nation's oldest ethnic historical center and is one of the oldest scholarly research centers in New York, ironic given that the American experience, when compared with that of Jews in Eastern Europe, Germany, and other places around the world, is one of the youngest. [13] American Jews, then, were the first to take seriously the notion that Jews needed to begin documenting not just their historic unity but also their historic diversity as a people that had ethnic and cultural distinctions based on the places they lived and on their roots in different places.

The Institute for Jewish Research, known as YIVO (*Yidishe visnshaftlekhe organizatsie*), was founded in Vilna, in 1925, as a scholarly home and repository for the particular cultural experience of Eastern European Jewry. In the tumult of World War II, many brave scholars and activists saved the YIVO archives and library and brought them to New York, where they serve as the world's central research facility on Eastern European Jewish history and culture. Scholars are not the only ones who use YIVO's research library. Many American Jews embarking on family history or genealogical projects contact YIVO daily. In this way, YIVO is part of American Jewry's memory-making landscape of New York.

German Jewish refugees and scholars who had fled Nazi Germany founded the Leo Baeck Archives, named after the famous German rabbi and philosopher, in 1955. The Yeshiva University established a museum at its upper Manhattan campus in 1973 and moved it downtown with the establishment of the Center. The junior partner, the American Sephardi Federation, was founded, in 1984, as a branch of the World Sephardi Federation and Zionist Association. Together, these five diverse institutions make up the core institutions at the Center for Jewish History.

The Center for Jewish History negotiates the tension between the Jewish interest in Jews' unity and the American focus on ethnic diversity. The Center's multiple institutions showcase diversity, but the Center then brings this diversity together in one research center and tries to create unity. Allan Nadler, YIVO's director of research, admitted that unity was the true success of the Center when he said, "This was not easy, to bring the organizations together when the trend in Jewish life is really the opposite. There is so much division in Jewish life today. It's so exciting . . . the possibility of unity in the American Jewish community, where you have so much factionalism along religious lines."[14]

In the first annual report, the chairman of the board, Bruce Slovin, also emphasized the need for "creating unity": "At a time when we face the simultaneous onslaughts of widening assimilation and deepening anti-semitism throughout the world, the continued growth and vitality of the Center is a source of Jewish pride and inner strength."[15] In his essay, Slovin uses the term "in the Diaspora" to describe both the location of the institution and the historical records it is preserving. Not in so many words, Slovin subtly suggests that documenting the history of Israel will not be a centerpiece of this institution, as there are other institutions devoted to this mission.[16] Like many other Jewish institutions that emphasize unity in times of crisis, the Center's chairman used the dual threats of assimilation and anti-Semitism to encourage readers of the annual report to continue financially supporting the Center. The Center, to Slovin, represents in institutional terms this dialectic between unity and diversity— the multicultural Jewish nation. What he doesn't mention is how the diversity of and differences among Jews, and the constant discussion of this diversity and difference, is a particularly American (Jewish) obsession.

Joshua Eli Plaut, then executive director of the Center, in 2001 came up with an even more interesting way to describe the dynamic tension of unity and diversity that marks the American obsession with collective identity. He uses the metaphor of "a tapestry, many threads woven together to create a whole. Five historical narratives converge at the Center. . . . There is great strength in both the unity of the five partner organizations and in their diversity."[17] Commentators even remarked on this tension before the institution's founding: "The center . . . is notable not just for the breadth of its exhibitions but also because it bespeaks a cultural unity—not to be confused with uniformity by any means—at a time when much attention is focused on the divide between secular and traditional Jews."[18] The question remains whether talking about unity in fact makes it so. Are the five institutions trying to create a cohesive narrative of Jewish life and of global Jewry, or is each one fostering the development of a particular narrative?

Located just off of Union Square on 16th Street between Fifth and Sixth Avenues, the site chosen to unite Jewish history and Jewish narrative is not far from the historic homeland of American Jewry—the East Village and the Lower East Side. As if words expressing unity were not enough, the building's architecture and construction also serve as a metaphor for the institution. The owners of the Center, the dominant partner among whom is YIVO, purchased six separate buildings and asked the architect, Richard Blinder, to combine them into one. Blinder described this as "the magic of physically bringing six disparate units into one cohesive whole." He went on to say, "We wanted the building to represent the old and the new as we moved to the new millennium. The building represents history and the future. The new building reflects a modern spirit and the old buildings are what they are: preservation of history. So we combined preservation of the old while introducing the new for a new century—and that will be the Center for Jewish History." Blinder recognized that the task of creating unity meant not just unifying diverse places but also collapsing time by bringing past, present, and future together under one roof. The Center is not just another museum dedicated to conserving, preserving, displaying, and documenting; not simply an educational institution serving the future generations of world Jewry; not simply a research center where scholars can create the future record of Jewish history and culture and American Jewish families can conduct genealogical research. It is all of these things—community center, educational institution, archive, library, and museum. Like the Skirball Museum in Los Angeles, which made architectural headlines, architects and engineers hailed the Center as a brilliant solution to the problem of unifying six buildings into one.[19]

The Center cost $55 million to create, rivaling the cost of Los Angeles's Museum of Tolerance and the $85 million required to construct the new Manhattan Jewish Community Center. The building alone cost $31.7 million. The Center was deemed important enough to American history that Congress gave it $4 million to help digitize its Jewish culture and history archives for placement on the Internet.[20] The New York State Legislature signed a law guaranteeing that the Center for Jewish History would receive $200,000 annually. In Governor George Pataki's words, "The Center for Jewish History will chronicle the greatness of Jewish Europe and the Yiddish-speaking world, so much of which was destroyed by the Nazis. . . . Jewish people have made enormous contributions to world civilization, and this facility will ensure the world always remembers their contributions."[21]

Not to be upstaged by the governor, on August 5, 1999, the day of the governor's announcement, Mayor Rudolph Giuliani announced $3 million in capital funding from the city budget. Giuliani said: "Outside of Israel, this will be the single largest research and cultural institution dedicated to the documentation, preservation, and protection of Jewish history. It's only appropriate that New York City, a place that has been so enriched by Jewish history, heritage, and culture, serve as the site for this institution."[22] It seems that everyone, from Slovin and Plaut to Pataki and Giuliani, views the Jewish world through a diasporic lens, comprising Israel and everywhere else.

Like the battle over public funding for the Museum of Tolerance, the granting of public funds to support the Center for Jewish History demonstrated the rootedness of the Jewish past in the American landscape, even a Jewish past that has nothing to do with the United States. Although Congress doesn't give money to Jewish organizations, synagogues, or schools in order to avoid breaching the separation of religion and state, the United States wants to see both Jewish ghosts and contemporary Jewish culture as part of its own past and present.[23]

Despite the hyperbole of commentators, founders, and employees alike, much of what drove the creation of the Center was pragmatic. Many of the component institutions had dwindling attendance, were short on space, and were low on financing. Of the five constituent institutions, YIVO, the Institute for Jewish Research, is by far the largest part-

ner. YIVO sold its pricey building on upper Fifth Avenue to buy the building in Chelsea. The Leo Baeck had long outgrown its space on East 73rd
Street, and the AJHS was located hundreds of miles from New York, in
Waltham, Massachusetts, at Brandeis University. The Yeshiva University
Museum was housed on the YU campus in Washington Heights and had
very few visitors. The move to the heart of Manhattan was a bonanza for
all four institutions.

The American Sephardi Federation is the odd partner in this unity project for several reasons. The ASF was not one of the founding institutions
and was incorporated only in 1998, nearly four years after the initial
founding of the Center. The late incorporation of the ASF shows that it
was not done for the same pragmatic reasons that brought Ashkenazic
Jewry together.

The ASF stands apart from the other organizations for many reasons.
First, and perhaps most significant, it is the one organization not connected
to Ashkenazic Jewry, whose roots are in Central and Eastern Europe. The
ASF is also an explicitly Zionist organization with ties to the World Zion-
ist Congress. None of the other groups has such an overt political stance,
except for YIVO's traditional base of support in socialist Yiddish culture.
More generally, the ASF was about community activism among Sephardic
Jews and was less about scholarship and documenting the past.

If the ASF has such a different mission from the four founding institutions, why include it? The late Leon Levy, the former president of the ASF,
put it bluntly: "No Center for Jewish History can be complete without
the inclusion of Sephardic history."[24] The Center, however, did not seem
to have a problem excluding Sephardic Jewry in its initial constitution. Including the ASF, then, was about making Jewish diversity institutionally
visible in the Center. Another response suggested that the inclusion of the
ASF was another way of rectifying the seeming divisiveness in the Jewish
world. "In a world divided by Orthodox, Conservative, and Reform
Jews, the ASF should take a leading position as an example organization
in the U.S. for which religious pluralism is not an issue because we share
a tradition of great tolerance and mutual respect."[25]

The ASF could also subtly bring Israel into this New York–based institution. The other four institutions all had specific charges to cover a
particular Jewish community defined by its geography and culture—
American Jewry, German Jewry, and Eastern European Jewry. No group
had Israel on its archival or library agenda. According to then executive
director of the ASF, Vivienne Roumani-Denn, the ASF could fulfill the

function of a collector of material about Israel because of Israel's large Sephardi population. In her words, "How can you have a Center for Jewish History without Israel? But we can't have a sixth partner. So Sephardic Jews should do it."[26]

At stake in the founding of the Center are competing claims to the Jewish map. We wonder why there is not yet an institute dedicated to the study of Israeli Jews as such. Is there an unarticulated assumption that Israeli Jewry functions differently than American or German Jewry? Whether it realizes it or not, the Center is playing a role in dismantling diaspora. It has made New York one of the most important repositories of Jewish history, but it does so in a very American way, with its union of diversity and unity. Whether stated or not, the Center is making New York the primary place to which people travel if they want to do research in Jewish history or simply discover their past. And in the future, perhaps there will be an institute for Israeli Jewry, institutionally breaking down the Israel-diaspora dichotomy and making the Center for Jewish History a truly global Jewish institution.

Where Past and Present Come Together: The Museum of Jewish Heritage

It in fact came as no surprise to us that New York's "Holocaust Museum" is not really a Holocaust museum. The Museum of Jewish Heritage is a beautifully designed, thoughtfully executed history museum that places the Holocaust in the context of modern Jewish history. This is not the Skirball Museum, nor is this a Museum of Tolerance. The Museum of Jewish Heritage—A Living Memorial to the Holocaust, to give its full title, is New York's most recent answer to the museum world, a combination history museum, memorial, and public cultural space that brings together past, present, and future in a most creative way—by using the voices of those who experienced the events described in the museum.

As with all other Jewish museums we write about, the Museum of Jewish Heritage has its own split personality. If the Museum of Tolerance–Bet Ha-Shoah looks inward and outward at tolerance and insular nationalism, if the Hebrew Union College Skirball Museum is at once triumphally Jewish and rhetorically universal, the MJH-LMH attempts to present modern Jewish history while making the claim that the Holocaust is the event that has most shaped modern Jewish history. The story of the founding, funding, and establishment of the MJH has been well told in Rochelle Saidel's *Never Too Late to Remember*.[27] In the late 1970s, former New York mayor Ed Koch recognized the lack of a Holocaust memorial and educational space in New York and mandated a group of wealthy donors to change that. It took nearly twenty years and many complicated debates about the museum's structure before the Museum of Jewish Heritage—A Living Memorial to the Holocaust opened its doors, in 1997.

In execution, however, it is not surprising to us that New York has produced the most original form of Jewish history/Holocaust museum either of us has visited. This is not to say that the artifacts at the MJH are the richest. The U.S. Holocaust Memorial Museum and *Yad va-Shem* possess richer troves of Holocaust artifacts, and each has a world-class research center. It is not even the broadest, most in-depth Jewish history museum. The Diaspora Museum in Israel tells more stories, and the Skirball has more on twentieth-century American Jews than does the MJH. But the MJH-LMH is one of the few museums to present modern Jewish history as a history of diversity and the story of the Holocaust as a piece of what happened to modern Jews. Unlike the U.S. Holocaust Memorial Museum, which opens its permanent exhibition with a picture of dead Jews at Ohrdruf, the MJH opens with a multimedia film and a photo-and-voice exhibition arguing that to understand Jews, one has to understand that there is no such thing as "a Jew." The three-dimensional film extravaganza talks about the many places Jews live, the many languages Jews speak, and the many ways Jews have moved around and settled in the modern world. In general, the permanent exhibition favors diversity over unity, talks about life more than death, an ironic statement in a Holocaust museum, and uses first-person voices as its primary narrative strategy. While the Museum of Tolerance presents pre-Holocaust Jewish history romantically, the Museum of Jewish Heritage has a multimedia exhibition that presents prewar European Jewry as an ideologically embattled group of people arguing passionately about socialism, Zionism, liberalism, and modern religious Judaism. The Museum of Tolerance uses voiceover and music, while the MJH uses contemporary readings of the original visionaries of Zionism, Bundism, and other Jewish movements of the twentieth century.

The museum takes a classic Holocaust education technique and puts it to new uses. In Holocaust education and in Holocaust museums, first-person storytelling has replaced third-person narrative as the way most people approach the Holocaust. The Museum of Jewish Heritage tells all of modern Jewish history through the lens of the first person by designing its exhibits around oral history, photographs, and personal artifacts. For this reason, the museum's focus is twentieth-century history, with the first floor dedicated to pre–World War II and Holocaust history, the second floor dedicated to the Holocaust, and the third floor describing postwar Jewish history from around the world. There is very little narration and almost no analysis. History unfolds through the stories, objects, and ephemera of those who experienced it. Director David Marwell was especially proud of the way the museum curators give life to inanimate objects by placing personal photographs of the owners next to the objects they possessed.[28] As museumgoers, we were both drawn into the stories of the documents, valises, hairbrushes, menorahs, and other artifacts of Jewish life through the photographs in ways that other museums' artifacts were not able to grab us.

The museum is perched on the southern tip of Manhattan, just steps away from the ferry to Ellis Island and from the ground zero memorial site. All museums occupy symbolic space. Since Los Angeles has very few ghosts to make certain spaces more meaningful than others, the Museum of Tolerance and the Skirball chose to locate themselves in the heart of living Jews' neighborhoods. But since New York is full of ghosts, there were plenty of opportunities to build a museum in haunted space. The museum was given a land grant just opposite Ellis Island, a place far away from any living Jewish neighborhood but deeply enmeshed in Jewish New York's ghostly landscape. Museum architects designed the vista over the river toward the Statue of Liberty and Ellis Island as a central element, and a visitor is never more than a few steps away from a reminder of the gateways to modern Jewish history, a history that, not coincidentally, places New York at the center of modern Jewish life.

As testament to its New York-centric vision of Jewish life, the central 2005 temporary exhibition was titled *New York: City of Refuge*. The exhibit documented the stories of Jewish immigrants to New York from the end of World War II to the present. Unlike the Ellis Island story of the poor huddled masses of Eastern Europe that so many American Jews presume to be the master narrative of American Jewish history, this exhibition showed that in the modern age, John F. Kennedy International Airport is the portal to America for modern immigrants, who have come from war-ravaged Europe, post-Communist Russia, Iraq, Iran, Ethiopia, Cuba, and Israel. Most museums narrate modern Jewish history as a story of the darkness of twentieth-century Europe leading to the light of modern Israel. Both in its permanent exhibition and in this temporary one, the Museum of Jewish Heritage suggests that history starts after the Holocaust, and, in this story, Jews *leave* an embattled Israel for the vibrancy and economic vitality of New York, even if they are no longer guided by the beaming light of the Statue's torch or walking the gauntlet of Ellis Island, both of which are visible from the temporary exhibition space. In the MJH's version, unlike every other narrative of Jewish migration to America, the original bronze gates of an old synagogue at JFK airport greet the museum visitor at the entrance to the modern Jewish migration story. Its location in New York gives the museum the confidence to show that, although the Holocaust scarred modern Jewish history, it did not mean the end of Jewish diversity. For the MJH, the lesson of the Holocaust is not that Jews now need guns to find safety in the modern world and that Jews must remain vigilant in the fight against anti-Semitism, which is the Museum of Tolerance's message. It is that Jews continue to live in many places, speak many languages, and find homes around the world, *despite* the scar of the Holocaust. And where do most Jews feel most at home? In this museum's worldview, Herzl and Ben Gurion got it wrong. New York is the city of Jewish refuge.

New York as a Real Homeland: The Diversity of New York Jewish Communities

Like Poland, New York may be a Jewish home because it has ghosts and Jews flock there to encounter them, but, like Israel, New York is a Jewish home also because it is the place in which many Jewish immigrants have chosen to settle. From nineteenth-century German Jews, early-twentieth-century Eastern European Jews, and postwar Hasidic Jews to post-Soviet Bukharan and Russian Jews and Israeli and Ethiopian Jews, New York, even more than Israel or Los Angeles, is the place Jewish migrants *choose* to call home. (Many Jewish migrants from Russia end up in Israel, because it is simply easier to gain residency rights there.)[29]

Russian immigrants have turned Brighton Beach into "Little Odessa" —even though most Jews are no longer from Odessa but are from Moscow, Petersburg, Kiev, and Minsk—and the Russian Jewish presence in New York has become so palpable that the *Forward* newspaper, the classic Yiddish socialist newspaper from the early twentieth century, now publishes a Russian-language edition that reflects the more conservative cultural and political tastes of the Russian immigrant community.[30] Israeli immigrants flock to Queens, Williamsburg, and, for those who can afford it, the Upper West Side, where Hebrew is almost as unremarkable as New York–inflected English on the streets of Jerusalem.[31] Like the turn of the twentieth century, when Eastern European Jewish immigrants turned New York into a Jewish polyglot, today immigrants from around the world are doing the same thing.

In 1990, immigrants made up just over 28 percent of the city's total population. And the foreign-born population is climbing again and may reach the numbers last seen in the pre–World War I period.[32] As for Jews, the 2002 UJA-Federation study on New York's Jewish population found that foreign-born Jews made up 27 percent of the New York area's Jewish population; the Russian-speaking Jewish community made up 20 percent of New York City's total Jewish population. There are more Russian-speaking Jews in New York than there are Jews in nearly every city in the country.[33] This diversity of Jewish ethnicity and the many layers of Jewish immigrant cultures affect New York Jews' sense of home and rootedness.

But New York Jews' sense of home and rootedness is not defined just by diverse ethnicities. It is also tied to degrees of Jewish observance, engagement with American political culture, and differing levels of embracing modernity. New York did not become a "Jewish city" until the mid- to late nineteenth century, even if Jews had lived there since 1654. It shocks many people to learn that the neighborhoods in Brooklyn that today are home to Hasidic Jews, who embrace modernity with ambivalence, originally became Jewish neighborhoods with the migration of middle- and upper-middle-class Reform and secular German Jews in the nineteenth century. To understand the history of living Jews in New York is an exercise in excavation and movement, of revealing the many layers of Jewish life in each place that make *all* places in New York haunted by ghosts even as they're inhabited by live people.

We have explored three institutional sites of Jewish memory making, nostalgia, and ghosts—the Lower East Side, the Center for Jewish History, and the Museum of Jewish Heritage. Now we turn to explore sites focused on the present: Crown Heights/Borough Park and Brighton Beach, two neighborhoods whose migrant influx occurred after the cataclysmic events of World War II and whose neighborhood character, languages, and customs challenge the assumptions and understanding of most American Jews. These communities do not integrate nicely into the well-established, Ashkenazi-dominated, nostalgia-driven, upper-middle-class culture of the Jews (particularly on the Upper West and East Sides, which we explore later in the chapter) who built, maintain, and visit the Center for Jewish History and the Manhattan Jewish Community Center. These are the Jews who live on the margins of American Jewish culture, as they are represented in mainstream media and the cultural displays in museums such as the Skirball in Los Angeles.

Jewish Tours: Seeing Crown Heights on a Hasidic Map

We use the metaphor of migration into, out of, or through a particular world intentionally to suggest that home and the Jewish map are not simply about physically moving around the world while bringing along one's roots. They are also defined by how different Jews see the world through different lenses. A recent convert to Hasidism, a *baal tshuvah,* may move physically miles away, a few blocks away, or not at all, but "home," "self," and "community" come to take on new meaning, and the process of getting there requires cognitive long-distance travel. The religious Zionists who work in the diaspora business as tour guides see Israel very differently from the organizers of the birthright israel/taglit program, even if they take American Jewish youth to the same sites. And the Orthodox Jews who run the Museum of Tolerance present a very different sense of Jewish rootedness from that presented by the Reform Jews who run the Skirball Cultural Center just miles up the road.

Those tourists who seek a lost, "authentic" past on the Lower East Side and nostalgically yearn to hear the strains of Yiddish, Hebrew, and Russian spoken on the street need only take the F train to Brooklyn.[34] There, in the neighborhoods of Crown Heights, Borough Park, Williamsburg, and Flatbush, Yiddish thrives as a living language. On the streets of these places, travelers and tourists can see versions of Jewish life that, for many more secular Jews around the world, represent Jewish authenticity and moral authority in the debates about "who is a real Jew."

Ironically, ultra-Orthodox and Hasidic historical claims to authenticity and space in Brooklyn are a relatively recent phenomenon, tied to the cataclysmic events and migrations of twentieth-century Jewish history. Hasidic Jews made New York their home in the years during and after World War II. Some have suggested that the Holocaust did not destroy the vibrant Hasidic communities of Poland but rather forced those that survived to migrate to a place that was open enough to maintain their separate ways of life. Regardless of interpretation, it is clear that the size and openness of New York, and, by extension, the pluralism of the United States, provided the refuge necessary to fully re-establish Hasidic communities in a postwar world shaken by genocide. They found that relatively welcoming space in the wide avenues and narrow row houses of Brooklyn. By now, Brooklyn has become the organizational and cultural locus of Hasidic Jewry, just as much if not more than the Hasidic neighborhoods of Bnei Brak and Meah She'arim in Israel. With its infrastructure of *yeshivot*, synagogues, girls' schools, welfare associations, baby networks (*gmachim*), bookstores, and kosher restaurants, bakeries, and butchers, Hasidic Brooklyn is a world unto itself, and many an anthropologist's dream fieldwork setting.[35]

If the Jewish geography of New York weren't complicated enough, the Hasidic geography of Brooklyn is itself as complicated. Each sect derives its name from the town in Poland from which its rebbe's court originated, and different communities settled in different parts of Brooklyn. Williamsburg is dominated by the reclusive Satmar Hasidim, the anti-Zionist and antisecular Hasidic movement that does not do outreach to those not already part of the community. Borough Park is dominated by the Bobover Hasidim. Crown Heights is dominated by the largest and most visible Hasidic sect in the world—Lubavitcher Hasidism, also known as Chabad. Chabad, known for its strategy of "*kiruv*," outreach to secular and marginally observant Jews, sends out *shlichim* (messengers) to establish Chabad houses on college campuses and in far-flung cities with few or predominantly assimilated Jews.[36] Passionate and extroverted young men staff Mitzvah Mobiles, teaching other Jewish men how to wear prayer shawls and phylacteries on the street, in airports, on campuses, and in other public spaces where they might find random Jews. (David has been approached by young men working in Chabad outreach in such diverse places as Jerusalem, Berkeley, Budapest, Moscow, Paris, London, New York, and Los Angeles. Chabad men generally do not approach Jewish women on the streets, so Caryn never has experienced such unsolicited, public encounters.) In cities across the United States and around the world, Chabad *shlichim* organize large Hanukkah displays, host *Shabbat* dinners every Friday night, and conduct highly successful telethons on major television stations, with major Hollywood stars imploring viewers to donate. These telethons have raised millions of dollars, often from Reform and Conservative Jews, for Chabad's various projects and organizations. In Crown Heights, the gray-bearded visage of Rabbi Menachem Mendel Schneerson, the leader who preached the imminence of the messiah and coaxed Chabad into a worldwide phenomenon of outreach and recruitment, has decorated car bumpers, living room walls, storefront windows, and banners proudly hung at the entrances of major *yeshivot*.[37] In our final visit, in January 2005, one store in Crown Heights had a full array of Rebbe memorabilia, including refrigerator magnets and trading cards.

In a twist on the New York–Israel connection, the Chabad Lubavitch headquarters in Kfar Chabad Israel are actually an exact replica of the somewhat shabby and dilapidated beehive of activity located in Crown Heights. Like the Museum of Tolerance, which is sending American Jewish visions of tolerance back to Israel, Chabad sends its visions of religious Jewishness back to Israel. One new project is the construction of a Hasidic Discovery Center on Eastern Parkway in the hope of attracting tourists and potential "migrants" into the world of Lubavitch Hasidism. In financial terms alone, the Chabad empire is big business for the local economy in Brooklyn and a major powerhouse in the world of Jewish fund-raising and organizational strength.

We want to situate Hasidic Jews on the Jewish map of New York and show how they complicate the notion of home. What does home mean, in a social and cultural world so far removed from the elite, postmodern, deeply nostalgic, and memory-obsessed culture of Manhattan's non-Orthodox and secular Jews? In a world only a short subway ride away from the Center for Jewish History, is Brooklyn the "Promised Land" for Chabad, more so than Jerusalem? To explore this part of the New York Jewish map, we explored these neighborhoods on foot and online.[38]

From Caryn's field notes on a Friday:

> We arrive in Crown Heights by mid-morning, just in time for the collective rush to prepare for *Shabbat*. The streets are congested with people doing last minute shopping in markets, bookstores, and bakeries with signs in Yiddish, Hebrew, and English. In many ways, the street scene is reminiscent of Friday mornings in downtown Jerusalem (and to a lesser extent, the Upper West Side in Manhattan), with the sense of urgency in the air of people trying to get everything done before *Shabbat* preparations begin by midafternoon. In a bakery on a busy corner, the service area is packed with women of all ages, several baby strollers, men avoiding eye contact with women, and young kids under five with little *payes*

[side curls]. The bakery staffers run back and forth from the counter to the wall stocked with columns of challot, rugelach and other baked goods, as the customers jostle to get closer to the front of the counter. It feels like organized pandemonium, so when we finally get our bag of goodies to bring to a *Shabbat* dinner for that evening, we quickly hustle out onto the relative spaciousness of the street.

We pass by a bookstore selling papers in Yiddish, posters and cards with the face of Rabbi Schneerson, rows and rows of books published by Art Scroll [an Orthodox publisher in Brooklyn], and a table stocked with educational toys, including a hilarious if unintentionally campy alarm clock in the shape of a young Orthodox boy, which features a chorus of boys singing the morning prayer "Modeh Ani" to the accompaniment of a tinny-sounding rock band.

Dressed in jeans and jackets, we clearly stand out in the neighborhood as outsiders, and yet both of us look distinctly Jewish—it's odd to feel at home and not at home simultaneously. How many times a year can one say they feel somewhat self-conscious for not looking or feeling "Jewish enough"? David was tempted to put on a *kippah* while wandering the streets to blend in better, but the Barney's bag carrying a fancy digital camera, notebook, and tape recorder gave him away as a modern, less-observant Jew.

Home has multiple meanings and political claims here. It is the staking of physical "territory" in urban Brooklyn and transforming it into indisputably Jewish spaces through the establishment of *yeshivot, shuls,* and businesses. It is about politics and ensuring that elected officials draft and vote on legislation and public policy that benefits and reflects the interests of the neighborhoods. But home is also about constructing and interpreting what Jewish identity means through specific lenses of ideology and history. Chabad plays with the tensions of modernity and tradition, the universalist welcoming of strangers and tourists as opposed to the particularism and insularity of the neighborhood's daily rhythms. In their organization, public street culture, politics, and vision, Crown Heights and Borough Park diverge starkly from most other American Jewish communities in defining "home." And yet, in its outreach strategies and discourse of universal access to Judaism, Chabad epitomizes savvy entrepreneurial instincts. Chabad harnesses distinctly postmodern technologies, such as Web sites, twenty-four-hour "Kotel Cams," online discussion groups, and other media to distribute its message. This clash of modernity and tradition "is very, very New York," says an official at the New York Tourism Bureau. "Our greatness as a city is its cultural diversity."[39] Chabad is its own global community within a community with its headquarters, not unlike global Jewry's, in New York, specifically at 770 Eastern Parkway in Brooklyn, where it is currently building a massive brick-and-mortar center.

In the virtual world, Chabad's Web site has two virtual tours. Its outreach Web site, www.jewishtours.com, provides a marketing video for its tours, described as pilgrimages without the long plane flights across the Atlantic. Chabad provides online tourists with a brief introduction to Chabad and claims rather boldly, "The Hasidic movement transformed European Jewry into a spiritual oasis in a relatively short period of time. In fact, over 60% of European Jewry became adherents to Hasidic ideals by the beginning of the second World War." The second virtual tour is called "Building the Future of Jewish Life in America." Images of the World Trade Center and the Statue of Liberty flash on the screen, juxtaposed with classic images of bearded rabbis, who represent the public (and almost always masculine) face of Orthodoxy. The virtual tour invites participants to watch a scribe at work on writing a Torah and to see people wearing "real Jewish clothing." In the words of Bob Swacker, of the Multinational Institute of American Studies at New York University, "It's a museum community of live people." This suggestive metaphor neatly highlights the contradictions and paradoxes of contemporary Chabad. Whereas museums have traditionally housed the artifacts and material culture of people and places lost and subjected to or plundered by colonialism, the Chabad virtual and neighborhood tours give participants a tiny glimpse into the living, complicated, and insular world of a thriving Jewish culture that actively seeks more Jewish adherents in the quest to bring about the Messiah.[40] One of the rabbis on the site argues, "This is as American as apple pie," suggesting that Chabad, though it eschews the temptations of popular culture and many aspects of modernity, is quintessentially and intrinsically an American social phenomenon, an integral part of the multicultural mix of the United States, even as the movement has become thoroughly global.

However much one might claim Crown Heights as a living museum of exotic subjects, bus and walking tours portray this religious community as a welcoming place for all interested Jews.[41] In fact, this marketing of accessibility is exactly what makes Chabad attractive to the many nonreligious Jews who come to Crown Heights to gawk at the "strangeness" of this world, to recover or reinvent their Jewish roots through *yeshiva* study, or to nostalgically remember a fictive past never personally experienced. Rabbi Epstein, the primary talking head in the promotional videos, explains that Chabad is always trying to improve "how to most effectively inspire Jewish people and non-Jewish people." Discussing his vision in front of a construction site for the future Hasidic Welcome Center, Rabbi Epstein explains, "I see the Center as a homecoming area that would have food facilities and overnight staying facilities. People know there is always a place where they can feel *heymish*. We're talking about hundreds of thousands of people. It's not just another Jewish center. It's literally a world welcome center for all nations for all people to really be inspired in a positive way." Rabbi Epstein's vision roots the "ground zero" (or, perhaps, ground Zion) of global Jewish homecoming smack in the center of Brooklyn—not Israel—and frames that welcoming specifically as a place for "all people" and "all nations," presumably including both Jews and non-Jews. Where else would thoroughly postmodern Hasids create a global welcome center for the multicultural masses, if not in Brooklyn?

Chabad's outreach has taken on new form with the opening of the Jewish Children's Museum, in January 2005. Unfortunately, the eight-story glass, steel, and stone museum was not yet open to the public during our January visit, so we were able only to hear several stories about the inside of this lavish museum. The $30 million children's Jewish funland sits in the heart of Crown Heights, not too far from the epicenter of the Crown Heights riots and literally next door to 770 Eastern Parkway. The museum is dedicated to Ari Halberstam, who was killed in 1994 by a Lebanese gunman on the Brooklyn Bridge. His name is imprinted on the vibrant, colorful mural of children's faces that adorns the steel façade of the museum.

With a mock-kosher supermarket and bigger-than-life-sized challah for children to play on, it is no wonder that the Jewish Children's Museum proved a hit with young children at a special public relations event in December 2004. Chabad invited New York City school children to the museum's special opening, which included such notables as Senator Hillary Clinton, Mayor Michael Bloomberg, and former mayor Rudolph Giuliani. The wave of press about the opening emphasized the museum's mission of tolerance through education, and images projected on NBC News showed happy African American children pushing shopping carts, collecting kosher food products, and gazing up at the stars through a *sukkah,* as the children learned about Sukkot.[42] Like the Museum of Tolerance, the Jewish Children's Museum claims to be geared to children, both Jewish and not. Channah, a young Orthodox girl who attended the opening, said she liked that Jewish and non-Jewish kids could play together, but in Jewish space. "You see other people and get to socialize and be together."[43] Of course, as a Chabad institution, its primary target audience is non-Orthodox Jewish children. Unlike the Museum of Tolerance, which shows Jews to be different because of their victimhood, the Jewish Children's Museum shows all children how Jews are different because of their rituals and practices.

From David's field notes:

> I was excited to speak Yiddish on the streets of Borough Park, even if many Hasids are suspicious of young, clean-cut American Jews' newfound interest in Yiddish. For these Jews, Yiddish is not about nostalgia or about accessing radical, socialist Jewish culture. It is about maintaining boundaries between a traditional Jewish culture and the American culture in which it exists that constantly seeks to encroach on its cultural and social separateness. My Yiddish violated that boundary. As I turned a corner, I noticed something I wasn't expecting to see—signs in Russian, deep in the heart of the Hasidic neighborhood. To me, Russian stood for Soviet émigrés, Jews whose connection to Jewish identity was ethnic and political, not spiritual. What would Russian immigrants be doing in Borough Park? To answer that question, I got back on the F train and headed to the end of the line—Brighton Beach.

Taking the Q Train South: From One Jewish Community with Its Own Map to Another

Brighton Beach is a classic American immigrant neighborhood. Like the Lower East Side at the turn of the twentieth century, Brighton Beach is filled with relatively poor and working-class Jewish immigrants from Russia who speak their native language (Russian now, not Yiddish), maintain independent community networks, and remain on the periphery of the established New York Jewish world. Despite their social and cultural marginality in New York, some high estimates suggest a Russian-speaking Jewish population in the New York area of 350,000, nearly a third of the total Jewish population.[44] If it weren't for the mass in-migration of young, upper-middle-class American Jews who move in droves to New York, Russian Jews, like their Lower East Side counterparts, would eventually dominate the New York Jewish landscape. But, as we show in our exploration of the Manhattan Jewish Community Center, they don't.

The cultural context today is very different from that which faced those who came at the turn of the twentieth century. The melting-pot narrative has been replaced by a celebration of American multiculturalism and diversity. Airplanes that traverse the distance between Moscow, Tel Aviv, and New York in nine hours have replaced steamships that took weeks to cross the Atlantic. Kennedy International Airport has replaced Ellis Island, which now serves as a memory site for the descendants of Russian immigrants from past generations.[45] Brighton Beach Jews can now share information and culture instantly with Russian Jews scattered across the world. They can and do spend the holidays traveling within their transnational community, across vast time and space in ways that earlier immigrants could not and did not.

Some predict that Brighton Beach will go the way of the Lower East Side. It will empty out and refill with other poor, non-Jewish immigrants, or it will gentrify. Second-generation Russian Jews will speak English, move to Manhattan or the suburbs, and "leave the ghetto," a story brilliantly told by the young Russian Jewish immigrant writer Gary Shteyngart.[46] However, this analogy works only so far; the impoverished, cramped ghettos and garment industry sweatshops of the turn-of-the-century Lower East Side hardly reflect the tidy bungalows and row houses in Brighton Beach and the service-economy businesses that line the working-class retail corridors. Others think that because the international Russian Jewish community has become truly transnational, New York's Russian Jews will be able to maintain independent Russian-language communities that are shaped by the particular national context in which they exist, whether in Russia, Ukraine, Israel, Germany, or the United States. Both are in fact true to a certain extent, which shows that New York is both what it was to the Jewish world in the twentieth century—an immigrant destination—as well as the center of a new Jewish world that has many easily traversable centers in the twenty-first century.

The neighborhood at the end of the F line is just a hop, skip, and jump from Coney Island, the early-twentieth-century hub of American Jewish entertainment. Brighton Beach had been a Jewish neighborhood since the 1920s, and diverse and vibrant Jewish communities had lived there through and shortly after World War II. This Jewish past and the elderly

Jews who continued to live there made it a desirable location to settle the new wave of immigrants from the Soviet Union. Only after the wave of Jewish emigration from the Soviet Union in the 1970s, however, did Brighton Beach become a Russian, as opposed to a general Eastern European Yiddish-speaking, enclave. By 1980, it was the largest Soviet émigré outpost in the world, home to more than thirty thousand Soviet Jews. It very quickly became known as Little Odessa because of the Ukrainian roots of many of the migrants.[47] The 1980s Soviet restrictions on emigration, which came to be known in the United States as the refusenik crisis, slowed the influx of new immigrants and helped fix Brighton Beach culture in the 1970s. It was not until a massive wave of Russian Jews came to the United States in the late 1980s and 1990s that Brighton Beach had a new set of Jewish immigrants bringing a *perestroika*-era and post-Soviet Russian culture to Brighton Beach. These newer immigrants had a decidedly different outlook and perspective on the meaning of home from their émigré predecessors.

Since the late 1970s, there have also been conflicts between the Russian Jewish immigrants and the more established Jews in Brooklyn and Manhattan, who do not understand Soviet Jewish identity adequately. Religious American Jewish organizations seeking new members among Russian immigrants have had a hard time making inroads into a community whose collective identity developed around Jewishness as an ethnicity, not a religion. In fact, some Soviet Jews see no contradiction between being Jewish and converting to Christianity, which many of them do.[48] According to Arkady Kagan, most American Jews still see Russian Jewish immigrants as charity cases needing to be helped, not as equal partners in the development of Jewish life in America.[49] Chabad, in Brooklyn, sponsored a radio program, *Gorizont* (Horizon), hosted by Alexander Sirotin, a playwright and director from Moscow, as a way of mediating the distance between religious and Soviet ethnic identities.

As a nearly flawless speaker of Russian, David can pass as a Russian immigrant when he strolls into the shops in Brighton Beach asking for pirogi.

From David's field notes:

I almost got lost looking for Brighton Beach. Asking for directions was proof of my outsider status. Any Russian Jew in New York (and even in Moscow and Tel Aviv) knows the way to Brighton Beach, but this Russian-speaking L.A. suburban Jew had to ask directions to the nearest pirogi shop. I didn't know what I was looking for. I knew that I was writing about a living but marginalized community in New York, one that proved New York's status as a Zion of the contemporary Jewish world. But how to prove that? The ads for the upcoming visit of a popular Russian singer? I wanted to show that the Brighton Beach landscape looked just like a fusion of a Moscow landscape with an American twist. (Or, in the words of Robin Williams, Moscow on the Hudson). Sure, the dress looked like that of Muscovites from the Brezhnev era, the food was similar, many of the products in stores were imported from Russia.

But next to the preserved peppers from Bulgaria and Ukraine were kosher soups from Israel and kosher wine next to the trendiest Russian vodka. In my many years in Moscow, I rarely saw Israeli products in stores, although in the late 1990s it became more common. But here, Russian Jews can bring Moscow culture and Israeli Jewish culture together. Russian Jews buy and sell Israeli kosher soup, not because Russian Jews keep kosher but because most Russian immigrants see their connection to Israel as an integral part of their Jewish identity. On the bottom shelf in the same store, I saw a big can of pork, a little piece of Russian culture in this Russian Jewish store.

As Brighton Beach's second generation of younger Russian Jews settles in, they now relate to this place very differently. Recent immigrants from Moscow who grew up in a post-Soviet Russia with shopping malls, bustling cafés, and high fashion do not see Brighton Beach as their immigrant "soft landing." In the 2000s, Russian Jewish immigrants frequently settle in Bensonhurst and suburban New Jersey, instead of in the older Russian Jewish enclave.[50] To many of these younger immigrants, Brighton Beach is a place frozen in time, "a world full of sour looks, suspicion, and hopelessly outdated fashion."[51] Like second-generation Jews who used to go to the Lower East Side for the best pickles, the bookshops, and the reminders of their childhood, new Russian immigrants who live in New York go to Brighton Beach for the Russian-language bookshops, bakeries that sell real black bread, and a fix of Soviet nostalgia. The question remains: How will this new nostalgia compete with the very alive relationship older immigrants have to Brighton Beach when this generation of 1970s immigrants passes away? Will the area go the way of the Lower East Side and become some other group's immigrant soft landing? Or will the nonstop flights from Moscow and the long-term maintenance of an international Russian-speaking community in Moscow, Tel Aviv, and

New York force Brighton Beach to become a Jewish home of both the ghostly nostalgic past and the vibrant, very living future? This question is already being answered in the Lower East Side when, on a Saturday, American Jewish tourists visiting the Tenement Museum compete for space on the sidewalks with the new Jewish hipsters and young modern Orthodox families that are "re*jew*venating" the area. Perhaps Brighton Beach will go the same way as migration continues from Russia and Ukraine; as the "Russification of Jewish New York," to use the words of Annelise Orleck, continues, it will continue to be a Jewish home of the past, present, and future.[52]

Re-Imagining the Center: The New Jewish Community Center in Manhattan

Taking the train literally and metaphorically back from Brooklyn to Manhattan, we now turn to the Upper West Side, to circle back to our original questions about New York, Jews, and the sense of place. Arguably in 2005 the most visibly recognized Jewish neighborhood in the country, the Upper West Side is flanked by Lincoln Center to the south and by the academic conglomerate of the Jewish Theological Seminary, Barnard College, Columbia University, and Teacher's College to the north. Along the way from one end to the other are the oldest synagogue in New York (Congregation Shearith Israel, established in 1654), the famous Zabar's, H & H Bagels, kosher delis and restaurants, Judaica bookstores, the Drisha Institute (a feminist *yeshiva*), and countless *minyans* representing every shade and nuance of denominationalism, from Hasidic *shtibels* to egalitarian and queer-friendly Renewal congregations.[53] Unlike many other ostensibly Jewish neighborhoods across America, it's not unusual to see groups of young, nattily dressed Jews in *kippot* and long skirts walking down Broadway to and from synagogue on a Friday night or Saturday morning. In the multicultural tumult of New York City, the Upper West Side, for all its diversity, feels distinctly and undeniably Jewish.

In the middle of all of this political liberalism, cultural cosmopolitanism, and Jewish pluralism sits the new Jewish Community Center, a flagship institution of the Upper West Side, but only recently established in the past fifteen years. The JCC deftly embodies the contradictions of the multicultural New York Jewish landscape, serving as a space to explore the tensions of modernity and tradition, unity and diversity, past and present. And somehow, the JCC manages to provide both physical and social space to house organizations and agendas that at first glance might seem hopelessly at odds with each other.

The first thing you notice is the building. It rises from Amsterdam Avenue at 77th Street, a sleek gray steel and concrete structure with grace notes of sky reflected off glass. Construction took more than a decade and cost $85 million; today the new JCC, according to its Web site, "is a building that houses our collective desires." Designed to meet the needs of contemporary, notoriously busy, and overscheduled New Yorkers, the JCC functions as an anchor in a neighborhood steeped in more than four generations of American Jewish culture. Not only is the JCC a source of constant activity and programming for the wider community, but it also represents a stunning achievement of successful politicking, savvy fundraising, and innovative construction in its dense urban neighborhood. A quick glance at the donor list of its most recent programming guide reveals substantial financial support from the City and the State of New York, from familiar Jewish philanthropists such as Barbara Dobkin, Samuel Bronfman, and the Tisch family, and even from corporate sponsors such as Exxon Mobil Corporation.[54] One glowing review from an Israeli delegate to the World Congress of Jewish Community Centers wrote:

> It began 11 years ago with a committee, one room, a secretary and a director and a small budget of $300,000. The founders wanted to create a creative model of a JCC where Jews from all walks of life would be not only welcomed but truly integrated into the decision making process. Seeing the JCCs as a bridge builder institution, pluralistic, cutting across economic status, gender, and concentrating on the people who make the JCC. For example, the JCC tried to create an open board where you did not have to be a donor in order to be influential. Interestingly, Debbie [Hirschman, the former executive director] attributes the current success to the fact they operated without walls for a decade and created a sense of community and true partnership with synagogues and other institutions.[55]

The obvious question is: Why would the most Jewish neighborhood in New York not establish a Jewish community center until the late twentieth century, and then only after years of organizing, politicking, and fundraising? Why did it take so long to create what functions as a foundational Jewish institution in so many other communities across the country? Is it because Jewish New York has other community centers, such as the 92nd Street Y, on the Upper East Side, and the Sol Goldman Y, on 14th Street? Or was there always too much competition with other organizations, programs, and activities for Jewish New Yorkers to care?

With programs and centers ranging from a Jewish feminist resource center to a state-of-the art gym facility to a center for Jewish meditation, the JCC provides a glimpse into the not-so-distant future of how the Jewish establishment recognizes, responds to, and incorporates cultural innovation and social change. For whom and how does the JCC reflect the unique character and culture of New York Jews? How much does the JCC serve as a model for other similar institutions around the country? And how does the JCC straddle the tensions engendered by a pluralistic, fractious New York Jewish community that includes, among others, feminists, Orthodox Jews, Buddhist-Jews, peaceniks, families with young children, and queers? The answer is in its organizational history, which has always accepted a broad interpretation of Jewish identity to welcome as many people through its institutional doors as possible.

Flexible Notions of Jewish Identity: The History of the JCC Movement

The Jewish Community Center in Manhattan is part of the wider movement of JCCs, which began in 1854, when the first Young Men's Hebrew Association opened in Baltimore to provide social services for Jewish immigrants from Eastern Europe and Russia. These early precursors of the contemporary Jewish community center were vehicles for assimilation and citizenship by offering classes in English language instruction and practical tips for how to navigate American culture. The centers also offered social activities and a venue to cultivate a sense of Jewish community independent of any religious denomination or synagogue setting.[56] After the First World War, the YMHAs merged with the Jewish Welfare Boards, which were charged with meeting the community needs of Jewish military personnel, to create the Jewish community center movement.

As American Jews' sense of home changed with assimilation, upward mobility, and white flight to the suburbs, so too did the JCCs, which moved along with the Jews in the 1950s and 1960s and expanded their facilities to meet the demands of postwar baby boomer families. Although many New York Jews left the Lower East Side and other areas of Manhattan to move to the outer boroughs, Long Island, and New Jersey, the Manhattan JCC stayed put in its physical home on Amsterdam Avenue. As a neighborhood anchor, it continues to reflect the changing kaleidoscope of New York Jewish culture. Indeed, secularism, pluralism, and a deliberate avoidance of the divisions that characterize most other areas of the American Jewish landscape are the hallmark of official JCC policy. Its mission statement reads:

> The vision of the JCC Movement is to maximize the use of the programs and services, the position in the community, and the accessibility of the Jewish Community Center to welcome all Jews, to help each Jew move along a continuum of Jewish growth, and to build Jewish memories. The ultimate goal is to create a community of learning Jews who are consciously Jewish; who are respectful of Jewish differences; and who are knowledgeable of and committed to Jewish values and practice; who participate in synagogue life and in Jewish communal and cultural life; who make Israel a central component in their identities as Jews; and who manifest their Jewishness in lifestyle, life choices, and life commitment, thus creating a Jewish community capable of continuing creative renewal.[57]

The mission statement raises interesting questions of interpretation. What constitutes "Jewish growth" and "Jewish memories"? These obviously mean different things to different people. Is a secular, atheist Jew who uses the JCC simply for its pool and gym facilities someone who is "manifesting her Jewishness in lifestyle"?

The JCC is seen by its donors and constituents as a center for "being and doing" Jewish, but for whom? Perhaps not for Russians in Brighton Beach or for the Chabad Lubavitch in Brooklyn, but, from observations of people in the lobby, pool, and meeting rooms, we found that the "clientele" reflects the population of the Upper West Side. During two visits in the fall of 2003, it was hard not to notice the frenetic bustle of activity and people coursing through the space. At mid-morning, the lobby was filled with strollers and young children, well-dressed moms and nannies imploring children to put on their raincoats and drink from their sippy cups. Seniors were meeting in conference rooms for discussion groups and pizza, while a group of Modern Orthodox men were studying in the Bet Midrash during their lunch hour. And, in a coincidence that could happen only in New York, we ran into Shaul Kelner, a thirty-something fellow social scientist who provided much insight for the earlier chapter on American Jewish teen travel and birthright israel, dropping off his daughter for a playgroup.

Apparently, this question—acknowledging the politics of Jewish unity and diversity—is something that JCC rebuilders sought to address from the very beginning of the process. Hirschman and her colleagues began meeting with rabbis representing all denominations, and they continue to meet every six to eight weeks. "It's an extraordinarily strong partnership."[58] According to former executive director Debbie Hirschman, the JCC now has more than eleven thousand members from across the communal spectrum. Rabbi Joy Levitt, the director of programming, explains: "A lot of lay leaders felt the need for a pluralistic institution that brought together people from the Upper West Side and beyond without regard for denomination or family structure. They sought to reflect the community and wanted markers of Jewishness to be extended—to include services and swimming, with a real strong neighborhood feel."

Like the Skirball, in Los Angeles, the JCC in Manhattan recognizes that the future lies in ecumenicalism and in embracing change as a way to remain relevant to its constituents. In many ways, its strategy is the opposite of Chabad's, which embraces tradition, rather than change, as its path into the future. Both the Skirball and the JCC celebrate the universal while providing programming for particularistic groups, and both implicitly celebrate how secular American culture influences Jewish cultures and creates flourishing hybrids. While the Skirball might curate an exhibit on Persian Jews to reflect the particular migration histories of the L.A. region, the JCC hosts programming with Edah, a Modern Orthodox group, Ma'yan (The Jewish Women's Project), and Congregation Beth Simchat Torah, one of the oldest and largest LGBT synagogues in the country. A recent program reflected the multiculturalism of Jewish New York and the changing understanding of "who is a Jew." The program, called "Jews of Color Speak Out," included a panel composed of a Korean/Ashkenazi cantor and rabbi, an Orthodox African American, a gay Mexican American, and a Jewish woman adopted from Thailand. The program, which was sponsored by CBST, Kulanu, Jews for Racial and Economic Justice, and Swirl, drew a crowd of more than two hundred people.

The JCC is also an incubator for innovative projects and a reflection of where the Jewish community is headed. Both Ma'yan and Makom: The Center for Mindfulness are products of Jews involved in secular social movements (feminism, New Age spirituality) who have influenced how Jews imagine themselves and create community—literally by establishing office and program space in the JCC. In a recent interview with Rabbi Jill Hammer, program director of Ma'yan, she explained that the project was envisioned as a way to change how the Jewish community responds to feminism and gender inequality. Rabbi Hammer said that as a marker of how much things have changed, Ma'yan originated the now-famous and much-replicated "Feminist Seder," which draws an average of two thousand people over three nights of Passover to reinterpret the seder from a feminist perspective. It's no accident that this innovative ritual started on the Upper West Side in New York City, and now feminist seders have become a standard part of communal programming in Jewish communities across the country.

Like the Center for Jewish History, the JCC bridges seemingly untenable differences among Jews by embracing diversity as a virtue, without any particular religious ideology to bind together the people who use its facilities, and by bringing this diversity together in a unity—a single building and a single mission of creating one home for all Jews. This tactic, the bedrock institutional mission of the JCC, allows it to successfully sidestep some of the issues, debates, and political sand traps that consistently and predictably create discord among segments of Jewish communities.

As central institutions, the Center for Jewish History and the Jewish Community Center in Manhattan project a broad, diverse vision of Jewishness in America. Both emphasize how Jews and Jewishness have changed in America generally, and in New York specifically. They emphasize diversity within American and global Jewry even as they show how this very diversity reflects Jews' own similarity to America. Jews, like Americans, are a diverse people bound together by abstract notions of unity. Like the Skirball, these two Jewish institutions project a liberal, rooted, diverse Jewish community. Whether New York is a melting pot, a kaleidoscope, or a tapestry, these Manhattan Jewish institutions show how rooted American Jews are in American soil, and how central New York is to this diverse Jewish world.

Chabad takes a different approach to rooting itself in America. When one of the rabbis on the virtual tours says that touring Crown Heights is "as American as apple pie," he does not mean that Hasidic Jews are a diverse people brought together by abstract notions of unity. He is emphasizing that the ability for this group to maintain such a visible degree of separation, to live in a "world apart" from the American landscape, could happen *only* in America because of its ideology of tolerance and freedom of (and freedom from) religion that governs American life. There is no embrace of diversity, only an embrace of American tolerance—leave us alone and we'll leave you alone. (The Museum of Tolerance in Los Angeles also relies on this laissez-faire approach to American diversity.) Chabad, then, is quintessentially American, because only in the United States are people allowed to maintain such separate lives. The global headquarters of this seemingly antimodern community *has* to be in the United States, specifically in New York, precisely because of America's and New York's ability to serve as home to radically diverse groups of people.

Even though there are many Hasidic Jews there, Chabad's global home is not in Israel. As Noah Efron has shown in his recent book, *Real Jews,* what makes Israel such a strife-ridden place for religious and nonreligious Jews alike is precisely the lack of an ideology of tolerance and a separation of synagogue and state. Precisely because there is no freedom of, or freedom from, religion, Israeli politics puts pressure on the insularity of Hasidic Jews. Although Efron focuses on how religious Jews encroach on the secularism of Israeli society, the reverse is also true. The Israeli state constantly encroaches on Hasidic Jews' ability to lead separate lives, and the issue has only become more strained as the government considers lifting the exemption on military service for religious students. Ironically, then, institutions for radically Americanized Jews and those for deeply separatist Jews both call America home, and both see New York as their Zion, the place where both can craft the kind of lives they choose. And, even more ironic, many secular Israelis, tired of the political conflict with the Palestinians and the religious conflicts with ultra-Orthodox Jews, are migrating to the new Zion of New York as a more tolerant, pluralistic alternative to the original "Promised Land."

We saw this same dialectic between separation and integration, between public and private, on our ethnographic research in diverse Jewish neighborhoods throughout New York. Unlike institutions, neighborhoods are not managed by boards, professional staffs, and mission statements. They are defined by the people who live in them and by the ghosts of the past. And neighborhoods, unlike many more impersonal institutions, are where people enact the intimacies of Jewish life—through cooking *Shabbat* meals in small apartments, shopping for groceries, creating families—in other words, neighborhoods are where people actually practice Jewish culture. New York is a new Zion because it is both an institutional and communal center of Jewish life. In Brighton Beach we found an odd synthesis of Russian-émigré American culture that makes Israel a key component of its Jewish identity, while on the Lower East Side we saw ghosts of the first wave of Russian Jewish immigrants competing with new modern Orthodox families and young secular Jews for space. Both the relatives of the old immigrants and the new settlers call this place "home."

It is New York's ability to embrace diversity and to allow for separateness, to allow the past, present, and future to mingle in a dynamic tension, that makes the city home to global Jewry. It is its radical wealth and its dire poverty, its giant temples to American Judaism and its run-down prayer houses in Borough Park, its scrappy innovation and its august establishments that has made New York Zion. Even though property prices have pushed many to Long Island, New Jersey, and Westchester County, with the creation of new institutions and the revitalization of new neighborhoods, New York seems poised to be Zion for religious queer Jews in Manhattan, secular Israelis in Williamsburg, *klezmer* musicians on the Lower East Side, insular Hasids in Crown Heights, and everyone in between for a long time to come.

Epilogue
The End of the Jews

After a few glasses of wine in a dingy airport bar, a place we found ourselves all too often while doing research for this book, Caryn jokingly said, "I've got the title! Trust me, it will create conversation." She grinned mischievously. "How about *Israel: Who Needs It?* It's perfect!" After talking her down from her giddy excitement, David suggested that such a polemical title might scare too many people off. Not to mention that this potential title simply put Israel back at the center of the Jewish map.

The question is not "Who needs Israel?" Each chapter of this book engages with Israel in deep and important ways. Moscow's Jews sought refuge there and now maintain connections to Israel that would have been unimaginable forty years ago. American Jews (among other new Jews) relate to Israel through philanthropy, travel, politics, and culture. For us, the point is that Jews could change their collective identity and self-perception if we recognize that the Jewish world is more complex than the simple diaspora-Israel dichotomy suggests. As we have shown, there are many Jewish homes, and Jews would be better off recognizing their ethnic, linguistic, political, and sexual diversities and embracing them rather than ignoring or suppressing those differences.

The Jewish map would certainly change if, for example, American Jewish organizations did what Israeli queers do by bringing Israeli high school students to the United States to learn about Jewish religious and cultural pluralism, rather than sending American Jews to Israel to develop a sense of Jewish nationalism. In fact, several programs—Building Bridges for Peace and Seeds of Peace—do just that by bringing Palestinian and Israeli kids to the United States each summer to learn about diversity and tolerance. The Jewish map might look different if we recognized that Russian Jews everywhere have different conceptions of Jewishness and if we trained people in Russian language skills to be Jewish leaders worldwide. Imagine if the Hebrew Union College started a program for Russian-speaking Jewish leaders to train to become rabbis in New York or Moscow. The map would look different if Jewish Studies programs in the United States sent as many students to study abroad in London, New York, Moscow, Buenos Aires, or Prague as they do to Jerusalem, Tel Aviv, Haifa, and Beersheva. It would look different if, when Jewish organizations did send Jewish youth to Israel, they did not simply use Israel as a historic backdrop on which to become "better American Jews" but actually discovered the living, breathing, amazingly diverse and complicated society that Israel is. This might mean spending less time at places like *Yad va-Shem* and the Western Wall and encouraging our students to study Arabic and Russian as well as Hebrew so that they could better communicate with all Israelis.

The first time either of us presented this material to an audience and posed the idea that this might be the end of the Jewish diaspora, the conversation became very heated. At one point, one of the participants anxiously asked: "Are you telling me that this is the end of the Jewish people?" He passionately argued that there was some sense of comfort or security, both metaphorically and physically, in the idea that Jews were a nation with a state in Israel. Were we challenging that notion? Does the end of diaspora signal the end of the Jewish people?

Quite the contrary.

In each chapter, we have shown that new Jews are creating new homes and futures in intimate, symbolic, and national ways. We first explained the process by which Jews around the world became attached to modern Zionism, to the idea that Jewish collective survival is dependent on the concept of a unified home in a nation-state. The subsequent chapters showed many ways that Jews complicate the binary of Zion and diaspora. In the chapter on Moscow, we found that most Moscow Jews have family or friends living in Israel, New York, or Los Angeles and are simultaneously crafting their own forms of Jewish identity rooted in a post-Soviet context. The chapter on identity tourism and the diaspora business showed how American Jews use Israel and Eastern Europe not as a longed-for homeland or a place of nostalgic memory but as backdrops for teaching their children to be better, more strongly committed American Jews. In Los Angeles, both the Skirball Cultural Center and the Museum of Tolerance serve as venues for addressing contemporary social problems and as sites of nostalgia and historical memory. But each museum approaches these questions differently depending on its interpretation of Judaism, modernity, and pluralism. We argued that queer Jews see the Jewish map differently by suggesting that connections to intimate and symbolic places (such as San Francisco and Jerusalem) do not just come from one's past and family but are also about creating new communities, sexualities, and the future.

And, in New York, we show how all Jewish places, both institutions like the Manhattan Jewish Community Center and the Center for Jewish History and neighborhoods like Crown Heights, the Upper West Side, and Brighton Beach, become home because of ghosts from the past, communities in the present, and visions of the future. This tension between what different Jews see in different places is what makes Jews establish roots in these places. It's the classic tension between global and local, and the cosmopolitanism Jews exhibit comes from the constant circulation of people and culture among Jews' many homes.

In the introduction, we asked the question "What does a working-class second-generation Sephardic Jewish woman in Bnei Brak have in common with an upper-middle-class Ashkenazi Jewish woman in Beverly Hills?" The simple answer is that they both have the word "Jew" in their list of identities. But, as we've shown, there are some Jews, namely some secular Israelis, who do not identify as Jews but see themselves as Israelis. It's only when these secular Israelis travel to other global Jewish communities and engage with other Jews that the "Jewish question" arises. In fact, in a recent *New York Times* article, Edward Rothstein discusses recent public academic conversation about whether the Jewishness of Israel's statehood is no longer necessary. He quotes Haim Hanegbi, an Israeli leftist, who said on the page of *Haaretz,* Israel's highbrow daily, "A Jewish state can no longer exist here." And an Israeli academic, Meron Benvenisti, went one step further, stating, "The Zionist revolution is over."[1] In our experiences as professional Jews and as Jewish studies professors, we find that these statements seem blasphemous to most American Jews, who see the Jewishness of Israel as one of the key ideas that bind Jews. But Israelis have been bandying about the question of the Jewish future of Israel for years. And for many Israelis, the idea of "the Jewish people" is less important than the challenges of living in a state of constant conflict and tension.

In a recent sociological study of Jews in the former Soviet Union, respondents were asked about their connections to Jews of different ethnicities throughout the former Soviet Union and the world.[2] Ashkenazi Russian Jews claimed to feel a closer kinship to Russian non-Jews than to Israeli Jews. In other words, post-Soviet Jews question the very notion of a singular, unified Jewish people. So, in fact, what some of us think, feel, and do already reflects the end of diaspora. But Jews are reluctant to abandon this idea, despite the reality that it no longer reflects who Jews have become and, more important, who we are to one another.

The present and future of Jewish communities means traveling ideas, people, and cultural forms throughout the world, constantly engaging in dialogue with each other, and changing the meaning of Jewishness in the process. The end of diaspora also means radically rethinking Jews' relationships to one another across these disparate communities and places. If the concept of "the Jewish people" means that Jews are all one, that we speak with one voice, that we inherently share a common understanding and vision of the world, then our emphatic answer to that anxious man's question is yes, this is the end of "the Jewish people," and this development is good for the Jews. If this is how we understand "the Jewish people," then it is no longer a useful concept for describing Jewish life.

But, as many Jews around the world are discovering, "the Jewish people" means not that all Jews are one but, rather, that all Jews share one thing and one thing alone—they identify as Jews, whatever that may mean. It is a postmodern—some might even say an empty—definition of Jewish identity, which makes the definition of Jewishness completely subjective and slippery. But, in fact, the only thing that Jews have in common is the fact that they self-identify as Jews. This may mean that Israelis who do not identify as Jews may no longer want to be part of "the Jewish people," an ironic twist of Zionist fate that has created a Jewish state that unmakes Jews. Rather than bemoan the demise of a unified people, we think it is the very slipperiness of Jewish identity that provides so much fertile potential for creativity, innovation, and adaptation in all the places Jews call home. By abandoning the confines of nationalistic and diasporic constraints for a more nuanced, flexible understanding of Jewish identity that embraces difference and differences as core virtues, we as Jews can become better global citizens.

The move away from the binary of diaspora-homeland should be celebrated as evidence of Jews' ability to put down roots, to build houses and live in them, to plant gardens and eat of their fruit, as the prophet Jeremiah said more than two thousand years ago. It is evidence that Jews are a group of diverse peoples with many cultures, many homes, and infinitely creative ways of expressing what it means to be at home, as Jews.

Notes

NOTES TO THE PREFACE

1. For a relatively neutral account of how interfaith families contribute to Jewish communal life, see Sylvia Barack Fishman, *Double or Nothing? Jewish Families and Mixed Marriage* (Waltham, MA: Brandeis University Press, 2004).

NOTES TO THE INTRODUCTION

1. Stefan Helmreich, "Kinship, Nation, and Paul Gilroy's Concept of Diaspora," *Diaspora* 2(2) (1992), p. 245. Helmreich bases his definition of diaspora on the Oxford English Dictionary. See also Erich Gruen's *Diaspora* (Berkeley, Los Angeles: University of California Press, 2001), which examines the origins of the concept after the dispersions of Jews from the Kingdom of Israel first through the Hellenistic and then through the Roman Empires.

2. These definitions of the terms *galut* and *galuti* come from R. Alkalay, *The Complete Hebrew-English Dictionary* (Jerusalem: P. Shalom Publications, 1981).

3. The Boyarins cite Neturei Karta as an example of this new form of diaspora because of their rejection of Jewish political hegemony over the land. See Daniel Boyarin and Jonathan Boyarin, "Diaspora: Generation and the Ground of Jewish Identity," *Critical Inquiry* 19(4) (1993), pp. 724–25. For a fuller discussion of Neturei Karta's ideology and its conception of Jewish identity, see Mitchell Judah Heifetz, "Jewish Anti-Zionism: A Case Study in Political Ideology," M.A. thesis, Case Western Reserve University, 1972. For an ethnographic description of the Reb Arelach sect in Mea Shearim, see Sam Heilman, *Defenders of the Faith: Inside Ultra-Orthodox Jewry* (New York: Schocken, 1992).

4. See Immanuel Jakobovits, "Religious Responses to Jewish Statehood," *Tradition* 20(3) (fall 1982), p. 192, as cited in Bernard Wasserstein, *Vanishing Diaspora: The Jews in Europe since 1945* (Cambridge, MA: Harvard University Press, 1996), p. 86. As he grew older, Schneerson mellowed his religious anti-Zionist stance and supported Chabad activities in Israel.

5. Erich Gruen, "Diaspora and Homeland," in *Exiles and Diasporas: Vari-*

eties of Jewish Identity, ed. Howard Wettstein (Berkeley/Los Angeles: University of California Press, 2002), pp. 32, 36.

6. S. Y. Abramovitch, *Tales of Mendele the Book Peddler,* ed. Dan Miron and Ken Frieden (New York: Schocken, 1996), p. 307.

7. See Daniel Elazar, "Community," in *Encyclopedia Judaica,* CD-ROM version, 1997, or David Roskies, *The Jewish Search for a Usable Past* (Bloomington: Indiana University Press, 1999), ch. 7.

8. See Steven Aschheim, *Brothers and Strangers: The East European Jew in German and German Jewish Consciousness, 1800–1923* (Madison: University of Wisconsin Press, 1981); George Mosse, *German Jews beyond Judaism* (New York: Hebrew Union College Press, 1985).

9. For more on the formation of particularly American forms of Jewish religious identities in the nineteenth century, see Jonathan Sarna, *American Judaism: A History* (New Haven: Yale University Press, 2004).

10. Mary Antin, *The Promised Land* (New York: Houghton Mifflin, 1912), p. 141.

11. See Rebecca Kobrin, "Conflicting Diasporas, Shifting Centers: The Transnational Bialystok Émigré Community in the United States, Argentina, Australia, and Palestine, 1878–1949," Ph.D. diss., University of Pennsylvania, 2002.

12. See for example Irving Howe, *The World of Our Fathers* (New York: Schocken, 1976), p. 58. Howe cites the statistic that while two-thirds of the total number of immigrants to the United States in the years between 1908 and 1924 remained in the country permanently, 94.8 percent of Jews did so.

13. Deborah Dash Moore, "Jewish Migration in Postwar America: The Case of Miami and Los Angeles," in *A New Jewry? America since the Second World War: Studies in Contemporary Jewry,* ed. Peter Medding (New York/Oxford: Oxford University Press), p. 102. We would push Moore to ask why the most stable and secure Jewish community in the world is still "the diaspora."

14. See R. Stephen Warner and Judith G. Wittner, eds., *Gatherings in Diaspora: Religious Communities and the New Immigration* (Philadelphia: Temple University Press, 1998); Steven J. Gold, "Gender and Social Capital among Israeli Immigrants in Los Angeles," *Diaspora* 4(3) (1995), pp. 267–309.

15. Naama Sabar, *Kibbutzniks in the Diaspora* (Albany: SUNY Press, 2000), pp. 104–6.

16. In the early Zionist movement, there was much debate about whether the new Jewish homeland had to be on the same territory as the original Jewish homeland in Palestine or whether Jews could use any territory to create their home. The most famous non-Zionist proposal was the Uganda Proposal made by the British to give Jews territory in Africa for Jewish in-gathering. In 1903, the proposal was rejected in favor of a Zion-or-nothing platform. See Geoffrey Wheatcroft, *The Controversy of Zion: Jewish Nationalism, the Jewish State, and*

the Unresolved Jewish Dilemma (Reading, MA/New York: Perseus Books, 1996), pp. 108–10; Jonathan Frankel, *Prophecy and Politics: Socialism, Nationalism, and the Russian Jews, 1862–1917* (Cambridge/New York: Cambridge University Press, 1981), pp. 133–71.

17. Ella Shohat, *Dangerous Liaisons: Gender, Nation, and Postcolonial Perspectives* (Minneapolis: University of Minnesota Press, 1997); Yael Chaver, *What Must Be Forgotten: The Survival of Yiddish Writing in Zionist Palestine* (Syracuse: Syracuse University Press, 2004); Baruch Kimmerling, *The Invention and Decline of Israeliness: State, Society, and the Military* (Berkeley/Los Angeles: University of California Press, 2001).

18. The Supreme Court decision was handed down February 20, 2002. See the Israeli Foreign Ministry's Web site, www.mfa.gov.il/mfa, for details about the ruling.

19. Tom Segev, *Elvis in Jerusalem: Post-Zionism and the Americanization of Israel* (New York: Metropolitan Books, 2001), ch. 1.

20. Melvin Urofsky, *American Zionism from Herzl to the Holocaust* (Lincoln: University of Nebraska Press, 1995), pp. 312–13.

21. Jeffrey Shandler, "Producing the Future: The Impresario Culture of American Zionism before 1948," in *Divergent Jewish Cultures: Israel and America,* ed. Deborah Dash Moore and S. Ilan Troen (New Haven: Yale University Press, 2001), pp. 53–71.

22. David Ben Gurion and Jacob Blaustein, "An Exchange of Views," *American Jewish Year Book* 53 (1952): 564–68.

23. Wheatcroft, *The Controversy,* pp. 254–73.

24. Karen Brodkin, *How Jews Became White Folks* (New Brunswick: Rutgers University Press, 1998). On the relationship between American Jews and the idea of diaspora, see Naama Sabar, "Kibbutz L.A.: A Paradoxical Social Network," *Journal of Contemporary Ethnography* 31 (February 2002), pp. 68–94.

25. On the prestate material culture of American Zionism, see Shandler, "Producing the Future," pp. 58–61.

26. To read how Ahava invokes romantic images of Israel, see its Web site, http://www.ahava.com/general/about_us.asp.

27. Yael Zerubavel, *Recovered Roots: Collective Memory and the Making of Israeli National Tradition* (Chicago: University of Chicago Press, 1995).

28. Kevin Avruch, *Critical Essays on Israeli Society, Religion, and Government* (Albany: SUNY Press, 1997).

29. *Jewish Chronicle,* February 10, 1994.

30. See for example the work of the historians Benny Morris, Ilan Pappe, and Tom Segev and of sociologists such as Baruch Kimmerling and Meron Benvenisti.

31. On the idea of post-Zionism, see Lawrence Silberstein, *The Postzionism Debates: Knowledge and Power in Israeli Culture* (New York: Routledge, 1999).

32. Deborah Dash Moore and S. Ilan Troen, "Introduction," *Divergent Jewish Cultures: Israel and America* (New Haven: Yale University Press, 2001), p. 5.

33. David Biale, ed., *Cultures of the Jews* (New York: Schocken, 2003).

34. On North African Jewish communities in Israel, see Yoram Bilu, "Moroccan Jews, Shaping Israel's Geography," in Moore and Troen, *Divergent Jewish Cultures*, pp. 72–86; on Ivri-Nasawi, see Loolwa Khazoom, "United Jewish Feminist Front," in *Yentl's Revenge*, ed. Danya Ruttenberg (San Francisco: Seal Press, 2000). See the organization's Web site at http://www.ivri-nasawi.org/.

35. Howard Wettstein, ed., *Exiles and Diasporas: Varieties of Jewish Identity* (Berkeley/Los Angeles: University of California Press, 2002), p. 2.

36. Lawrence Silberstein, ed., *Mapping Jewish Identities* (New York: NYU Press, 2000).

37. See Larry Tye, *Homelands: Portraits of the New Jewish Diaspora* (New York: Owl Books, 2000); Howard Sachar, *Diaspora: An Inquiry into the Contemporary Jewish World* (New York: HarperCollins, 1985); and James Ross, *Fragile Branches: Travels through the Jewish Diaspora* (New York: Riverhead, 2001).

38. Boyarin and Boyarin, "Diaspora," pp. 712–13.

39. Ibid., p. 711.

40. Ibid., p. 714.

41. Richard Marienstras, *Être un peuple en diaspora* (Paris: F. Maspero, 1975), and his "On the Notion of Diaspora," in *Minority Peoples in the Age of Nation-States*, ed. G. Chaliand (London: South Asia Books, 1990), pp. 119–25.

42. James Clifford, "Diasporas," *Cultural Anthropology* 9(3) (1994), p. 303.

43. Leah Garrett, *Journeys beyond the Pale: Yiddish Travel Writing in the Modern World* (Madison: University of Wisconsin Press, 2003), pp. 170–71.

44. A few methodological notes: We have given pseudonyms to the informants who appear in the book to protect their privacy. Our statistics in each chapter come from a variety of sources, as noted. When it comes to debates about Jewish demographics, statistics are particularly politicized. Israeli government officials want immigration statistics to be higher; American Jews want the Jewish population of the United States to increase; and those who think Eastern Europe is dead want to show tiny numbers in Moscow and other major Eastern European cities. It is impossible to extricate oneself from these problems; therefore, we try to provide ranges, to give several sources, or, when we are feeling polemical, to offer a statistic that supports our point while showing that it is one of many possible statistics. For more on the problem with statistics, see Joel Best, *Damned Lies and Statistics: Untangling Numbers from the Media, Politicians, and Activists* (Berkeley/Los Angeles: University of California Press, 2001).

45. On how Jewish philanthropies use a language of unity to encourage donation, see Kerri Steinberg, "Contesting Identities in Jewish Philanthropy," in Wettstein, *Exiles and Diaspora*, pp. 253–78.

46. Barbara Kirschenblatt-Gimblett, "Spaces of Dispersal," *Cultural Anthropology* 9(3) (1994), p. 342. See also her book *Destination Culture: Tourism, Museums, and Heritage* (Berkeley/Los Angeles: University of California Press, 1998).

47. Ibid.

48. Zvi Gitelman, "The Decline of the Diaspora Jewish Nation," *Jewish Social Studies* 4(2) (1998), p. 127.

49. Kirschenblatt-Gimblett, "Spaces of Dispersal," p. 342.

50. Biale, *Cultures of the Jews,* p. xxix.

51. Yair Sheleg, "A Pan-Jewish Jewish Approach," *Haaretz,* May 11, 2004.

52. "Jewish College Students," a special report for the National Jewish Population Survey, 2000–2001, p. 19.

53. The official name of the program uses lower-case letters for "birthright" and "israel." The word "taglit" means discovery, in this case a double entendre in that students on the program are supposed to discover both Israel and their Jewish selves.

54. See Sam Kliger, "Russian Jews in America: Status, Identity, Integration," paper presented at conference "Russian-Speaking Jewry in Global Perspective," Bar Ilan University, June 2004. Kliger estimates the number of Russian Jews in New York at 350,000. In 1999, Mark Kupovetsky, a leading historian of Soviet Jewry, estimated the core Jewish population of Moscow at 320,000, although other sources put the number at closer to 250,000. The only survey to put Moscow's Russian-speaking Jewish population higher than New York's is that by the Federation of Jewish Communities of the Commonwealth of Independent States (FJC), which claims that there are 500,000 Jews in Moscow, despite the 2002 census figures, which showed 120,000. See www.fjc.ru/news/newsArticle.asp?AID=108529.

55. As peace prospects improved in 2005 after Yassir Arafat's death, student interest in taglit/birthright israel programs increased.

56. That said, the umbrella organization for French Jewry, Le Conseil Representif des Institutions juives de France (CRIF), condemned only the fighting between France and Israel, not the specific comment by Sharon, and said that it is up to the individual or the family to decide whether or not to move to Israel. For the CRIF press release, see www.crif.org (in French).

57. "Ex-chief rabbi: European Jewry has no future," *J: The Jewish News Weekly of Northern California* 108(49) (December 10, 2004), p. 21a.

NOTES TO CHAPTER 1

1. Gabriele Freitag, *Nächtstes Jahr in Moskau! Die Zuwanderung von Juden in di sowjetische Metropole 1917–1932* (Göttingen: Vanderhoeck & Ruprecht, 2004).

2. Mordechai Altshuler, *Soviet Jewry on the Eve of the Holocaust* (Jerusalem: Yad va-Shem, 1998).

3. Bernard Wasserstein, *Vanishing Diaspora* (Cambridge, MA: Harvard University Press, 1997); Zvi Gitelman, *Century of Ambivalence* (Bloomington: Indiana University Press, 2001); Yuri Slezkine, *A Jewish Century* (Princeton: Princeton University Press, 2004).

4. Jewish population figures for the former Soviet Union are notoriously difficult to determine, since there are such competing definitions of who is a Jew. Estimates of the Jewish population of the Russian Federation range from 400,000 to 800,000; for Ukraine, from 300,000 to 500,000; and for Belarus, from 50,000 to 100,000. This makes the former Soviet Union the third largest Jewish population in the world, no matter which figures are used, behind the United States and Israel.

5. Wasserstein, *Vanishing Diaspora*. The book's title suggests the line of argument he is taking. He focuses on the persistence of anti-Semitism throughout Europe in the final two chapters. He shows that, even though Jews in Western Europe tend to feel at home, anti-Semitism, particularly connected to Middle Eastern politics, has cast a pall on Jews' continued integration into European societies. Wasserstein sees no possibility of Jews feeling at home in Eastern Europe and dismisses the statistics about Jewish revival. Wasserstein concludes: "Demographic, social, religious and cultural trends over the past half-century point inexorably towards the dissolution of the Diaspora, at any rate in Europe."

6. All interviews with informants in Moscow were conducted in Russian.

7. See David Shneer, *Yiddish and the Creation of Soviet Jewish Culture* (New York: Cambridge University Press, 2004).

8. For more on the history of Jews in the Soviet Union, see Zvi Gitelman, *A Century of Ambivalence: The Jews of Russia and the Soviet Union, 1881–Present* (Bloomington: Indiana University Press, 1988, 2001).

9. One of the earliest expressions of post-Stalinist Soviet Jewish identity came in a *samizdat* (unofficial Soviet publication) pamphlet that was eventually published in English by the Academic Committee on Soviet Jewry. Many of the articles in this pamphlet suggest that Soviet discourse about ethnic and religious identity significantly shaped Soviet Jews' identities. See Aleksandr Voronel and Viktor Yakhot, *I Am a Jew: Essays on Jewish identity in the Soviet Union* (New York/Tel Aviv: Anti-Defamation League of B'nai Brith, 1973).

10. Petrus Buwalda, *They Did Not Dwell Alone: Jewish Emigration from the Soviet Union, 1967–1990* (Baltimore/London: Johns Hopkins University Press, 1997), pp. 29–31.

11. Ibid., pp. 31–32.

12. Wasserstein, *Vanishing Diaspora*, p. 198.

13. Buwalda, *They Did Not Dwell Alone*, p. 15.

14. See for example Richard Cohen, ed., *Let My People Go* (New York: Pop-

ular Library Press, 1971). The idea of seeing Russian Jewry living the Exodus story has continued long after the Soviet Union died. For example, the International Hillel organization, which has invested resources in creating social organizations for Jewish students and youth in the former Soviet Union, sponsors an annual Pesach project. The project brings American Jews and Jews from the former Soviet Union together to put on a Passover seder. Some of the American students who participate view the experience as a second Exodus story. In the words of one participant, "Our exit from Egypt that is relived each year, it is not an analogy. It is truth and circumstance." To read more firsthand narratives from the Pesach project, see http://hillelnet.org.il/articles/index.html.

15. Buwalda, *They Dwelt Alone*, pp. 129–35.

16. See Gloria Deutsch, "Former Soviet Refusenik Ida Nudel: Where Is She and What Is She Doing?" *Jerusalem Post,* January 11, 2002, p. 14.

17. Jack Kugelmass, "The Rites of the Tribe: The Meaning of Poland for American Jewish Tourists," in *Going Home, YIVO Annual 21*, pp. 395–453; Barbara Myerhoff, *Number Our Days* (New York: Touchstone, 1980).

18. Wasserstein, *Vanishing Diaspora*, p. 199.

19. See Zvi Gitelman, *A Century of Ambivalence: The Jews of Russia and the Soviet Union, 1881 to the Present* (Bloomington: Indiana University Press, 2001), p. 185.

20. For more on the reasons for emigration, see Victor Zaslavsky and Robert Brym, *Soviet Jewish Emigration and Soviet Nationality Policy* (New York: St. Martin's Press, 1983).

21. Gitelman, *A Century of Ambivalence*, pp. 188–95.

22. Wasserstein, *Vanishing Diaspora*, p. 254.

23. Buwalda, *They Dwelt Alone*, pp. 163–66.

24. For an incredibly detailed demographic analysis of 1991 Jewish emigration to Israel, see Yoel Florsheim, "Immigration to Israel from the Soviet Union in 1991," in *Jews and Jewish Topics in the Soviet Union and Eastern Europe* 3(9) (1992), pp. 5–15.

25. There is little agreement on migration statistics. Ours are based on several sources, including the National Council for Soviet Jewry (www.ncsj.org/stats.shtml), the Israeli government (www.mfa.gov.il), the German Ministry of the Interior's Bureau of Statistics (www.bamf.de), and several scholars' own statistics.

26. Gitelman, *A Century of Ambivalence*, p. 218.

27. See for example Anatoly Medetsky, "Chief Rabbi Calls for Stronger Community" [Russian], *Vladivostok News,* November 2, 2000, available at vn.vladnews.ru.

28. http://www.chabad.org/global/about/article.asp?AID=244380.

29. "Present-day Situation and Prospects," *East European Jewish Affairs* 32(1), p. 22.

30. See www.chabad.org.

31. The most up-to-date information on Chabad can be found on its highly sophisticated Web site, www.chabad.org, where one can witness, among other things, a simultaneous Hanukkah candlelighting via streaming video.

32. See http://www.beytenu.aha.ru/russia_1.htm.

33. See "Dnepropoetrovsk: Lifting the Iron Curtain," chapter 2 in Larry Tye, *Homelands: Portraits of the New Jewish Diaspora* (New York: Henry Holt, 2001).

34. Interview with Berl Lazar, "*V Rossii nevozmozhno dolga byt' inostrantsem*," *Rodina* 4/5 (April 2002), pp. 202–4.

35. See *The Russia Journal*'s coverage of Jewish institutional in-fighting and Putin's role in supporting Chabad, especially Sam Greene, "Kremlin Seen Behind Jewish Community Rift," *Russia Journal*, July 1, 2000.

36. "Etot svet razgoniaet liuboi mrak: o vtopom s'ezde FEOR," *Pravda*, November 19, 2001 [Russian]. See also lechaim.ru.

37. Ibid.

38. See Andrei Zolotov, "Jewish Leaders Plagued by Kremlin Politics," *Moscow Times*, June 8, 2000.

39. Interview with Rabbi Adolf Shayevich, "Ostavaias' evreiami, byt' rossianami," *Rodina* 4/5 (April 2002), pp. 38–40.

40. Interview with Rabbi Chaim Ben Yaakov, who was at the time the chief rabbi for Progressive Judaism in Russia, October 1999.

41. See *Rodina: Rossiiskii istoricheskii illiustrirovannyi zhurnal*, Special edition, *Jews in Russia*. The journal is an organ of the Russian federal government.

42. In 2003, the Union of American Hebrew Congregations changed its name and became the Union of Reform Judaism.

43. See http://www.reform.org.il/russian/default.htm.

44. Interview with Rabbi Chaim Ben Yakov, October 1999. Ben Yakov is also on the faculty of the Jewish University of Moscow.

45. Interviews with Chaim Ben Yakov and conversations with several *machon* students, 1999. See also the World Union of Progressive Judaism Web site (www.wupj.org) for information about the *machon* program.

46. Erin Arvedlund, "A Russian Rabbi Teaches Jews, First Off, to Be Jews," *New York Times*, December 18, 2004, p. 4.

47. David Kaufman, *Shul with a Pool: The "Synagogue-Center" in American Jewish History* (Waltham, MA: Brandeis University Press, 1999).

48. Sue Fishkoff, *The Rebbe's Army: Inside the World of Chabad-Lubavitch* (New York: Schocken, 2003), p. 163.

49. Roman Shipov, "Lev Levaiev Honors His Father's Memory," *Ne sekretno*, January 24, 2003. See also Or Avner's Russian-language Web site, www.oravner.com.

50. Lev Levaiev, *Lekhaim* 2 (82) (1999) [Russian].

51. Betsy Gidwitz, "Jewish Life in Ukraine," *Jerusalem Letter* (Jerusalem: Jerusalem Center for Public Affairs), April 1, 2001.

52. "JCDF Goals and Criteria for Funding," available at www.ajws.org/jcdf.

53. Alexander Osipovich, "Reverse Exodus: Why are So Many Jews Returning?" *Russia Profile* 4 (October 2004), p. 36.

NOTES TO CHAPTER 2

1. Our notion of *diaspora business* was informed by, among others, Aihwa Ong, *Flexible Citizenship: The Cultural Logics of Transnationality* (Durham: Duke University Press, 1999); James Clifford, *Routes: Travel and Translation in Late Twentieth Century Culture* (Cambridge, MA: Harvard University Press, 1997); Arjun Appadurai, *Globalization* (Durham: Duke University Press, 2001).

2. For one conceptualization of this form of heritage travel, see Barbara Kirschenblatt-Gimblatt, *Destination Culture: Tourism, Museums, and Heritage* (Berkeley/Los Angeles: University of California Press, 1998).

3. See Linda Basch, Nina Glick Schiller, and Cristina Szanton Blanc, *Nations Unbound: Transnational Projects, Postcolonial Predicaments, and Deterritorialized Nation-States* (New York: Routledge 1994).

4. See Andre Levy, "To Morocco and Back: Tourism and Pilgrimage among Moroccan-Born Israelis," in *Grasping Land: Space and Place in Contemporary Israeli Discourse and Experience*, ed. Eyal Ben-Ari and Yoram Bilu (New York: SUNY Press, 1997).

5. Shaul Kelner, "Almost Pilgrims: Authenticity, Identity and the Extra-Ordinary on a Jewish Tour of Israel," Ph.D. diss., City University of New York, 2002, pp. 17–27.

6. Deborah Dash Moore and Ilan Troen, eds. "Introduction," *Divergent Jewish Cultures: Israel and America* (New Haven/London: Yale University Press, 2001), p. 10.

7. See Lynn Davidman and Shelley Tenenbaum, "Introduction," *Feminist Perspectives on Jewish Studies* (New Haven: Yale University Press, 1996).

8. Kelner, "Almost Pilgrims," pp. 27–40.

9. See Caryn Aviv, "Home-making: Gender, Emotional Zionism, and American Immigration to Israel," Ph.D. diss., Loyola University, Chicago, 2002.

10. Jeffrey Shandler, "Producing the Future: The Impresario Culture of American Zionism before 1948," in *Divergent Jewish Cultures: Israel and America,* ed. Deborah Dash Moore and S. Ilan Troen (New Haven: Yale University Press, 2001), pp. 53–71.

11. See the Rothberg School's Web site, www.overseas.huji.ac.il.

12. Kelner, "Almost Pilgrims," p. 13.

13. From the Jewish Agency's Web site, www.jafi.org.il: "*Shlichim* are sent for various reasons: some to work with local Jewish communities and Federa-

tions, some to teach in Jewish day schools, and some to lead the members of a Zionist youth movement. All of them live in a Jewish community and provide a living link to Israel."

14. See the Livnot U'lehibanot Web site, www.livnot.org.il, for the mission of livnot trips. Livnot now partners with birthright israel to provide free Livnot experiences to all eighteen- to twenty-six-year-olds who have not been on an organized Jewish trip to Israel before.

15. Michelle Wolkomir, "Emotion Work, Commitment, and the Authentication of the Self: The Case of Gay and Ex-Gay Christian Support Groups," *Journal of Contemporary Ethnography* 30(3): 305–34.

16. "Charedi" is a term used to denote "ultra-orthodoxy." The range of definitions, descriptions, labels, and microdifferentiation is subject to intense scrutiny and debate among insiders.

17. For example, there are programs designed specifically for seniors or for Bar/Bat Mitzvah adolescents, gay and lesbian educational tours, programs to reach out to unaffiliated Jews searching for spirituality, extremely expensive "deluxe" programs for wealthy philanthropists, and on and on. Segmenting to target a key audience for specific programs is crucial in staking out a claim in a crowded field.

18. See www.birthrightisrael.com.

19. Dina Kraft, "Winners of Charlie Awards Show How Birthright Is Having an Impact," Jewish Telegraph Agency, January 12, 2004.

20. In the former Soviet Union, Hillels are not necessarily connected with a university but serve as Jewish community centers for Jewish youth. We have visited Hillels in Moscow and Kiev.

21. See Barbara Kirschenblatt-Gimblett, "Imagining Europe," in *Divergent Jewish Cultures: Israel and America,* ed. Deborah Dash Moore and S. Ilan Troen (New Haven: Yale University Press, 2001).

22. For more on the meaning of travel to Poland for American Jews, see Jack Kugelmass, "Why We Go to Poland: Holocaust Tourism as Secular Ritual," in *The Art of Memory: Holocaust Memorials in History,* ed. James Young (New York: Prestel, 1994), pp. 175–84.

23. Deborah Findling, "A Hermeneutic Exploration of the Past as Present and Future: The March of the Living as Text," Ph.D., diss., University of San Francisco, 1999, p. 1.

24. The largest operation for capturing the testimony of survivors is Steven Spielberg's Shoah Visual History Foundation (www.vhf.org).

25. Findling, "A Hermeneutic Exploration," p. 35.

26. Jack Kugelmass, "The Rites of the Tribe: The Meaning of Poland for American Jewish Tourists," in *Going Home, YIVO Annual* 21, pp. 395–453.

27. Students come from all points in the global Jewish community, including

North America, Latin America, South Africa, Australia, Eastern and Western Europe, Russia, and Israel.

28. The Web site is www.motl.org.

29. Stephen Helmreich, "The March of the Living: A Follow-Up Study of Its Long-Range Impact and Effects," unpublished manuscript, cited in Findling, "A Hermeneutic Exploration," p. 38.

30. On preparing students for the March, see Oren Stier, *Committed to Memory: Cultural Mediations of the Holocaust* (Amherst: University of Massachusetts Press, 2003), pp. 154–57.

31. James Young, *The Texture of Memory: Holocaust Memorials and Meaning* (New Haven: Yale University Press, 1994).

32. Jackie Feldman, "It Is My Brothers Whom I Am Seeking: Israeli Youth Pilgrimages to Poland of the Shoah," *Jewish Folklore and Ethnology Review* 17(1–2) (1995), pp. 57–66.

33. Findling, "A Hermeneutic Exploration," p. 100.

34. Stier, *Committed to Memory,* pp. 176–78.

35. Chaim Waxman, *American Aliya: Portrait of an Innovative Migration Movement* (Detroit: Wayne State University Press, 1989), and his more recent *Jews in Israel: Contemporary Social and Cultural Patterns,* co-edited, with Dr. Uzi Rebhun (Waltham, MA: Brandeis University Press, 2004). The film *A Time of Favor,* made by Joseph Ceder, an American immigrant originally from Silver Spring, Maryland, explores the intensely emotional and nationalist subculture of *yeshivot* in the West Bank.

36. Lynn Davidman discusses similar programs run by Chabad Lubavitch that critique modernity and provide immersion experiences in her book *Tradition in a Rootless World: Women Turn to Orthodox Judaism* (Berkeley, Los Angeles: University of California Press, 1993). However, the major distinctions between programs run in the United States and those run by similar organizations in Israel are that the State of Israel generously subsidizes such programs, and their activities are heavily laden with emotional Zionist appeals to "redeeming the Land of Israel."

37. See, among others articles, Susan Thomson, "War Chills Israeli Study Programs Here: University of Illinois, Missouri University No Longer Send Students," *St. Louis Post-Dispatch,* April 5, 2002, p. B1. Many other universities were not sending students during the height of the Al Aksa intifada, including the University of California.

38. Deborah Sontag, "Israelis Angry at Foreign Jews Cancelling Visits," *New York Times,* June 11, 2001, p. A6.

39. Dina Kraft, "Funding Cuts Have Sponsors Worried about Birthright's Future," Jewish Telegraphic Agency, January 11, 2004. Other organizations eventually stepped in and filled the financial gap.

40. Dina Kraft, "Avi Chai Foundation to the Rescue: $7 Million Grant Could Save Birthright," Jewish Telegraph Agency, February 17, 2004.

41. See Diane Fuss, *Essentially Speaking: Feminism, Nature, and Difference* (New York: Routledge, 1990).

42. The Diller Fellows Program of San Francisco's Bureau of Jewish Education, a year-long teen leadership development program, now sends its participants either to Israel or to Argentina.

43. In addition to Eastern Europe's new vitality, a recent study commissioned by the National Foundation for Jewish Culture showed that a large majority of diverse leaders in American Jewish communities think that the Holocaust "is an insufficient and diminishing factor in American Jewish identity formation." See Richard Siegal, ed., "Commission Report on the Future of Jewish Culture in America: Preliminary Findings and Observations," *National Foundation for Jewish Culture,* October 2002, p. 10.

44. For example, in 2004, the Rocky Mountain Hebrew Academy, the non-denominational Jewish high school in Denver, Colorado, sent high school students to New York for Jewish identity travel. New Yiddish programs are springing up around the globe in places as diverse as Vilnius, Lithuania, and Strasbourg, France, and existing programs in New York and Amherst are expanding. *Klezmer* concerts, camps, and festivals have been trendy now for more than ten years globally. And we have not even touched on the new interest in Sephardic and Mizrahi cultures that inspires adult Jewish tourists to visit places like Turkey.

NOTES TO CHAPTER 3

1. Deborah Dash Moore, as quoted in Reed Johnson, "Museum Is Mirror for American Jews," *Los Angeles Daily News,* May 11, 1997, p. D5.

2. For more on the proliferation of memory sites, such as museums, in the 1970s and 1980s, see A. Huyssen, "Monument and Memory in a Postmodern Age," in *The Art of Memorials in History,* ed. James Young (Munich: Prestel-Verlag, 1994).

3. Richard Cohen, "Self-Image through Objects: Toward a Social History of Jewish Art Collecting and Jewish Museums," in *The Uses of Tradition: Jewish Continuity in the Modern Era,* ed. Jack Wertheimer (New York/Jerusalem: Jewish Theological Seminary, 1992), p. 209.

4. Ibid., p. 215.

5. Ibid., pp. 216–17.

6. Ibid., p. 223.

7. Ibid., p. 224.

8. This precedes the annual state-mandated commemoration of the Holocaust in Israel known as Yom Ha-Shoah (Holocaust Remembrance Day). Yom

Ha-Shoah was established by the Israeli Knesset in 1953 and officially incorporated into the Israeli calendar of observance in 1959. See Don Handelman and Elihu Katz, "State Ceremonies of Israeli Remembrance Day and Independence Day," in Don Handelman, *Models and Mirrors: Towards an Anthropology of Public Events* (Cambridge: Cambridge University Press, 1990).

9. James Young, *The Texture of Memory: Holocaust Memorials and Meaning* (New Haven: Yale University Press, 1993), p. 287.

10. Bet Ha-Shoah literally means "House of the Holocaust."

11. Edward Norton, "Yes and No to the Holocaust Museums," *Commentary* 96/2 (August 1993), p. 23.

12. See Neil Gabler's *An Empire of Their Own: How the Jews Invented Hollywood* (New York: Anchor Books, 1989).

13. Max Vorspan and Lloyd Gartner, *History of the Jews of Los Angeles* (Philadelphia: Jewish Publication Society, 1970), p. 17.

14. Bruce Phillips, "Los Angeles Jewry: A Demographic Profile," in *American Jewish Year Book, 1986* (New York: American Jewish Committee, 1986), p. 132.

15. Deborah Dash Moore, "Jewish Migration in Postwar America: The Case of Miami and Los Angeles," in *A New Jewry? America since the Second World War: Studies in Contemporary Jewry*, ed. Peter Medding, *An Annual VIII* (New York/Oxford: Oxford University Press), p. 104.

16. Ibid., p. 109.

17. Vorspan and Gartner, *History of the Jews of Los Angeles,* p. 267.

18. Moore, "Jewish Migration," p. 112.

19. Simon Greenberg, "Some Reflections," *Women's League for Conservative Judaism* 58 (Summer 1988), as cited in Moore, "Jewish Migration," p. 111. In her book-length treatment of L.A. Jewry, Moore reveals that, in 1947, when the University of Judaism was founded, Greenberg was initially one of those indeed trying to import denominational divisions. His later reflections from 1988 show how his opinions changed.

20. Shoshana Feher, "From the Rivers of Babylon to the Valleys of Los Angeles: The Exodus and Adaptation of Iranian Jews," in *Gatherings in Diaspora: Religious Communities and the New Immigration,* ed. R. Stephen Warner and Judith G. Wittner (Philadelphia: Temple University Press, 1998), pp. 71–94.

21. David Mittelberg and Mary Waters, "The Process of Ethnogenesis among Haitian and Israeli Immigrants in the United States," *Ethnic and Racial Studies* 15 (July 1992), pp. 412–35.

22. Naama Sabar, *Kibbutzniks in the Diaspora* (Albany: SUNY Press, 2000).

23. It's interesting to note that an Orthodox Jew began this project, coming from a community that usually insulates itself from outsiders and that, for the most part during the social movements of the 1960s, avoided joining multiracial political coalitions.

24. Interview with Adaire Klein, March 30, 2002.

25. Sheldon Teitelbaum and Tom Waldman, "The Unorthodox Rabbi," *Los Angeles Times Magazine,* July 15, 1990, p. 6.

26. Norton, "Yes and No," p. 23.

27. Rachel Abramowitz, "Opinions That Count for a Lot: When It Comes to Jewish-Themed Projects, the Views of the Simon Wiesenthal Center Staff Matter Too Much, Some Filmmakers Say," *Los Angeles Times,* April 15, 2001, Calendar, p. 5.

28. Nicola Lisus, "Misplacing Memory: The Effect of Television Format on Holocaust Remembrance," M.A. thesis, University of Toronto, as cited in Oren Baruch Stier, "Virtual Memories: Mediating the Holocaust at the Simon Wiesenthal Center's Beit Hashoah-Museum of Tolerance," *Journal of the American Academy of Religion* 64 (4), p. 833.

29. Stier, "Virtual Memories," p. 837. See also Edward Linenthal, "Locating Holocaust Memory: The United States Holocaust Memorial Museum," in *American Sacred Space,* ed. David Chidester and Edward T. Linenthal (Bloomington: Indiana University Press, 1995).

30. Oren Stier, *Committed to Memory: Cultural Mediation of the Holocaust* (Amherst: University of Massachusetts Press, 2003), ch. 4.

31. Over the course of two years, we visited the museum four times.

32. The terms reflect the binary language of social science group relations theory that emerged in the mid-1950s. A more contemporary and provocative linguistic strategy might ask visitors to choose between "racist" and "antiracist."

33. Peter Novick, *The Holocaust in American Life* (Boston/New York: Houghton Mifflin, 1999), pp. 13–15.

34. *Beit Hashoah,* brochure produced by the Museum of Tolerance, pp. 8–9.

35. Norton, "Yes and No," p. 24.

36. Tom Tugend, "Wiesenthal Museum for Paris Announced," *Jerusalem Post,* May 16, 2002, Jewish World, p. 7B. See also http://www.wiesenthal.com/about/NYTC2.pdf.

37. Ibid.

38. "Travel in Brief," *The Gazette* (Montreal), January 18, 2003, p. 16. See also "He'll Be Back," *Jerusalem Post,* May 7, 2004, p. 8.

39. Tom Tugend, "Wiesenthal Center Unveils Plans for Jerusalem Museum of Tolerance in Los Angeles," *Jerusalem Post,* May 4, 2000, p. 4.

40. Tom Tugend, "Wiesenthal Center's Plan for New Museum Met With Skepticism," *Jerusalem Post,* May 30, 1997, Features, p. 20.

41. Susan Freudenheim, "Large Gift to Help Wiesenthal Center Build Israel Facility," *Los Angeles Times,* May 10, 2000, Metro, Part A, p. 1.

42. Tugend, "Wiesenthal Center's Plan for New Museum Met with Skepticism."

43. Quoted in Bernard Weinraub, "Jewish History Museum Opening in Los Angeles," *New York Times,* April 21, 1996, Travel, p. 3.

44. Reed Johnson, "Museum Is Mirror for American Jews," *Los Angeles Daily News,* May 11, 1997, Living, p. D5.

45. Herbert Muschamp, "Architecture of Light and Remembrance," *New York Times,* December 15, 1996, Arts and Leisure, p. 1.

46. Michael Schuman, "Skirball Museum Illuminates Jewish Life in America," *Boston Herald,* December 24, 2000, Travel, p. 49.

47. Johnson, "Museum Is Mirror."

48. Over the course of three years, we visited the Skirball four times.

49. Diane Haithman, "Take the 405 to Utopia: Fourteen Years in the Making, the Hebrew Union College Skirball Cultural Center Will Open in April without Fanfare, or Debts," *Los Angeles Times,* November 19, 1995, Calendar, p. 3.

50. Dr. Uri Herscher, "Message from the President," Skirball Cultural Center Web site (www.skirball.com).

51. Haithman, "Take the 405 to Utopia."

52. See, for example, Leon Whiteson, "Monument to Identity: New Skirball Cultural Center Seeks to Hold on to Jewish Heritage," *Los Angeles Times,* August 5, 1996, Real Estate, p. 1.

53. Muschamp, "Architecture of Light and Remembrance."

54. Sephardic and German Jews migrated before the establishment of Ellis Island in 1894, when the federal government centralized immigration regulations. See Alan Kraut, *The Huddled Masses: The Immigrant in American Society* (New York: Harlan Davidson, 1982), and, on Jews and immigration, see Alan Kraut and Richard Breitman, *American Refugee Policy and European Jewry: 1933–1945* (Bloomington: Indiana University Press, 1987).

55. Beverly Beyette, "Filmmaker, Philanthropist: For Ex-Rabbi Skirball, Life's a Big Production," *Los Angeles Times,* November 17, 1985, View part 6, p. 1.

56. Robin Rauzi, "Celebrating Jewish Life: New Skirball Museum's Goal Is to Reflect Old and New of Proud Culture," *Los Angeles Times,* April 19, 1966, Metro, p. 1. See also Johnson, "Museum Is Mirror."

57. On the location of the Skirball, see Tom Tugend, "Hillside Heritage," *Los Angeles Times,* April 5, 1996.

58. Ibid.

59. Ibid.

60. Haithman, "Take the 405 to Utopia."

61. Muschamp, "Architecture of Light and Remembrance."

62. Ibid.

63. Rauzi, "Celebrating Jewish Life," p. 1.

64. Jan Breslauer, "Skirball's Vision for All Visitors: Museum Aims to

Broaden Focus on Jewish Culture," *Los Angeles Times,* April 20, 1996, Calendar, p. 1.

65. Ibid.

66. Haithman, "Take the 405 to Utopia." Herscher could also have been saying this because the museum opened not long after the passage of Proposition 187, also known as the anti-immigrant proposition, which restricted illegal immigrants' access to medical care, education, and other basic social services. The proposition was declared unconstitutional.

67. Whiteson, "Monument to Identity."

68. Karen Stein, "City on a Hill," *Architectural Record* (August 1996), p. 94.

69. Norton, "Yes and No," p. 31.

NOTES TO CHAPTER 4

1. We use the term "queer" as a means of incorporating all those who do not fit normative sexual and gender norms. This includes lesbian, gay, bisexual, transgender, and even intersex Jews. Although each of these groups has its own communities and political issues, the term "queer" allows us to bridge the strict distinctions among these groups. For more on our use of the term "queer," see the introduction to David Shneer and Caryn Aviv, eds., *Queer Jews* (New York: Routledge, 2002). Also, note that, for the most part, when we refer to Israeli queers, we are referring to Jewish Israeli queers. We talk about the complications of non-Jewish Israeli queers later in the chapter.

2. See Raz Yosef's *Beyond Flesh: Queer Masculinities and Nationalism in Israeli Cinema* (New Brunswick: Rutgers University Press, 2004).

3. David Weinberg, "Educating against Zionism," *Jerusalem Post,* April 23, 2000, p. 6.

4. See Tom Segev, *Elvis in Jerusalem: Post-Zionism and the Americanization of Israel* (New York: Owl Books, 2003).

5. Andrew Holleran, *Nights in Aruba* (Harmondsworth, UK: Penguin, 1991), p. 116.

6. Wayne Myslik, "Renegotiating the Social/Sexual Identities of Places: Gay Communities as Safe Havens or Sites of Resistance," in *BodySpace,* ed. Nancy Duncan (London: Routledge, 1996).

7. On the formation and segmentation of Castro as a gay ghetto, see Manuel Castells, *The City and the Grassroots* (London: Arnold, 1983), pp. 138–69.

8. Alexander Osipovich, "Reverse Exodus: Why Are So Many Jews Returning?" *Russia Profile* 4 (October 2004), p. 36.

9. Overt homophobia among senior members of the government and municipal officials still occurs frequently. In the squabble over the 2003 Pride March, Rabbi Haim Miller, the deputy mayor of Jerusalem claimed, "I think they have a

problem, they have a perversion, it is a disgrace." June 10, 2003. Available at www.BBC.com.

10. The Jerusalem Pride Parade was billed as a march of tolerance and diversity. However, few Palestinians attended, given the context of several recent suicide bombings and their fear of being outed among Palestinians, who exhibit severe homophobia.

11. In fact, the Bush administration has repeatedly nominated candidates with overt antipathies toward queer people for offices and judgeships, much to the dismay of liberal and queer civil rights groups.

12. See, among others, Shneer and Aviv, *Queer Jews*; Lawrence Schimel, *Found Tribe* (Santa Fe: Sherman Asher, 2002); Melanie Kaye-Kantrowitz and Irena Klepfisz, eds., *Tribe of Dina: A Jewish Women's Anthology* (Boston: Beacon Press, 1989).

13. See Rebecca Alpert, Sue Levi Elwell, and Shirley Idelson, eds., *Lesbian Rabbis: The First Generation* (New Brunswick: Rutgers University Press, 2001).

14. Alix Wall, "Queer Jews with Local Ties Make No Apologies in Anthology," *Jewish Bulletin of Northern California*, August 23, 2002.

15. It's no accident that most of the student leaders of *Keshet* are straight-identified, as openly gay students would automatically be asked to leave the rabbinical school, given the Conservative movement's current policy. However, more queer-identified students are opening the doors of the closet by telling close friends of their orientation, and more students in the educational school and other graduate divisions are coming out, as they do not face the same discriminatory policy as rabbinical students. Personal communication with Jeremy Gordon, *Keshet* coordinator, March 2003.

16. Shneer and Aviv, "Introduction," *Queer Jews*.

17. John D'Emilio, *Sexual Politics, Sexual Communities* (Chicago: University of Chicago Press, 1998).

18. Lee Walzer, *Between Sodom and Eden: A Gay Journey through Today's Changing Israel* (New York: Columbia University Press, 2000), p. 16.

19. Dan Izenberg, "Supreme Court Gives Lesbian Couple Right to Adopt Each Other's Children," *Jerusalem Post*, January 11, 2005, p. 1.

20. Walzer, *Between Sodom and Eden*, p. 6.

21. See Raz Yosef, *Beyond Flesh*, p. 1.

22. See Ruti Kadish, "Israeli Gays and Lesbians Encounter Zionism," in Shneer and Aviv, *Queer Jews*, pp. 224–37. Also see G. Herdt and B. Koff, *Something to Tell You: The Road Families Travel When a Child Is Gay* (New York: Columbia University Press, 2000).

23. Kadish, "Israeli Gays and Lesbians Encounter Zionism," p. 226.

24. See Susan Martha Kahn, *Reproducing Jews: A Cultural Account of Assisted Conception in Israel* (Durham: Duke University Press, 2000), ch. 2.

25. "First Out-of-the-Closet Gay Man Elected to Tel Aviv City Council," available at www.gaymiddleeast.com.

26. The Open House adopts the language used in 1970s social science on intergroup relations in its byline, "Advancing the Cause of Social Tolerance," which implies diversity and difference but, at first glance, does not explicitly spell out the kind of tolerance being advanced.

27. As reported in Karen Hawkins, "Israeli LGBTs Get U.S. Support for Center," *Windy City Times,* May 30, 2001.

28. Larry Luxner, "Oy Vey, Soy Gay," JTA News, April 3, 2005.

29. Walzer, *Between Sodom and Eden,* p. 7.

30. "The Agudah Reaches Out," *World Congress Digest* (Spring 2001).

31. Interview with Meirav Yaron, former director of programming at the Israel Center, San Francisco, April 28, 2003.

32. See Shaul Kelner, "Almost Pilgrims: Authenticity, Identity, and the Extra-Ordinary on a Jewish Tour of Israel," Ph.D. diss., CUNY, for a discussion of the taglit-birthright israel trips to Israel.

33. Interview with Meirav Yaron, April 28, 2003.

34. T. J. Michels, "S.F. Supe Has Gay Ol' Time on Israeli 'Journey of Pride,'" *Jewish Bulletin of Northern California,* May 11, 2001.

35. Matt Lebovic, "Gay MIT Student Resolute about Israeli Flag," *Bay Windows,* September 2, 2004.

36. See T. J. Michels and Ali Cannon, "Whose Side Are You On? Transgender at the Western Wall," in Shneer and Aviv, *Queer Jews,* pp. 84–99.

37. See Ilan Sheinfeld, "Zehut sheli," in his collection of poetry, *Karet* (Tel Aviv: Shufra Publishing, 1997), p. 55. The translation is our own.

38. Amir Fink and Jacob Press, eds., *Independence Park: The Lives of Gay Men in Israel* (Stanford: Stanford University Press, 1999), p. 89.

39. See www.365gay.com/newscono4/12/123104israel.htm.

40. This information is based on an e-mail exchange with Aeyal Gross. See also his article, "Challenges to Compulsory Heterosexuality: Recognition and Non-Recognition of Same-Sex Couples in Israeli Law," in *Legal Recognition of Same-Sex Partnerships: A Study of National, European and International Law,* ed. Robert Wintemute and Mads Andenas (Oxford, UK/Portland, OR: Hart, 2001).

41. Lesléa Newman, "The Writing on the Wall: On Being a Jewish Writer, a Lesbian Writer, and a Jewish Lesbian Writer," in Shneer and Aviv, *Queer Jews,* p. 34.

42. Walzer, *Between Sodom and Eden,* p. 16.

43. "Rafi Niv," *Independence Park,* pp. 65–90.

44. On Filipino queer guest workers in Israel, see Nurit Wurgaft, "Foreign Workers, and Gay, Too. It Isn't Easy," *Haaretz,* December 17, 2002.

45. Ahmar Mustikhan, "Group Fight for Palestinian Gays' Safety," at www.planetout.com, April 5, 2003.

46. See Tony Kushner and Alisa Solomon, *Wrestling with Zion: Progressive Jewish-American Responses to the Israeli-Palestinian Conflict* (New York: Grove Press, 2003).

47. See the Silk Road Theatre Project's Web site at www.srtp.org.

NOTES TO CHAPTER 5

1. See Jyl Lynn Felman, "Lost Jewish (Male) Souls," in *Queer Jews,* ed. David Shneer and Caryn Aviv (New York: Routledge, 2002). Also see www.storahtelling.org for a description of founder Amichai Lau-Lavie's attempt to meld Jewish and queer drag queen sensibilities into performance art through his character "The Shabbes Queen."

2. However, New York's Jewish cultural diversity is not necessarily reflected in the roster of major organizations and institutions, which continue to be dominated by the Ashkenazic descendants of German and Eastern European immigrants.

3. Susan Glenn, *Daughters of the Shtetl: Life and Labor in the Immigrant Generation* (Ithaca: Cornell University Press, 1991).

4. *Jewish Population Study, 2002* (New York: United Jewish Appeal, 2002), pp. 30–31. The total number of Jews living in New York City was given as 972,000. The greater New York area's Jewish population, however, remained stable as many people left the city for New Jersey and Long Island.

5. Miles Kronby recently founded a Web site, www.talkingstreet.com, which offers thirteen self-guided tours entitled "The Lower East Side: Birthplace of Dreams." Adam Baer, "Tramping Immigrant Byways with a Whisper in Your Ear," *New York Times,* September 25, 2003, Circuits section, p. 3.

6. Jeffrey Shandler, Beth Wenger, and Hasia Diner, "Introduction," in Diner et al., *Remembering the Lower East Side,* p. 7.

7. Ibid.

8. Jack Kugelmass, "Turfing the Slum: New York City's Tenement Museum and the Politics of Heritage," in Diner et al., *Remembering the Lower East Side,* p. 182.

9. Ibid., p. 198.

10. The bold claim of the Center may also have been a response to an institution in Israel, the Zalman Shazar Center for Jewish History, named for the labor Zionist leader and third president of Israel and Israel's first Minister of Education and Culture. With two "Centers of Jewish History," one in New York, the other in Israel, the Jewish historical world was developing at least two global research centers.

11. See, among other sources, "Lieutenant Governor Hails $2 million for Center for Jewish History," at www.state.ny.us/governor/ltgov/press99/aug05_99.htm.

12. The Association for Jewish Studies moved from Brandeis University to the Center late in 2003, following the American Jewish Historical Society's move almost ten years earlier. See *AJS Perspectives* for more on the Association's reasons for moving.

13. Richard Shepard, "Archives of Jewish History, Now under One Roof," *New York Times,* April 28, 1997, p. B6.

14. Allan Nadler, *YIVO Annual Report,* 2002.

15. Ibid., p. 2.

16. For example, the research institutions at The Hebrew University of Jerusalem and Tel Aviv University both house extensive scholarly collections documenting the histories and cultures of the State.

17. Joshua Eli Plaut, *Center for Jewish History Annual Report,* New York, 2002.

18. Richard Shepard, "Archives of Jewish History, Now Under One Roof," *New York Times,* April 28, 1997, p. B6.

19. David Chartock, "Development Team 'Steels' Show: Making One Building out of Six," *New York Construction News* 48(2) (September 1999), p. 19.

20. Timothy Burger, "Pols Win New York Cut of Federal Budget Pie," *Daily News,* October 23, 1998.

21. "Governor Announces $200,000 to the Center for Jewish History," New York State Governor's Office Press Release, available at www.state.ny.us/governor/press/aug20_4_98.htm.

22. "Mayor Giuliani Announces Funding for the Center for Jewish History," available at www.ci.nyc.ny.us/om/html/99b/pr309-99.html.

23. In the building of the Museum of Jewish Heritage in lower Manhattan, at least $22 million of the $60 million budget came from the New York City budget, with $5 million more pledged by the City Council. The State Assembly and Governor Pataki's office provided additional amounts, with the remainder coming from private donations. See Ralph Blumenthal, "The Museum of Jewish Heritage Begins Work on $60 Million Wing," *New York Times,* October 27, 2000, Arts and Leisure, p. 10.

24. American Sephardi Federation Archives, Series 2, Subseries 2, Box 9, Administration. See also Folder #2, Center for Jewish History, 1998. Fund-raising letter to Dr. Raphael, Mr. Lerner, and Mr. Zukrow, March 27, 1998. Several other letters had the same text.

25. ASF Archives, Box 1, Series 1, Board of Directors Meeting, November 1997. Board member Joel Marcus's speech.

26. Interview with Vivenne Roumani Denn, March 18, 2003.

27. Rochelle Saidel, *Never Too Late to Remember: The Politics behind New York City's Holocaust Museum* (New York: Holmes and Meier, 1996).

28. Interview with Dr. David Marwell, January 15, 2005. We visited the museum two times.

29. In 1989, the United States stopped recognizing Soviet Jews as refugees, making it much more difficult for them to come to the United States than to Israel. See chapter 2.

30. For a satirical fictional look at Russian Jewish immigrants in New York, see Gary Shteyngart, *The Russian Debutante's Handbook* (New York: Riverhead, 2002).

31. Jennifer Bleyer, "A Diaspora of Young Israelis, Decompressing," *New York Times,* October 5, 2003, Sunday Styles, p. 6.

32. Eric Homberger, *The Historical Atlas of New York: A Visual Celebration of Nearly 400 Years of New York City's History* (New York: Henry Holt, 1994), pp. 162–63.

33. United Jewish Appeal, *Jewish Population Study.*

34. We each visited Crown Heights and Borough Park three times.

35. For ethnographic studies of New York's Hasidic communities, see Stephanie Wellen Levine, *Mystics, Mavericks, and Merry-Makers: An Intimate Journey among Hasidic Girls* (New York: NYU Press, 2003); Lis Harris, *Holy Days: Inside the World of a Hasidic Family* (New York: Touchstone Press, 1995); and Samuel Heilman's classic, *Defender of the Faith* (Berkeley: University of California Press, 1999).

36. See Sue Fishkoff, *The Rebbe's Army: Inside the World of Chabad-Lubavitch* (New York: Schocken, 2003).

37. A recent *New York Times Magazine* article explored the controversies currently raging in the Chabad community between messianic and antimessianic Lubavitch adherents. See Jonathan Mahler, "Waiting for the Messiah on Eastern Parkway," *New York Times Magazine,* September 21, 2003, p. 42.

38. Caryn lived in Crown Heights for two years in the 1990s.

39. Fran Reiter, New York Tourism Bureau, as quoted in Jewish Tours virtual tour (jewishtours.com).

40. Some might argue that Chabad inverts the traditional museum metaphor of displaying legacies and artifacts of colonization by actively recruiting (colonizing) Reform Jews and introducing them to practices and observances that Reform Judaism long ago abandoned. We think this line of argument is a bit overstated but have heard it voiced among some Jewish communal professionals who worry about Chabad "stealing" away potential organizational clients and community participants.

41. The racial/ethnic and migration history of Crown Heights is less romantic than these trips suggest. Crown Heights has periodically erupted in violence and tension between groups, most famously in the early 1990s over the deaths of

Gavin Cato, an African American boy, and Yankel Rosenbaum, an Australian *yeshiva* student.

42. WNBC, "Jewish Children's Museum Opens," December 9, 2004.

43. E. B. Solomon, "In Area That Once Saw Race Riots, Kids Museum Teaches Tolerance," Jewish Telegraph Agency, December 13, 2004.

44. Sam Kliger, "Russian Jews in America: Status, Identity, Integration," paper presented at conference "Russian-Speaking Jewry in Global Perspective," Bar Ilan University, June 2004.

45. On the symbolic importance of an immigrant's point of entry, see Nancy Foner, *From Ellis Island to JFK: New York's Two Great Waves of Immigration* (New Haven: Yale University Press, 2002).

46. Shteyngart, *The Russian Debutante's Handbook* (New York: Riverhead Books, 2002).

47. Annelise Orleck, "Soviet Jews: The City's Newest Immigrants Transform New York Jewish Life," in *New Immigrants in New York,* 2nd ed., ed. Nancy Foner (New York: Columbia University Press, 2001), p. 112.

48. See Judith Deutsch Kornblatt, *Doubly Chosen: Jewish Identity, the Soviet Intelligentsia, and the Russian Orthodox Church* (Madison: University of Wisconsin Press, 2004).

49. Rachel Pomerance, "Russian Jews in America: From 'Clients' to 'Partners': Ties among Jews Are Changing," Jewish Telegraph Agency, March 30, 2004.

50. Nancy Foner, "Introduction," *New Immigrants in New York,* 2nd ed. (New York: Columbia University Press, 2001), p. 16.

51. Sabrina Tavernise, "To Young, a Russian Enclave Is Too Much Old Country," *New York Times,* October 8, 2003, pp. A1, A27.

52. Orleck, "Soviet Jews," p. 138.

53. See Peter Salwen, *Upper West Side Story: A History and Guide* (New York: Abbeville Press, 1989).

54. Program Schedule, Jewish Community Center of Manhattan, Fall 2003.

55. From the Web site of the World Congress of Jewish Community Centers (www.wcjcc.org).

56. From the Web site of the Jewish Community Center Association (www.jcca.org).

57. Ibid.

58. Sandee Brawarsky, "The Upper West Side: Cross-Section of Jewish Life," *Jewish Week,* July 26, 2002.

NOTES TO THE EPILOGUE

1. Edward Rothstein, "Seeking an Alternative to a Jewish State," *New York Times,* November 22, 2003, p. B11.

2. See Valeriy Chervyakov, Zvi Gitelman, and Vladimir Shapiro, "Religion and Ethnicity: Judaism in the Ethnic Consciousness of Contemporary Russian Jews," *Ethnic and Racial Studies* 20(2) (April 1997), pp. 280–305. For the specific comment about Russian Jews' affinity for others, see Gitelman's broader article, "The Decline of the Diaspora Jewish Nation: Boundaries, Content, and Jewish Identity," *Jewish Social Studies* 4(2) (1998), p. 121.

Index

Abram, Ruth, 143
Abramov, Sergei, 38
Abramovitch, S. Y., 5
Activism, 119, 121, 122–124
African Americans, 85
Agudah (Society for the Protection of Personal Rights), 119, 122–123, 124–125
Ahava company, 13
Aliyah (ascension to Israel): diminished importance to Zionists, 55; immigration surge after the 1967 War, 14; religious nationalism and identity travel, 65–67; Soviet Jews, 33
Allen, Woody, 137
American Civil Liberties Union (ACLU), 89
American Friends of the *Agudah* (AFA), 123
American Friends of the Jerusalem Open House, 123
American Jewish Historical Society (AJHS), 144, 148
American Jewish World Service, 48
American Sephardi Federation, 145, 148–149
Anglo-Jewish Exhibition, London, 74
Anti-Semitism: affecting Jewish integration into European society, 182n. 5; Center for Jewish History, 145; homophobia and, 118;

Moscow, 27–29; Museum of Tolerance exhibits, 85; Russia's public decrying of, 35
Antin, Mary, 7
Architecture: Center for Jewish History, 146–147; Museum of Jewish Heritage, 151; Skirball Cultural Center, 92, 94; Winnick Institute Jerusalem, 90–91
Art and music: evoking meaning and memory of Israel, 13; *klezmer* music, 16; Moscow's Jewish community, 27; queer Jews, 139; Skirball Museum exhibit on values, 103–104
Ascent program, 50–51
Ashkenazic Jews: America as Jewish homeland, 7–8; dominating New York organizations and institutions, 195n. 2; homelands and diasporas, 6; New York immigrants, 152–154; Skirball Museum exhibits, 101. *See also* German Jews
Assimilation: Ashkenazic Jews, 8; Center for Jewish History, 145; Russian Jewry, 31, 40; Skirball's message, 100, 101
Association for Jewish Studies, 144, 195–196n. 12
Atlit, 64
Auschwitz, 63

Babylonian Exile, 4
Bar and Bat Mitzvah ceremonies, 104
Bat Shalom/The Jerusalem Link, 119, 135
Bathhouses, ritual, 6, 36
Belarus: population statistics, 182n. 4
Ben Gurion, David, 11–12
Ben-Yakov, Chaim, 43, 47
Berenbaum, Michael, 76
Berman, Nancy, 99
Bet Chaverim, Congregation, 115–116
Beth Ha-Shoah–Museum of Tolerance. *See* Museum of Tolerance
Biale, David, 16
Birkenau, 63
birthright. *See* taglit/birthright israel programs
Bisexual Jews. *See* Queer Jews
Blaustein, Jacob, 11–12
Blinder, Richard, 146
Bookstores, 46
Borough Park. *See* Crown Heights/Borough Park
Boyarin, Daniel and Jonathan, 17–18, 23, 177n3
Brief Travels of Benjamin the Third, The (Abramovitch), 5
Brighton Beach, New York, 152–154, 160–164
Brooklyn, New York. *See* Brighton Beach, New York; Crown Heights/Borough Park, New York
Brown, Charles, 78
Bush, George W., 37, 193n. 11

Cannon, Ali, 126–127
Carter, Jimmy, 80
Cato, Gavin, 197–198n. 41
Ceder, Joseph, 187n. 35
Cemeteries, 5–6

Center for Jewish History, New York, 143–149, 169, 195n. 10, 195n. 12
Central Council of American Rabbis, 113–114
Chabad Lubavitch: connecting with Russian Jewish immigrants, 162; Crown Heights community, 155–160; diaspora business, 50–51, 52; Levaiev's financing Russian Jewish programs, 47; Moscow outreach, 36–38; Moscow's Marina Roshcha Jewish Community Center, 44–45; Moscow's non-Chabad Orthodox community, 39–41; programs as museum metaphor, 197n. 40; rooting itself in America, 169–170
Charedi, 186n. 16
Charlie Awards, 59
Children: Jewish Children's Museum, 159–160; Museum of Tolerance, 82–85; Skirball Museum's exhibits, 100, 104
Chlenov, Mikhail, 39
Citizenship, 129–130. *See also* Right of Return
Civic religion, support for Israel as, 12–15
Civil rights movement, 32
ClaF (Lesbian Feminist Community), 119
Clergy: ordination of queer Jews, 114
Clifford, James, 18
Cohen, Richard, 73–74
Community: Brooklyn's Hasidic community, 154–160; queer Jews in the United States, 113; queer politics in Israel, 117–118; queers in Israel, 107–109
Community centers: Hasidic Welcome Center, 159; Jewish Community Center movement, 166–169; Man-

hattan Jewish Community Center, 147, 164–166; Moscow's first centers, 44–47

Congress of Jewish Religious Organizations and Communities of Russia (CJROCR), 39

Conseil Representif des Institutions juives de France, Le (CRIF), 181n. 56

Conservative Jews: diaspora business, 55; sexuality and diversity issues, 114–115

Crisis of continuity, 56

Crown Heights/Borough Park, New York, 139, 153–160, 197–198n. 41

Culture, Jewish: Skirball Museum exhibits focus on, 98–99; Soviet Yiddish culture, 31

Cultures of the Jews (Biale), 16

Dayan, Yael, 120

Dead Sea, 13

Death camps, 62, 63

Diaspora: *aliyah* versus, 66–67; celebration of, 17–18; defining and describing, 2–6; dismantling, 20–22; identity as diasporic tension, 17–18; mythic return to the homeland, 8; public perceptions of, 1–2; Skirball Museum's message, 97–98; Zionism and the Exile, 9–12

Diaspora business: aims of, 52; Eastern Europe, 61; ensuring the perpetuation of the Jewish people, 57–58; history of Jewish youth travel, 53–56; intifada and violence in Israel, 68–70; religious nationalism and identity travel, 65–67; renewing Jewish spirituality, 57; taglit/birthright israel programs, 58–59, 68–70, 125, 181n. 53, 181n. 55, 186n. 14; tailoring travel

to specific groups, 186n. 17; violence curtailing Israel travel, 68–69, 188n. 42

Diaspora Museum, Tel Aviv, 97, 150

Diller Fellows Program, 188n. 42

Discrimination against gays, 110

Diversity and unity: American Sephardi Federation, 148–149; Chabad's failure to embrace diversity, 169–170; dynamic tension between diversity and unity, 16; Israeli queers' identity, 108; JCC movement, 168–169; Jerusalem Open House, 194n. 26; Jewish identity as diasporic tension, 17–18; New York's Ashkenazic domination, 195n. 2; New York's Upper West Side, 164–166; post-Zionism, 15–16; questioning unified Jewish identity, 19–20; uniting queer Jews, 121–122, 199n. 26; unity as theme for Center for Jewish History, 145–146. *See also* Queer Jews

Dubowski, Sandi, 131–132

Eastern Europe: identity tourism, 51–52, 61–65; secular Jewish identity, 16; Skirball's portrayal of immigrants, 99; YIVO, 144–145. *See also* Ashkenazic Jews; Yiddish language; *individual countries*

Echoes That Remain (film), 86–87

Eden, Michal, 121

Education: encouraging *aliyah*, 67; establishing traditional schools, 5–6; homophobic hiring practices in Jewish education, 113–115; identity tourism, 52, 57–58; Jewish Children's Museum, 159–160; Joint Distribution Committee's mission in Russia, 48; Moscow's Jewish community, 36; Moscow's para-rabbinic

Education (*Continued*)
training program, 43–44; Museum of Jewish Heritage, 150–151; Museum of Tolerance, 80–88; schools in the Soviet Union, 34–35; straight Jews' support of queer rights, 193n. 15; study-abroad programs in Israel, 54–55; violence curtailing study-abroad programs, 68–69, 188n. 42; Winnick Institute Jerusalem, 91
Efron, Noah, 170
El-Ad, Hagai, 121–122
Ellis Island, 96, 151, 152, 161
England: Anglo-Jewish Exhibition, 74
European Jewry, modern, 24
European Museum of Mutual Respect, 90
Even, Uzi, 121
Exile: crafting home and diaspora, 4–5; defined and described, 17; Zionism and, 9–12
Exodus, reliving, 182–183n. 14

Family: immigration issues for queer Jews, 129–130; Israeli lesbians, 120; queer Jews in the United States, 113–114
Feldman, Jackie, 64
Feminist organizations, 119–120
Feminist Seder, 169
film industry, 95
financial support: American Jews and early Zionism, 11; American support of Israel through travel programs, 54; Center for Jewish History, 147; Chabad programs, 155–156; Manhattan's new Jewish Community Center, 165; Museum of Jewish Heritage, 150, 196n. 23; Museum of Tolerance, 81, 89; queer Jews organizing across na-
tional boundaries, 122–124; Russian Jewish communities, 45–49; UJA, 15–16; Winnick Institute Jerusalem, 90–91
Findling, Debbie, 61–62
First Temple Period, 4
Forward, 152–153
Foxman, Abraham, 91
France, 24, 181n. 56
French Hill, Jerusalem, 91–92

Galut (diaspora), 3
Garrett, Leah, 18
Gay rights: immigration to Israel and the United States, 129–130; Israel's progressive stance, 118–119
Gehry, Frank, 90, 91
Gender: private spaces constructing community, 6. See also Queer Jews; Women
Genocide, 85
German Jews: homelands and diasporas, 6; identifying with Germany, 7; Leo Baeck Archives, 145; New York immigrants, 152. See also Ashkenazic Jews
Ghetto fighters Kibbutz, 64
Gitelman, Zvi, 21, 35
Giuliani, Rudolph, 147
Glasnost, 34
Global Jews, 19, 21–22, 36–38
Gluz, Mikhail, 38
Going west, 109–110
Goler, Jonathan, 125
Gorizont (radio program), 162
Great Britain, 15
Greenberg, Simon, 79, 189n. 19
Gross, Aeyal, 129
Group relations theory, 190n. 32

Halberstam, Ari, 159
Hammer, Jill, 169

Hanukkah celebrations, 38, 103

Ha'shomer Hatza'ir (The Young Guard), 53

Hasidic Jews. *See* Chabad Lubavitch

Hasidic Welcome Center, 159

Hebrew language building an American Jewish identity, 14

Hebrew Union College–Skirball Cultural Center. *See* Skirball Museum

Hebrew University, 54–55

Hellenistic Jews, 4

Herscher, Uri, 94, 95, 97–98, 192n. 66

Herzl, Theodore, 10

Hesder yeshivot (education and military training program), 58

Hier, Martin, 79–81, 83, 91

Hillel organization, 182–183n. 14, 186n. 20

Hineini, Congregation, 41–42

Histadrut (Labor Zionist trade union), 54

Holleran, Andrew, 109

Holocaust: history of Holocaust commemoration, 75–77, 188–189n. 8; identity tourism, 52; immigration of German Jews, 6; March of the Living, 61–65; Museum of Jewish Heritage, 149–152; Museum of Tolerance exhibits, 86–88; post-war Zionist discourse, 12–15; role in American Jewish identity formation, 188n. 43; Skirball Museum's exhibits, 98; survivors organizations, 186n. 24

Holocaust in American Life, The (Novick), 86

Holocaust Memorial Museum, 76, 82, 89, 150

Holocaust Remembrance Day *(Yom ha-shoah)*, 105

Holocaust (television program), 79–80

Homeland: America as Ashkenazic Jews' homeland, 7–8; constructing and rooting in, 18; Crown Heights, 156–160; defined by attitude and identity, 154–155; historical perspective on, 3–5; Israel and queer Jews, 128; Israel and the rise of Zionism, 9–12; New York as Jewish homeland, 141–143, 152–154; queer Jews' ambivalence about Zionism, 133; Soviet Union as, 60

Homophobia, 114–115, 192n. 9, 193n. 11

Homosexual Jews. *See* Queer Jews

Human rights issues, Soviet persecution of Jews, 32

Hymietown, 137

I Am a Jew (Soviet Jewish publication), 31

Identity: alternatives to travel to Israel, 70–71; American obsession with collective Jewish identity, 145–146; constructing a modern secular Jewish identity, 12–13; as diasporic tension, 17–18; evolution of Russian Jewish identity, 31; former Soviet Union's Jewish communities, 35, 182n. 9; German Jews identifying with Germany, 7; home and space for queer Jews, 109–112; Los Angeles Jews shaping their own identity, 78–79; March of the Living, 65; Moscow's anti-Semitism shaping Jewish identity, 27–29; Moscow's Jewish community, 27, 39–41, 47–48; Museum of Tolerance's failure to include non-Jewish narrative, 88–90; museums as synagogues, 72–73; museums' portrayal of, 105–106; national and sexual identities, 129–131; New York's

Identity (*Continued*)
  Russian Jewish immigrants, 162;
  post-Zionism and alternatives to
  Zionism, 16–17; queer Jews' ambivalence about Zionism, 133–136;
  queer Orthodoxy, 132; religious Soviet Jews, 34; Sheinfeld's "My Identity," 128; transgender experiences,
  126–127; Zionism building an
  American Jewish identity, 13–14.
  See also Diaspora business
Identity tourism. *See* Diaspora business
Imagined communities, 18
Immigrants and immigration: California's Proposition 187, 192n. 66; from
  the former Soviet Union, 35; German
  Jews' exile from the homeland, 6–7;
  growth of JCC movement, 166;
  growth of Los Angeles Jewish community, 77–79; movement from Israel to Russia, 48–49, 110; New
  York's history of, 140–143; New
  York's Tenement Museum, 143;
  1920s growth of Moscow's Jewish
  community, 26–27; portrayed at the
  Museum of Jewish Heritage,
  151–152; queer politics across national borders, 129–130; Right of
  Return, 10–11; Russian immigrants
  in Brighton Beach, 152–154,
  160–164; settling in New York,
  152–154; Skirball's exhibits, 96, 99;
  Soviet Jews, 29–30, 32–34, 197n. 29.
  See also *Aliyah* (ascension to Israel)
Impresario culture, 11
Institute for Jewish Research (YIVO),
  144–148
Integration of queer Jews into community life, 116–117
International Hillel organization,
  182–183n. 14
Intifada, 15, 68–70

Israel: American Sephardi Federation,
  148–149; as answer to crisis of
  continuity, 56–57; Chabad headquarters, 156; diaspora and homeland, 9–12; early Zionists choosing
  a homeland site, 178n. 16; homophobia, 192n. 9; identity tourism,
  50–56; intifada, 68–70; Israelis and
  sexual identity, 107–108; lack of
  tolerance and synagogue/state separation, 170; March of the Living,
  62–65; New York immigrants, 153;
  Orthodox Jews' failure to acknowledge Jewish sovereignty, 4; post-
  statehood Zionist discourse, 12–15;
  queer Jews' ambivalence about
  Zionism, 133–136; queer Jews organizing across national boundaries, 122–124; queer Jews traveling to, 124–129; queer Orthodoxy,
  131–132; queer politics across national borders, 129–131; queer politics in Israel, 117–122; as refuge
  for Soviet Jews, 32–34; religious
  nationalism and identity travel,
  65–67; replacing diaspora with
  global Jews concept, 20–22; Russian emigration, 35; as safe space for
  queers, 109–112; San Francisco-Is-
  rael LGBT Alliance, 116–117;
  Wiesenthal Center's expansion to,
  90–91; Zalman Shazar Center for
  Jewish History, 195n. 10. *See also*
  Diaspora business; Zionism
Israel Center (San Francisco), 116,
  124–125
It is Called Genocide (film), 85
IVRI-Nasawi, 16

Jackson, Jesse, 137
Jackson-Vanik Amendment (1974),
  32, 34

JCC. *See* Jewish Community Center movement
Jeremiah (prophet), 4
Jerusalem Link, The, 119
Jerusalem Open House (JOH), 111, 121–123, 125–126, 194n. 26, 199n. 26
Jerusalem Pride March, 111, 120–121, 192n. 9, 193n. 10
Jewish Agency (Israel), 35, 48
Jewish Children's Museum, 159–160
Jewish Chronicle, 74
Jewish Community Center, New York, 164–166
Jewish Community Center movement, 166–169
Jewish Community Development Fund (JCDF), 48
Jewish Fascism, 28
Jewish Theological Seminary (JTS), 114–115
Jewish Welfare Boards, 166
John F. Kennedy Airport, 151–152
Joint Distribution Committee (JDC), 45, 48
Journey of Pride, 116, 124–125

Kadish, Ruti, 119
Kagan, Arkady, 162
Keep Not Silent (Alexander), 131–132
Kehilah lesbit feministit (Lesbian Feminist Community), 119
Kelner, Shaul, 55, 168
Keshet Argentina, 122
Keshet (rainbow) group, 114, 115, 193n. 15
Kfar Chabad Israel, 156
Khoury, Jamil, 135–136
Kibbutz Lochamei Getaot (Ghetto fighters Kibbutz), 64
Kibbutz movement, 53
Kibbutz Program Center, 55

Kirschenblatt-Gimblett, Barbara, 20–21
Kirschner, Robert, 99
Klein, Adaire, 80, 81
Klezmer music, 16
Kliger, Sam, 181n. 54
Knesset, 10, 188–189n. 8
Koch, Ed, 150
Kogan, Zinovy, 34
Kol Dor, 21–22
Koret Foundation, 116
Kronby, Miles, 195n. 5
Kugelmass, Jack, 62, 143
Kushner, Tony, 119

Land: Jews rooting themselves in, 5–6
Landsmanshaftn (community self-help groups), 7, 78
Language: diaspora, 3; New York's Lower East Side, 142; Reform services in Moscow, 42; Soviet Jews' self-identifying through, 34; West Los Angeles, 80. *See also* Hebrew language building an American Jewish identity; Yiddish language
Lappe, Benay, 114–115
Lau, Israel Meir, 24
Law of Return. *See* Right of Return
Lazar, Berel, 37, 40, 46–48
Legal issues: gay rights and politics, 113, 118
Leo Baeck Archives, 144–145, 148
Leo Baeck Temple, Los Angeles, 97
Lesbian Jews, 132. *See also* Queer Jews
Lesser, Joshua, 115–116
Levaiev, Lev, 47
Levitt, Joy, 168
Levy, Leon, 148
LGBT Alliance (San Francisco organization), 116, 123, 125
LGBT issues. *See* Queer Jews

Libraries, 46
Lieben, Salomon Hug, 75
Little Odessa. See Brighton Beach,
New York
Living Bridges Program, 124–125
Livnot u'Lehibanot (Chabad outreach
program), 50–51, 57, 65–66, 186n.
14
Los Angeles, California: growth of
Los Angeles Jewish community,
77–79; New York museums' ties to
Los Angeles museums, 138–139.
See also Museum of Tolerance;
Skirball Museum
Lower East Side, New York, 140,
141–143; cell-phone tours, 195n. 5

Ma'ayan, 168–169
Machon (para-rabbinic training pro-
gram), 43–44
Majdanek, 63
Makom: The Center for Mindfulness,
168–169
Manhattan Jewish Community Cen-
ter, 147, 167–168
March of the Living, 51–52, 61–65,
68–70, 87, 186n. 27
Marienstras, Richard, 18
Marina Roshcha Jewish Community
Center, Moscow, 44–47
Marriage: queer Jews' immigration to
Israel and the United States,
129–130; same-sex marriage,
113–114
Marwell, David, 151
Masada, 13
Melitz: The Center for Jewish-Zionist
Education, 55
Memories of Israel, reinventing, 13
Mercaz Hamagshimim, 67
Meretz party, 135
Messier, Jean-Marie, 90

Mezuzah (doorpost), 6
Michaelson, Dafna, 62
Michels, TJ, 126–127
Mikva'ot (ritual bathhouses), 6, 36
Military training, 58
Miller, Haim, 192n. 9
Minsk, Belarus, 34, 44
Mircaz Keshet (The Rainbow Center),
116
Moore, Deborah Dash, 8, 16, 73,
189n. 19
Mosaic: The National Jewish Center
for Sexual and Gender Diversity,
116
Moscow, Russia: anti-Semitism in,
27–29; battle over Jewish identities
and communities, 39–41; building a
Jewish homeland, 30; community
centers, 44–47; emergence of Reform Judaism, 41–44; evolution of
Jewish identity from 1917 to the
present, 30–35; funding Jewish
communities, 47–49; global Jews in,
36–38; Russian Jews in New York
and Moscow, 181n. 54
Most-favored-nation trading status,
32
Multiculturalism, 121–122, 168,
199n. 26
Muschamp, Herbert, 92, 96, 98
Museum of Jewish Heritage–A Living
Memorial to the Holocaust,
149–152, 196n. 23
Museum of Tolerance: establishment
of, 79–81, 189n. 23; exhibits,
82–88; identity and victimization,
76–77; international campuses,
90–92; laissez-faire approach to
diversity, 170; mission of, 88–90;
Museum of Jewish Heritage and,
150; nativization of the Holocaust, 104–105; New York con-

nection, 139; Skirball's ambiance and, 94

Museums: Center for Jewish History, New York, 143–149, 169, 195n. 10, 195n. 12; Chabad's programs as museum metaphor, 197n. 40; Holocaust commemoration, 75–77; Jewish Children's Museum, 159–160; Museum of Jewish Heritage, 149–152, 196n. 23; Museum of Tolerance, 82–86; New York museums' ties to Los Angeles museums, 138–139; origins of the Jewish museum phenomenon, 73–75; as synagogues, 72–73; Tenement Museum, 143. *See also* Museum of Tolerance; Skirball Museum

Music. *See* Art and music

"My Identity" (Sheinfeld), 128

Myslik, Wayne, 110

Nadler, Allan, 145

Nationalism: religious nationalism and identity travel, 65–67; secular Israeli queer identity, 134; tension between sexual identity and, 130–131; Zionism and, 17

Nationality, Jewishness as, 31

Necropornography, 86, 87

Neturei Kartah, 4, 177n. 3

New York: City of Refuge (MJH exhibit), 151–152

New York City, New York: cell-phone tours of the Lower East Side, 195n. 5; Center for Jewish History, 195n. 10; as center of Jewish culture and life, 137–139; Crown Heights Hasidic community, 154–160; ethnic diversity of the Jewish communities, 152–154; Hasidim in Crown Heights/Borough Park, 139, 153–154, 154–160, 197–198n. 41;

history of Jewish presence, 139–141; Jewish Community Center and the JCC movement, 164–169; as Jewish homeland, 7, 152–154; Jewish organizations and institutions, 143–149; Museum of Jewish Heritage, 149–152; population statistics, 195n. 4; revisiting the Lower East Side, 141–143, 195n. 5; Russian Jews in Brighton Beach, 152–154, 160–164; Russian Jews in New York and Moscow, 181n. 54

Newman, Lesléa, 130

Nights in Aruba (Holleran), 109

Nikitskai Jewish Community Center, Moscow, 45–46

1967 War, 13–14

Niv, Rafi, 128, 133

Nonprofit organizations, 123. *See also* Philanthropy

North American Jewish Federation, 48

Novick, Peter, 86

Or Avner Chabad Lubavitch Fund, 47

Ordination of queer Jews, 114

Organizations and institutions: American Jewish Historical Society, 144, 148; American Sephardi Federation, 145, 148–149; Ashkenazic Jews' dominating New York's, 195n. 2; Center for Jewish History, 143–149, 169, 195n. 10, 195n. 12; Israel's historical and cultural collections, 196n. 16; JCC movement, 166–169; Leo Baeck Archives, 144–145, 148; Los Angeles's self-help organizations, 78; Moscow's Jewish community, 34–35; Museum of Jewish Heritage, 149–152, 196n. 23; Yeshiva University Museum, 144, 145, 148; YIVO, 144–148

Orthodox Jews: making *aliyah*, 65–67; Moscow's alternatives to Chabad, 39–41; Museum of Tolerance, 76–77, 79–81, 89–90, 189n. 23; queer Jews' identity and space, 112; queer Jews' opportunities in New York, 139; queer Orthodoxy, 131–132; refusal to acknowledge Jewish sovereignty in Israel, 4. *See also* Chabad Lubavitch

Otzma program, 58

Outreach programs: Chabad community in Crown Heights, 155–160; Chabad programs in Moscow, 36–38; Jewish Children's Museum, 159–160; Russian Jewish Congress, 39

Palestine: Israel-Palestine women's activism, 119; Jerusalem Pride Parade, 193n. 10; lack of political choice, 23; queer Israelis' peace advocacy, 134–136

Passover: feminist seders, 169; Skirball programs and exhibits, 96, 103; Soviet Jews reliving the Exodus, 182–183n. 14

Pataki, George, 147

Peace organizations, 119, 135

"Peaceful Warriors" exhibit, 83

Persian Jews, 79

Philanthropy: funding and organizing queer communities and programs, 115–116, 123; funding Russian Jewish organizations, 47–49; Manhattan's new Jewish Community Center, 165; politicization of support for Israel, 15; taglit/birthright israel, 58–59

Piccolo Bar, Tel Aviv, 118

Pink vote, 121

Plaut, Joshua Eli, 145–146

Poland: March of the Living, 63–65; roots of New York's Hasidic communities, 154–155

Politics: criticism of Zionism, 14–15; early Zionism, 10; Moscow's two chief rabbis, 40–41; political violence and tourism, 68–70; protesting Soviet persecution of Jews, 32; queer and Jewish American politics, 112–117, 193n. 11; queer identity in Israel, 107–108; queer politics across national borders, 129–130; queer politics in Israel, 117–122

Popular culture, 139

Population statistics. *See* Statistics and demographics

Post-Zionism, 15–20

Postcolonialism, 17

Prague Museum, 75

Precious Stones (Khoury), 135–136

Pride Parades, 111, 120–121, 192n. 9, 193n. 10

Promised lands, 109–110

Proposition 187, 192n. 66

Protocols of the Elders of Zion, The, 28–29

Putin, Vladimir, 37, 38

Queer Jews: ambivalence about Zionism, 133–136; Israel as safe space, 109–112; Israeli queer identity, 107–108; New York's opportunities for, 139; nomenclature of sexual identity, 192n. 1; queer and Jewish American politics, 112–117, 193n. 11; queer Orthodoxy, 131–132; queer politics across national boundaries, 122–124, 129–131; queer politics in Israel, 117–122; travel to Israel, 124–129

Rabbinic Period, 5
Rabin, Yitzhak, 86
Rainbow Center, The (*Mircaz Keshet*
), 116
Ramo synagogue, 63
Real Jews (Efron), 170
Reb Arelach, 4
*Recovered Roots: Collective Memory
and the Making of Israeli National
Tradition* (Zerubavel), 13
Reform Jews: curtailing travel during
political violence, 69; diaspora busi-
ness, 55; emergence of Russian Re-
form Judaism, 41–44; queer Jewish
communities and politics in the
United States, 113–114. *See also*
Skirball Museum
Refugees, 197n29
Refusenik movement, 34, 162
Religious observance: Chabad's Russ-
ian outreach programs, 37–38;
making *aliyah*, 65–67; tailoring
identity tourism, 57–58. *See also*
Conservative Jews; Orthodox Jews;
Reform Jews
Rescue efforts in Moscow's Jewish
community, 27
Right of Return, 10–11, 32–33, 129
Rituals remembering the homeland,
5–6
Rocky Mountain Hebrew Academy,
188n. 44
Rodina (Russian publication), 41
Roots, Jewish, 59
Rosenbaum, Yankel, 197–198n. 41
Rothberg School for Overseas Stu-
dents, 54–55
Roumani-Denn, Vivienne, 148–149
Royal Albert Hall, London, 74
Russia: Hillel organization, 186n. 20;
Hillel's annual Pesach project,

182–183n. 14; immigrants' return
from Israel to, 48–49, 110; Jewish
population in the former Soviet
Union, 182n. 4; New York immigrants, 152–154; queer Jews organizing across national boundaries,
122; Russian immigrants in
Brighton Beach, 152–154,
160–164. *See also* Moscow, Russia
Russian Conservatory, 27

Sabar, Naama, 127
Sacks, Jonathan, 15
Safdie, Moshe, 101
Safe haven, Israel as, 109–112, 128,
135
Same-sex marriage, 113–114
Samizdat (Soviet publication), 182n. 9
San Francisco, California: Jewish
queer politics, 116; Journey of Pride
to Israel, 124–125; as queer Zion,
109; as safe haven for queer Jews,
132
Satmar Hasidim, 155
Schimel, Lawrence, 112
Schneerson, Menachem Mendel, 4,
47, 156
Schools. *See* Education
Schuman, Michael, 96
Schwarzenegger, Arnold, 90–91
Second Temple Period, 4
Secularism: Chabad's outreach pro-
grams in Moscow, 38; cultural politics of the Diaspora, 18; funding
Russian Jewish organizations,
48–49; Israel's lack of tolerance and
synagogue/state separation, 170;
JCC projects, 169; Moscow's secular Jewish identity, 31; queer American Jews in Israel, 126; queer Is-
raelis, 108; queer Jews' ambivalence

Secularism (*Continued*)
about Zionism, 133–136; queer Orthodoxy, 132; Skirball Museum's goals and patrons, 95, 100; tension between religious and secular Israeli queers, 121; Winnick Institute Jerusalem, 91

Security and safety: identity travel and, 68–70; Israel as safe space, 110; Museum of Tolerance, 82

Self-help organizations, 78

Separation and integration dialectic, 170–171

Sephardic Jews: American Sephardi Federation, 145, 148–149; creating a new secular Jewish identity, 16; homelands and diasporas, 6; Skirball Museum exhibits, 101

September 11, 2001, 138

Sexuality. *See* Queer Jews

Sha'ar Zahav, Congregation, 119

Shabbat preparation in Crown Heights, 156–157

Shalom, Chaya, 119

Shandler, Jeffrey, 11, 141–142

Sharon, Ariel, 24, 181n. 56

Shayevich, Adolf, 39, 40

Shazar, Zalman, 195n. 10

Shefa Fund, 115

Sheinfeld, Ilan, 128

Shlichim (messengers or cultural attachés), 56, 155, 185–186n. 13

Shoah Visual History Foundation, 186n. 24

Shteyngart, Gary, 161

Shulman, Nelly, 44

Shvydkoi, Mikhail, 38

Silberstein, Lawrence, 17

Silk Road Theatre Project, 135–136

Simon Wiesenthal Center. *See* Museum of Tolerance

Sirotin, Alexander, 162

Skirball, Jack, 95

Skirball-Kenis, Audrey, 95

Skirball Museum: architecture of, 146–147; atmosphere of, 94; ecumenicalist agenda, 168; ethnic makeup of visitors, 100; impetus for establishing, 75; message of, 97–100; mission of, 92–97

Slovin, Bruce, 145

Society for the Protection of Personal Rights, 119

Solidarity missions, 69

Solomon, Alisa, 119

Soviet Union: Chabad Lubavitch outreach programs in, 36; evolution of Jewish identity, 30–35; Jewish migration to Israel and the United States, 32–34; Soviet Jews' refugee status, 197n. 29; youth tourism, 60

Space and place: Israel as safe space for queers, 109–112; Jews' establishment of, 5–6; queer American Jews in Israel, 125–126

Stalinism, 31

Statistics and demographics: former Soviet Union's Jewish population, 182n4; New York's immigrant Jewish population, 153; New York's Jewish population, 195n. 4; New York's Russian immigrant population, 160–161, 181n. 54; political nature of, 180n. 44; Russia's Jewish population, 35, 181n. 54

Stephen S. Wise Temple, 97

Stereotypes, Jewish, 40–41

Stier, Oren, 65, 82

Stonewall Riots, 120–121

Streisand, Barbra, 138

Summer youth programs, 54

Svirsky, Gila, 119

Swacker, Bob, 158

Synagogue/state separation, 170

Synagogues: fate of the Soviet Union's, 40; growth of queer communities, 115–116; March of the Living, 63; Moscow's Congregation *Hineini,* 41–42; museums as synagogues, 72–73; Skirball Museum exhibit on values, 103

taglit/birthright israel programs, 58–59, 68–70, 125, 181n. 53, 181n. 55, 186n. 14
Technology: Museum of Tolerance's use of, 82–85; Skirball Museum's use of, 93–94
Tel Aviv queer community, 118, 120–121
Tenement Museum, 143
Terrorism, 68–70, 138
This is Called Genocide (Museum of Tolerance film), 99
Time of Favor, A (film), 187n. 35
Transgendered Jews, 126–127. *See also* Queer Jews
Travel and tourism: alternatives to Israel travel, 188n. 44; cell-phone tours of the Lower East Side, 195n. 5; Chabad's virtual tours, 158; the diaspora business, 51–53; history of youth travel, 53–56; intifada and violence in Israel, 68–70, 188n. 42; Journey of Pride, 116; Masada, 13; New York, 138, 140, 141–143; post-Cold War heritage travel to Eastern Europe, 61–65; queer Jews, 124–129; religious nationalism and identity travel, 65–67; taglit/birthright israel programs, 58–59, 68–70, 125, 181n. 53, 181n. 55, 186n. 14; use of literature of travel to envision the world, 18
Treblinka, 63

Trembling before G-d (Dubowski), 131–132
Troen, S. Ilan, 16
Tuneyadevka, 13
Twelfth Zionist Congress, 11

Uganda Proposal, 178n. 16
Ukraine: Jewish population, 182n. 4
Union of Religious Communities of Modern Judaism in Russia (URCMJR), 43
United Jewish Appeal (UJA), 15–16, 140
United Jewish Communities, 58, 70
United States: queer and Jewish American politics, 112–117, 193n11; queer Jews' ambivalence about Zionism, 133–136; queer Jews organizing across national boundaries, 122–123; Reform Judaism, 42; Soviet Jews' emigration to, 33–34. *See also* Los Angeles, California; New York City, New York
Unity. *See* Diversity and unity
University of Judaism, 79, 97, 189n. 19
University of Southern California, 94–95
Upper West Side, New York, 164–166, 167
Urban flight, 166–167
U.S. Holocaust Memorial Museum, 76, 82, 89, 150

Vaisman, German, 122
Vaisman, Igor, 34
Values, Skirball exhibit on, 102–104
Vanishing Diaspora (Wasserstein), 182n. 5
Vienna, Austria, 74–75
Violence, 68–70, 80, 197–198n. 41
Virtual tours, 158

"Visions and Values: Jewish Life from Antiquity to America" (Skirball exhibit), 93–94
Visions and Values (Skirball film), 98–99

Walzer, Lee, 118
Wasserstein, Bernard, 29, 33, 182n. 5
Wealth, Moscow's Jewish communal life and, 39–40
Web sites, 158
Weddings, Jewish, 103
Weizman, Ezer, 120
Wenger, Beth, 142
West, going, 109–110
Western Wall, Jerusalem, 58, 69, 126–127
Wideman, John Edgar, 96
Wigstock Riots, 120–121
Williamsburg, Brooklyn, 155
Winnick, Gary, 90–91
Winnick Institute Jerusalem, 90–91
Women: growth of Russian Reform Judaism, 44; Israeli lesbian organizations, 119–120; peace advocacy by queer Israelis, 134–135; Skirball Museum exhibits, 99
Women in Black, 119, 135
World Union for Progressive Judaism, 47
World War II stability of Moscow's Jewish population, 26–27
World Zionist Organization, 54
WorldPride Festival, 111, 122

Yad va-Shem (Israel Holocaust museum), 150
Yaron, Meirav, 124–125
Yediat ha'aretz (knowledge and love of the land of Israel), 53
Yeshiva University, 80–81
Yeshiva University Museum, 144, 145, 148

Yiddish language: cultural and religious separateness through, 160; Eastern Europe as source of secular Jewish identity, 16; Moscow's book collection, 46; as mythic symbol, 8; Soviet Jewish identity, 31
YIVO. *See* Institute for Jewish Research
Yom Ha-Shoah (Holocaust Remembrance Day), 105, 188–189n. 8
Yosef, Raz, 118
The Young Guard, 53
Young Judaea, 53, 54
Young Men's Hebrew Association (YMHA), 166
Youth and travel: history of youth travel, 53–56; Soviet Union, 60; taglit/birthright israel programs, 58–59, 68–70, 125, 181n. 53, 181n. 55, 186n. 14

Za'avah (horror; term used for diaspora), 3
Zalman Shazar Center for Jewish History, 195n. 10
Zellman, Reuben, 114
Zerubavel, Yael, 13
Zionism: American Sephardi Federation, 148; choosing a location for the homeland, 178n16; crafting a home and a homeland, 9–12; history of youth travel, 53–56; increasing criticism leading to post-Zionism, 15–20; March of the Living narrative, 64–65; metaphorical Zion for queer Jews, 109–112; post-statehood discourse, 12–15; queer Jews' ambivalence about, 133–136; religious nationalism and identity travel, 65–67; Soviet Jews expression of identity, 31; Zion as eternal Jewish home, 3–5
Zionist Factor, The, 28

About the Authors

Caryn Aviv is a Marsico Lecturer and an affiliated faculty with the Center for Judaic Studies at the University of Denver. She is a founder of Mosaic: The National Jewish Center for Sexual and Gender Diversity and editor of *Queer Jews* (Routledge, 2002). She is currently working on a book project about transnational peace camps for teens. Aviv has lived and worked in the United States and in Israel.

David Shneer is director of the Center for Judaic Studies and associate professor of history at the University of Denver. His previous books include *Yiddish and the Creation of Soviet Jewish Culture* (Cambridge, 2004) and *Queer Jews* (Routledge, 2002), and he is currently working on a book on Soviet Jewish photographers and World War II. Shneer has lived and worked in the United States, Germany, and Russia.